Dedicated to my mother, Grace.
1916 ~ 2008

A photographic and historical guide to the
Parish Churches
of
East Suffolk

as defined by the Archdeaconry of Suffolk in 1836

compiled and photographed
by
Adrian S. Pye

Coming next

West Suffolk

The parishes of West Suffolk as defined by the Archdeaconry of
Sudbury and other peculiars, 1836.

Preface

It is through being involved in family history that I started photographing the churches where my family, at one time or another, had lived. It is even more recently that I have taken an interest in the architecture and development of the parish church. I started gathering together a collection of local churches for my own interest and I eventually decided to photograph every church in Suffolk. A task that spanned three years. During my journeys through the county I have seen some very interesting churches and have met some wonderfully interesting people. It is to these un-named people that I owe my thanks for their encouragement and assistance in compiling this publication. Particularly to Ann Johnson and Bryan Samain for their invaluable assistance.

Every church has been photographed from the outside, however difficult this was at times. It is because of the difficulty in some cases of capturing the whole church that I decided to make a contemporary record. Hopefully before they were all surrounded by housing development, trees or had community centres and crèches built on the side of them. It is with regret that I did not start this endeavour 40 years ago, before the pressure of urban development took its toll. But in truth it is only since the development of the digital camera that I have been able to afford to take tens of thousands of photographs simply for the cost of a camera and a computer.

I would like to thank all the churches that were open to visitors and church crawlers such as myself and only wish there had been more. These days it is a risk to leave a church unlocked, but the risk has always been there: look at the size of some of the iron bound, triple-locked parish chests! Today's vandalism is nothing in comparison with the damage caused by the Puritans in the 16th century. It is arguable that an open church attracts visitors and therefore vandals are without opportunity. Unfortunately some churches receive only one or two visitors each week. But it has been said that 'a locked church is a dying church' and I do tend to agree. By discouraging visitors and expecting them to find a house a half a mile away in the hope that the key-holder is at home, or to call a telephone number without the benefit of an STD code. It causes frustration, to put it mildly.

Every church in this book was visited and photographed by me personally in an attempt to update the earlier writings and observations of others, but we are all fallible and I apologise in advance for any errors that may have crept into the text.

This is only intended as an easy to read guide to the parish church and is in no respect a complete reference. It is intended to be read by those who wish to pick out a church or churches they wish to visit whether for family history research or simple curiosity.

I found many delights in many churches; some took my breath away in pure admiration. I found many disappointments too, and occasionally my heart sank as I saw the work of so called restorers who had caused more damage than a shed full of vandals.

Having finished East Suffolk and well on my way through West Suffolk I have satisfied myself that the benefit justified the cost. I have decided to continue my mission into Norfolk and have already found that it too has some outstanding churches to offer the church crawler. As with Suffolk some are easier to photograph in their entirety than others, but every one is one step nearer to my goal of over 1300 churches in both counties.

Only the briefest of details have been included with each church and as previously mentioned is just a taste of what each one offers to the stranger and parishioner alike. The brevity of the notes does not necessarily indicate the parish has little to offer the enquirer, it is simply a matter of how much one can fit onto a page.

Because of my interest in family history the area covered is based on the Deaneries within the Archdeaconries of Sudbury and Suffolk as they were in 1836. All Suffolk parishes are now in the St. Edmundsbury and Ipswich Diocese unless stated to the contrary. The deaneries have changed too and are listed under Deanery 2000. Part of Lothingland is now in Norfolk but is included here as it once was part of Suffolk. Lothingland is in the Norwich Diocese.

Many Victorian churches have not been included as they are not the principal church of the parish. There are blank pages at the end of the book to include your personal notes.

The parishes are listed in alphabetical order and where a cardinal point precedes the name it is treated as part of the name. As South Cove, not as Cove, (South). Some parishes are prefixed with Little or Great others as Parva or Magna as a suffix, their listing depends on common usage.
The Ordnance Survey grid references are for the parish church, the village centre is sometimes a considerable distance away. Post codes are also given where available but do not always relate precisely to the church, as churches do not normally receive mail; sometimes the code relates to a house nearby.

A few parishes I have marked thus *****, as I commend them to the reader. In my own opinion they are especially interesting historically and architecturally and are always open or accessible during the day (or were at the time of writing).

I hope the reader enjoys reading this as much as I enjoyed gathering its contents; and if in some small way I have encouraged others to visit our ecclesiastical heritage I consider my labours worthwhile.

Adrian S. Pye.
Lowestoft, Suffolk. 2008

Table of Contents   page

In addition to his own researches, the author gratefully acknowledges information gleaned from the following sources: Whites Directory for Suffolk 1845; Suffolk Churches and their treasures (1938) by H. Munro Cautley; Guides in various churches. Ipswich & St Edmundsbury Diocese for the post codes and deaneries; Ordnance Survey for map grid references.

Whilst every effort has been made to ensure accuracy, the author apologises in advance for any errors that may have been made. No liability can be accepted for any loss or damage by following directions given for reaching the churches listed, or for visiting the sites and interiors of the churches listed.

Published by ASPYE.
aspye@talktalk.net

Printed by Micropress Printers Halesworth

ISBN 978-0-9558797-0-8

AKENHAM

Dedication:	St Mary
No of Bells:	1
Deanery 1836:	Claydon
Hundred:	Bosmere & Claydon
Union house:	Barham
Deanery 2000:	Ipswich

3 miles N of Ipswich between Claydon & Westerfield: from Thurleston Lane look for Bower Farm.
O.S. grid ref TM 147488
Post Code IP1 6TQ

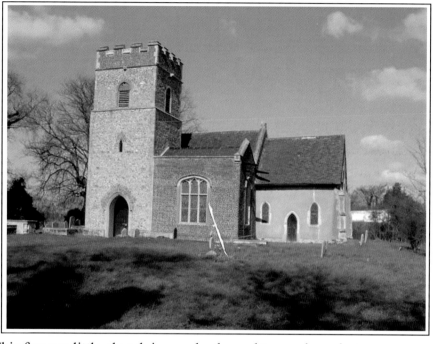

This famous little church is on a back-road to nowhere, but once you have found it be sure to go round to the north side and see the grave of little Joseph who died on his second birthday and because he hadn't been baptised was refused a burial in consecrated ground. The story was national news at the time and caused much dissent in the Church. The church itself has little else of interest and has been unused since 1972. The church dates from around the 14th c. and the south tower serves as a porch. There are still traces of the former church in the Norman slit window in the nave with pillared jambs. The south chapel is Tudor but has been dreadfully restored. The local farmer who lives in the farm at the rear of the church holds a key. Declared redundant 1976

ALDEBURGH

Dedication:	St Peter & St Paul
No of Bells:	8
Deanery 1836:	Orford
Hundred:	Plomesgate
Union house:	Wickham Market
Deanery 2000:	Saxmundham

7 m SE of Saxmundham on the mid Suffolk coast: there is a large car park west of the church on Victoria Road.

O.S. grid ref TM 463568

Post Code IP15 5BB

A feature of interest here is the south porch which extends right out to the road. By necessity there are arches in the east and west walls to allow processions to pass without having to leave the consecrated ground of the churchyard. The font is typical East Anglian type and a 15th c. piscina in the north chapel. The iron-bound parish chest is very large and the pulpit is dated 1632. There are a few interesting memorials: one to George Crabbe, the poet, another to 7 lifeboatmen who lost their lives trying to rescue sailors on a stormy December night in 1899. There is another beautiful memorial to Lady Henrietta Vernon who died in 1780 but is not buried here. Well worth an hour of your time.

ALDERTON

Dedication:	St Andrew
No of Bells:	1
Deanery 1836:	Wilford
Hundred:	Wilford
Union house:	Nacton
Deanery 2000:	Woodbridge

7 miles SE of Woodbridge between Shottisham & Bawdsey: junction of The Street & Woodbridge Road.

O.S. grid ref TM 342416

Post Code   IP12 3BT

Alderton is a peaceful little village with a church which has a dilapidated tower, which has been like this for two hundred years or more. The single remaining bell stands at the west end of the tower on a low gantry. The church itself is much restored. The chancel was completely rebuilt in 1862. The north porch and much of the north wall of the nave are of the original building. In the spandrils of the doorway are carved St. George one side and dragon the other. Septaria, a local brown stone, was used extensively in the original construction as in many other churches in the area. The arms of George III hang above the chancel arch. A simple 14th c. piscina is embedded in the south wall of the nave.

ALDRINGHAM   (cum THORPE)

Dedication:	St Andrew	
No of Bells:	1	
Deanery 1836:	Dunwich	
Hundred:	Blything	
Union house:	Bulcamp	
Deanery 2000:	Saxmundham	

1 mile S of Leiston between Leiston & Aldeburgh: look for Church Lane, off the B1353.

O.S. grid ref TM 451602

Post Code   IP16 4QT

Some distance from the village up a dusty trackway on the Thorpeness road is where you will find this charming little church. It was completely rebuilt as the painting inside the church will illustrate. It originally had a substantial square tower. Now a small bell turret with a single bell sits above the roof at the west end. Inside there is little to interest the historian but the font is 15th c. and the Holy table is of the Stuart period. In the churchyard there are a few interesting monuments, one of which is an unusual design of casket tomb with scroll decoration to Edward and Letitia Gannon who during their lifetime were notable benefactors to the poor. A lovely peaceful situation.

ASHBOCKING

Dedication:	All Saints	
No of Bells:	6	
Deanery 1836:	Bosmere	
Hundred:	Bosmere & Claydon	
Union house:	Barham	
Deanery 2000:	Woodbridge	

6 miles N of Ipswich between Helmingham & Witnesham: off the B1078, near Ashbocking Hall.

O.S. grid ref TM 169545

Post Code   IP6 9LG

Ashbocking has history dating back two thousand years with a Roman road and encampment. The church is in the grounds of the hall where the Bocking family once resided and is a 2½ mile walk from the village centre. The building is 13th c. but the square tower is Tudor. The font is Norman with a richly carved 15th c. cover. The early 14th c. iron-clad parish chest is 6 feet long with four locks. The Arms of Charles I hang on the south wall. On the same wall is some finely carved stonework surrounding a window. Curiously each side is completely different from the other, one seemingly fruit and flowers with the other vegetables possibly suggesting male and female undertones.

ASHBY

Dedication:	St Mary
No of Bells:	1
Deanery 1836:	Lothingland
Hundred:	Mutford & Lothingland
Union house:	Oulton
Deanery 2000:	Lothingland, Norwich

6 miles NE of Lowestoft between Lound & St Olaves: off Blocka Road by Ashbyhall Farm.

O.S. grid ref TM 489990
Post Code NR32 5NB

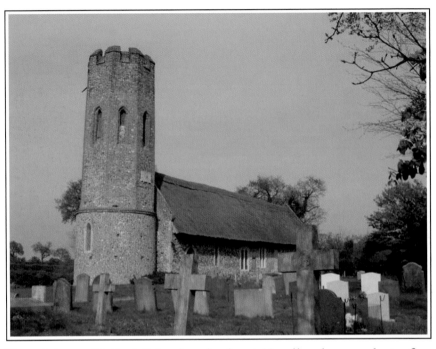

The visitor will find this church about ½ mile along a dusty farm track. The thatched roof is very fitting in this rural setting. The unusual tower has a rounded base with the upper two thirds octagonal which would suggest an almost total collapse at some time in the past. The 12th c. font has been badly mutilated and the simple 13th c. piscina is flanked by a window sill sedilia. In the graveyard almost next to the path to the south door is a memorial to James Leggett, who at the age of 16 was fatally injured by falling under the team of horses he was driving. A memorial plaque to Sarah, wife of John Sherwood, is on the south wall of the nave and a headstone to Hannah his second wife of 10 weeks, is close by.

ASHFIELD cum THORPE

Dedication:	St Mary	
No of Bells:	2	
Deanery 1836:	Claydon	
Hundred:	Thredling	
Union house:	Barham	
Deanery 2000:	Loes	

5 m W of Framlingham between Debenham & Earl Soham: in The Street, Ashfield.

O.S. grid ref TM 210626
Post Code IP14 6LX

This church was built in 1853. Nothing remains of the earlier church except some woodwork which has been utilised in the construction of an altar and prayer desk. It is an unattractive brick-built edifice, difficult to park near and even more difficult to photograph, being largely surrounded by mature trees. The earlier church stood in ruins for over 100 years and St Peter's chapel at Thorpe, which had been renovated in 1739, became the parish church and the place of worship until this, the present church was built. St Peter's then fell into decay. Nothing of real interest here I'm afraid.

(ASHFIELD cum) THORPE

Dedication:	St Peter	
No of Bells:	2	
Deanery 1836:	Claydon	
Hundred:	Thredling	
Union house:	Barham	
Deanery 2000:	Loes	

2 miles SE of Debenham
between Debenham &
Earl Soham: off the
A1120, into Thorpe Lane,
near Thorpe Hall.
O.S. grid ref TM 200622
Post Code IP14 6NE

The ivy-mantled flint and mortar ruins are a haven for wildlife and birds nest in the tranquillity of this lovely place. As mentioned on the previous page, this little round towered chapel-cum-church was the parish church of Ashby after St Mary's became ruinous in the 18th c.. St Peter's, which was recorded as ruinous in 1602, was rebuilt in 1739 by the local squire, and was used until the new church at Ashfield was completed in 1853. Burials however still took place at Ashfield St Mary's in the grounds of the ruinous church. It is situated in the lovely surroundings and garden of Thorpe Hall and access is available at all reasonable times. A few headstone memorials are still scattered around the ruins.

ATHELINGTON

Dedication:	St Peter
No of Bells:	3
Deanery 1836:	Hoxne
Hundred:	Hoxne
Union house:	Stradbroke
Deanery 2000:	Hoxne

5 miles SE of Eye
between Redlingfield &
Wilby: within the village
on a narrow country road.
Use the church car park.
O.S. grid ref TM 210708
Post Code IP21 5EH

The church was probably built in the reign of King Edward III as the corbel heads on the belfry doorway are representative of the period. Unfortunately however this quaint little church offers very little for the historian. The tower appears very slim but that is due to the lack of buttresses. The turret stairs to the belfry have a carved stone roof. The 15th c. font with traceried bowl carved from Aubingy stone is quite unusual. There is a Stuart holy table, and the carving on the benches are worth the visit. A few of them are reproductions, but the majority are of a very early date and of exceptionally fine craftsmanship. Every one worth a photograph, but alas, space forbids. Please use the church car park as the road is very narrow here.

BADINGHAM

Dedication:	St John the Baptist	
No of Bells:	5	
Deanery 1836:	Hoxne	
Hundred:	Hoxne	
Union house:	Stradbroke	
Deanery 2000:	Loes	

4 m NE of Framlingham between Peasenhall & Dennington: from the A1120, on Low Street, Badingham.
O.S. grid ref TM 305683
Post Code IP13 8JX

The church dates from Norman times, but only parts of the original construction can be seen today at the west side. Most of the building dates from the 15th c. Because it is built on a hillside near the source of the River Alde the floor rises 25 inches towards the chancel. This is not uncommon but it is quite noticeable here. The lovely octagonal font illustrates the seven sacraments. The nave has a single hammerbeam and arch-braced collar roof. Edward Rous left £3-6s-8d in 1506 for two clerestory windows to be added to admit more light onto the rood. There is, in the chancel, a substantial monument to the Cotton family which is dated 1611. Another monument to a member of the Carbonell family dated 1423 is on the opposite wall.

BADLEY

		2 miles S of Stowmarket
Dedication:	St Mary	between Stowmarket &
No of Bells:	3	Needham Market: on the
Deanery 1836:	Bosmere	B1113 turn west opposite
Hundred:	Bosmere & Claydon	Doveshill Cottages.
Union house:	Barham	O.S. grid ref TM 062559
Deanery 2000:	Bosmere	Post Code IP6 8RU

Made redundant in 1986 this is probably the most difficult church to get to in the whole county. I am surprised it wasn't abandoned many years ago. A book has been written about the village and the church and I will not detract from those who have the church's interests at heart. There is a 13th c. font and a late 12th c. door. The nave roof is of tie-beam and king-post construction. The pews are faded and bleached to a light shade of grey. The most admirable thing of interest is the west window in the tower. There is also a curious inscription in a floor slab to Dorothy Poley in the chancel. If you do visit, make sure it is open before driving the mile or so over a roadway that may cut your tyres to ribbons.

BARHAM   (and Claydon)   5 miles N of Ipswich
Dedication: St Mary & St Peter   between Claydon &
No of Bells: 4   Henley: in Church Lane,
Deanery 1836:   Claydon   off Norwich Road.
Hundred: Bosmere & Claydon
Union house: Barham   O.S. grid ref TM 136509
Deanery 2000:   Bosmere   Post Code   IP6 0PU

The entrance to the church is through the 14th c. south tower. The nave has a single hammerbeam roof with low arch-braced collar and clerestory windows. The church has little to offer the architectural student but the monuments and brasses are interesting to the historian. The family monuments represented here are Middleton, in the chapel north of the nave; and further to the north the Bacon monuments in their private chapel. On the north wall of the chancel is a fine Southwell monument dated 1640 and a brass on the floor nearby. There is also a 15th c. table monument with cusped and crocketted ogee arch and pinnacled side buttress. Since the church at Claydon was made redundant in 1977 (see page 61) St Mary's has the additional dedication of St Peter.

BARKING (with Barking Tye)

Dedication:	St Mary	
No of Bells:	now 6, before 1911, 5	
Deanery 1836:	Bosmere	
Hundred:	Bosmere & Claydon	
Union house:	Barham	
Deanery 2000:	Bosmere	

4 miles S of Stowmarket between Needham Market & Great Brickett: off the A1078 in Parson's Lane.

O.S. grid ref TM 076535
Post Code IP6 8HJ

The tower (unusually) has hexagonal buttresses. The south doorway is late 13th c. with 16th c. doors with the BVM cipher. The 14th c. roof is arch-braced with tie-beams and king posts. The font is elaborately carved with a decorative cover. There are 2 piscinas, a 13th c. example which has been restored and a cusped 14th c. example with a single sedilia beside. Hanging above this is a helmet and crest. The church still retains its charcoal braziers, serpent, bier and iron-bound parish chest which is enormous. The Royal Arms are of Charles II. In the north aisle one of the windows is a beautifully carved terra cotta reveal. In the tower arch hangs the clapper from the tenor bell, one of 5 bells which was melted down to create a new peal of 6 in 1911.

BARNBY

Dedication:	St John the Baptist
No of Bells:	1
Deanery 1836:	Lothingland
Hundred:	Mutford & Lothingland
Union house:	Oulton
Deanery 2000:	Beccles & S. Elmham

4 miles E of Beccles between Beccles & Lowestoft: on the A146, set back on a bend in the road with a layby.

O.S. grid ref TM 480899

Post Code NR34 7QN

The church is thatched and sits comfortably in its rural setting, hardly noticeable from the busy road hidden behind tall trees. Within the embattled tower, the single 15th c. bell is inscribed in Latin, "May the bell of St John resound for many years". An irregular shaped stoup is inside the blocked north door. The font is 13th c. and has a central pillar and eight detached brightly coloured, smaller ones equally spaced beneath the octagonal bowl, on the faces of which are shallowly carved arches. There are a number of wall paintings from the 15th c. and are well preserved. A very rare banner-stave locker is still maintained with its original door which is the only example in existence. The locker is roughly 80 inches high, 11 wide and 12 inches deep.

BARSHAM

Dedication:	Holy Trinity	
No of Bells:	5	
Deanery 1836:	Wangford	
Hundred:	Wangford	
Union house:	Shipmeadow	
Deanery 2000:	Beccles & S. Elmham	

2 miles W of Beccles between Beccles & Bungay: on the north side of the B1062, near The Old Rectory.

O.S. grid ref TM 396896

Post Code   NR34 8HA

The nave is thatched and the chancel is tiled. The round west tower is very slightly oval in its upper reaches and is certainly Saxon. As you enter the south door you cannot miss the signal flags up in the rafters, 'England expects every man this day to do his duty etc.'. Nelson's mother, Catherine Suckling was born here in 1725. Her father was the rector. On your right is a poor-box dated 1691 and a stoup. On the stairs to the pulpit there is part of the old altar rail dated 1636. In the Sanctuary there is the old square Norman font with crude chevron markings and next to it, the tomb of Edward Echingham 1527. He was responsible for the unique east window which you must appreciate from outside as well as inside. Keep looking, you will find more.

BATTISFORD

Dedication: St Mary
No of Bells: 1
Deanery 1836: Bosmere
Hundred: Bosmere & Claydon
Union house: Barham
Deanery 2000: Bosmere

3 miles S of Stowmarket
between Little Finborough
& Barking: in Church
Road, near The Hall.

O.S. grid ref TM 055544
Post Code IP14 2HF

Wander around the church before you enter and you will find a scratch dial on the quoins of the chancel south wall. Note the lack of buttressing and the little bell turret with its single bell sits comfortably on the roof at the west end of the nave. . The tower fell many hundreds of years ago, so many in fact the threshold in the porch is made from two of the tower gargoyles. The octagonal engaged columns of the porch doorway have slots cut in them (for some reason unknown to me). The font is 14th c. and has a traceried bowl, the holy table and rails are Stuart. The roof has arch-braced cambered tie beams with king posts and collar runners. The Royal Arms are those of Queen Anne. The serpent that once played to the singing in this church is now in Christchurch mansion, Ipswich.

BAWDSEY

Dedication:	St Mary the Virgin	
No of Bells:	1	
Deanery 1836:	Wilford	
Hundred:	Wilford	
Union house:	Nacton	
Deanery 2000:	Woodbridge	

8 miles SE of Woodbridge between Alderton & the coast: at the southern end of the B1083.

O.S. grid ref TM 346401

Post Code   IP12 3AH

Bawdsey was once a victim of a disastrous prank. On November 5th 1842 some boys decided to have a bonfire on the roof of the tower. By the following morning the top of the tower was lying on the ground with much of the nave and the chancel. Today the east side of the truncated tower reveals the original height of the nave roof and the chancel was never rebuilt. The east end of the nave now accommodates the chancel. The sanctus bell window (once inside the church) is six feet above the height of the present roof. What is left of the tower however, is 15th century. Inside there is little of interest as all historical artefacts were lost in the fire. While you are there have a look at the great sarcophagus tomb standing on a mound, west of the tower.

BAYLHAM

Dedication:	St Peter
No of Bells:	6
Deanery 1836:	Bosmere
Hundred:	Bosmere & Claydon
Union house:	Barham
Deanery 2000:	Bosmere

2½ miles S of Needham Market between Needham Market & Gt Blakenham: from the B1113, onto The Street then to Church Lane.
O.S. grid ref TM 102515
Post Code   IP6 8JS

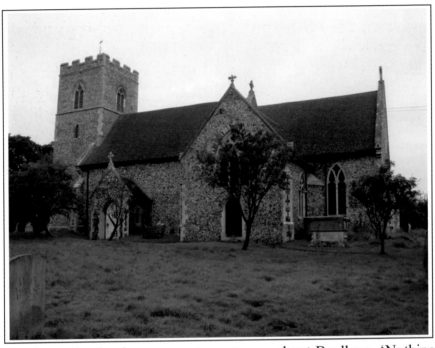

H. Munro Cautley has one sentence to say about Baylham. 'Nothing but a Norman door N. of nave, with square lintel and chequered tympanum above and a traditional font'. Unfortunately I cannot add much, except to say I thought the setting delightful. The tower is generally unchanged with its neat battlements. The Victorian restoration altered the church drastically and added north and south transepts which impair the outward appearance of the church. There is a 16th c. memorial to John Acton and family mounted on the north wall of the chancel. It depicts John, his wife, their three daughters and two sons kneeling at a prayer desk. The church was locked, which was most inconvenient, and so I do not know what other delights may be found inside.

BECCLES

		9 miles W of Lowestoft
Dedication:	St Michael	between Lowestoft &
No of Bells:	10 in tower, 1 in church	Bungay:
Deanery 1836:	Wangford	unmissable, in the town
Hundred:	Wangford	centre.
Union house:	Shipmeadow	O.S. grid ref TM 421904
Deanery 2000:	Beccles & S. Elmham	Post Code NR34 9HE

Beccles is the most difficult of all churches to photograph. Above is shown the west window, the undercroft community centre, below it. The headstones that were removed when this was built are lying face up in the nave, just inside the porch. Beccles church tower is no longer part of the church as it was sold to Beccles Borough Council for one penny in 1971. The 15th c. south porch, with every conceivable kind of decoration, is the feature most admired, it is built entirely of stone and 34 feet high including the chamber with a squint to the altar. Inside there is much to admire. The north porch is of the same date but of flint and stone. Badly damaged by fire in 1586 it has little to offer of its early history, except monuments to many famous Becclesians of the past. Take a look left of the altar.

19

BEDFIELD

Dedication:	St Nicholas
No of Bells:	6
Deanery 1836:	Hoxne
Hundred:	Hoxne
Union house:	Stradbroke
Deanery 2000:	Hoxne

4 miles NW of Framlingham between Monk Soham & Tannington: in Church Lane.

O.S. grid ref TM 227663

Post Code IP13 7JJ

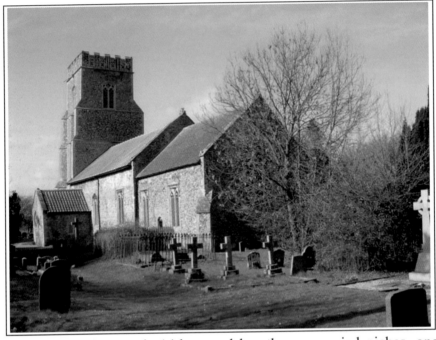

The embattled tower is 14th c. and has three canopied niches, one either side of the west window and one above it. The south porch is 14th c. and has a kingpost roof. The north door is 12th c. and has chevron patterns on the engaged shaft. An extension has been added to the nave and this can be clearly defined from the difference in the building methods used. The font is 14th c. with traceried panels to the octagonal bowl. The font cover is a splendid 66 inches high and was made in the 17th c., the lower part being octagonal and panelled, a pillar at each corner, above ogee braces converging on a finial. Each brace has arabesque decoration and terminates in a grotesque. Half the old roodscreen remains and the rood stairs are still open.

BEDINGFIELD

Dedication: St Mary
No of Bells: 1
Deanery 1836: Hoxne
Hundred: Hoxne
Union house: Stradbroke
Deanery 2000: Hartismere

4 miles SE of Eye
between Southolt &
Rishangles: on the four-
cross ways.

O.S. grid ref TM 179688
Post Code IP23 7QD

This fine 14th c. church is built of flint and stone but has been cement-rendered to the detriment of its appearance, with rusty stains running down the wall. The south porch roof is 15th c. and has pierced and traceried spandrils to the roof which although mutilated are still quite interesting. Inside, the nave has a double hammerbeam roof simple in its detail. Some of the seats are dated 1612 but some of the benches are perhaps 200 years earlier and, although nicely carved, have been badly mutilated. The holy table is early 17th c. and has an unusual leg configuration with three at each end and two more central on a longitudinal rail. The parish chest is large and heavily iron-bound. The font bowl is 15th c. sitting on an earlier base.

BELSTEAD		1½ miles E of Copdock
Dedication:	St Mary	between Wherstead &
No of Bells:	1	Copdock: best approached
Deanery 1836:	Samford	from the old A12, London
Hundred:	Samford	Road.
Union house:	Tattingstone	O.S. grid ref TM 126411
Deanery 2000:	Samford	Post Code IP8 3JT

The 14th c. south tower with 15th c. battlements, serves as a porch. Outside there are three scratch dials. Inside, the font is a traditional East Anglian type. You will also find a few moulded bench ends of 16th c. date. The pulpit is Stuart as is the holy table which is dated 1621 underneath. The lower part of the rood screen has painted figures on the panels which are mostly recognisable. They include St Sitha, St Ursula, St Margaret of Antioch, St Mary Magdalene, St Lawrence, St Stephen, St Edmund and St Sebastian. In the nave there are three 18 inches high figures on a brass to John Goldingham, who died in 1518, and his two wives. The arms are those of George III. The church is in a peaceful location only a short distance from Ipswich.

BELTON
Dedication: All Saints
No of Bells: 1
Deanery 1836: Lothingland
Hundred: Mutford & Lothingland
Union house: Oulton
Deanery 2000: Lothingland, Norwich

3 miles W of Gorleston
between Gorleston & River
Waveney: situated in
Church Lane, Bradwell.

O.S. grid ref TG 485029

Post Code   NR31 9JJ

The tower, although very early, is refaced and none of the original work can be seen from the outside. The body of the church is 14th c. A scratch-dial can be found on the nave buttress. The font is early 12th c. but is broken. A later 14th c. font is the one in use. In the sanctuary there is a 14th c. recessed tomb with a cusped ogee arch. The wall paintings are noteworthy but are faded. They are of St James the Great and St Christopher (who appears in almost every church that has wall paintings on display) and 'The three quick and the three dead'. John Ives, who wrote the history of Yarmouth is buried here.

BENACRE

Dedication:	St Michael	
No of Bells:	1	
Deanery 1836:	Dunwich	
Hundred:	Blything	
Union house:	Bulcamp	
Deanery 2000:	Halesworth	

4 miles S of Lowestoft between Henstead and the coast: turn east off the A12 at Benacre crossroads 1 m south of Kessingland.
O.S. grid ref TM 511844
Post Code NR34 7LL

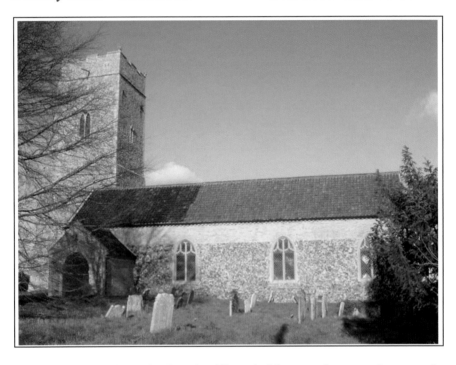

Benacre church is locked and will probably remain so as long as the key is held at nearby Benacre Hall. I have made repeated representations for entry but have had no success so far. Redundant since 1978 and owned by the estate, who tell me there is nothing of interest inside, this pleasant little church will continue to deteriorate. The south porch is built onto the south aisle which runs the complete length of the nave and chancel. It was burned down 200 years ago and restored and contains little of any real interest except Gooch monuments. The font has a typical 13th c. bowl. The Royal Arms are of George II. There is a story of Sir William Gooch's good manners as Governor of Virginia when he returned a salute from a slave.

BENHALL

		1 mile SE of Saxmundham
Dedication:	St Mary	between Saxmundham &
No of Bells:	6	Stratford St Andrew: at the
Deanery 1836:	Orford	southern end of Deadman's
Hundred:	Plomesgate	Lane.
Union house:	Wickham Market	O.S. grid ref TM 372619
Deanery 2000:	Saxmundham	Post Code IP17 1JL

Benhall is on the opposite side of the new A12 bypass to the village. It is signed from the road and is easily found. Once there you will find a tranquil place to open your picnic basket and enjoy the peace away from the traffic. While you are there take a look at the Norman south doorway. It is quite a large church for a relatively small parish, but it is filled with 19th c. box-pews. The Arms of George III hang on the wall and the pulpit is of Stuart origins. The font is more like a birdbath. For the brass enthusiast there are some to Edward Duke (1598), Dorothy his wife and their 16 children, and to Ambrose Duke (1610) and his wife Elizabeth. The only claim to fame is that Geoffrey Chaucer's daughter married the lord of the manor.

BENTLEY

Dedication:	St Mary	
No of Bells:	1	
Deanery 1836:	Samford	
Hundred:	Samford	
Union house:	Tattingstone	
Deanery 2000:	Samford	

6 miles SW of Ipswich between Capel St Mary & Tattingstone: in Church Road, Bentley.

O.S. grid ref TM 118381
Post Code IP9 2DA

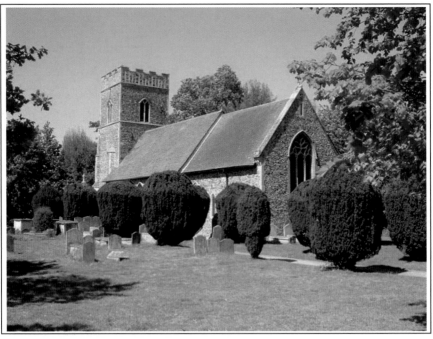

The church has been heavily restored over many years and very little of the original Norman workmanship remains today. The tower is 15th c.. There is a remade Norman doorway with one original stone worked into it and a Norman slit window in the north wall of the sanctuary. A 15th c. font has replaced the 13th c. original bowl but the purbeck base remains. Another 13th c. purbeck bowl has found its way into the north aisle but it doesn't match the base, perhaps it was brought in as a replacement and found unsuitable. There are two 15th c. benches with carved ends and buttressed arm rests and grotesques. The nave roof is a hammerbeam construction. Thankfully the trees that used to overwhelm the churchyard have been reduced to open the church to daylight and fresh air.

BLAXHALL

Dedication:	St Peter	
No of Bells:	6	
Deanery 1836:	Orford	
Hundred:	Plomesgate	
Union house:	Wickham Market	
Deanery 2000:	Saxmundham	

4 miles S of Saxmundham between Campsey Ashe & Snape: ¾ of a mile west of the village in Church Road.

O.S. grid ref TM 356569
Post Code IP12 2DP

Sheep were grazing in the churchyard, keeping the grass nicely trimmed. There are some signs of a much earlier church as there is a piece of 12th c. carved stone built into the west wall of the nave. This 500-year-old church is showing its age. The nave has an early 16th c. hammerbeam and arch-braced collar roof with carved spandrils. The font seems relatively modern; there was a lovely 13th c. font here a few years ago. The old rood stairs are still in the wall. The peace memorial is the work of local artist Ellen Mary Rope who lies in the churchyard. The east window is by another member of the Rope family, Dorothy. Michael Rope, brother of the artist, perished in the ill-fated R 101 airship at Beauvais in 1930. Marjorie Wilson, the literary genius, is yet another famous name from this remote parish.

BLUNDESTON

Dedication: St Mary
No of Bells: 2
Deanery 1836: Lothingland
Hundred: Mutford & Lothingland
Union house: Oulton
Deanery 2000: Lothingland, Norwich

4 miles NW of Lowestoft
between Somerleyton &
Corton:
off the B1074 in Church
Road.
O.S. grid ref TM 513972
Post Code NR32 5AJ

Blundeston is better known for David Copperfield than for anything else. Yet the church has attributes that generally go unnoticed. The tower is Norman and is the smallest in diameter anywhere, being only 8' 9" inside. The nave was enlarged to 29' many years ago giving it a strange lopsided appearance. There is still evidence of the Norman church here and there: in the south wall, for example, you will find the jambs of the old Norman door. In all probability the north wall still sits on Norman foundations. Inside the door is a stoup with a carved head below it. The Royal Arms are those of Charles II, 1673, but have been altered at some time. Outside near the chancel door is the font from Flixton St. Andrew which was left to fall down after it lost its roof in a hurricane in 1703.

BLYFORD

Dedication:	All Saints
No of Bells:	1
Deanery 1836:	Dunwich
Hundred:	Blything
Union house:	Bulcamp
Deanery 2000:	Halesworth

2½ miles E of Halesworth
between Holton &
Blythburgh:
on the B1123 opposite the
Queen's Head PH.
O.S. grid ref TM 424767
Post Code IP19 9JY

This neat little church stands very close to the road but is rarely visited. Opposite, is a public house which is reputed to be haunted, and has thousands of visitors. Both north and south doors are 12th c. Norman. The north being the most unusual inasmuch as it has two engaged shafts to each jamb both decorated individually. Carved cushion caps support an arch of three orders, two with chevron moulding. The font is 13th c. as is the piscina which is next to a dropped sill sedilia. The holy table is a fine Elizabethan example and has carved cushion legs. The banner stave locker is in use as a cupboard but the original door is lost. In 1494 Jane Taillour (Taylor) bequeathed wax to make candles for the 12 lights that lit the rood. Bishop Pollock of Norwich and Canon Moore are buried here

BLYTHBURGH *****

Dedication:	Holy Trinity	
No of Bells:	6	
Deanery 1836:	Dunwich	
Hundred:	Blything	
Union house:	Bulcamp	
Deanery 2000:	Halesworth	

4 miles W of Southwold between Halesworth & Southwold: just off the A12 in Church Road.

O.S. grid ref TM 450753
Post Code   IP19 9LP

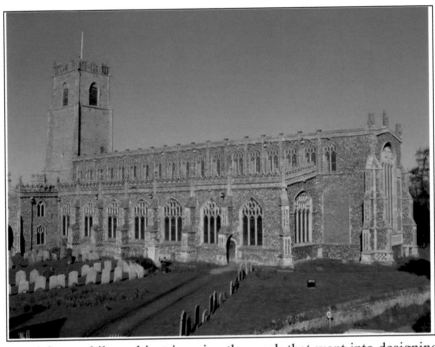

Stand for a while and just imagine the work that went into designing and building this grand church. Look at the symmetry and the graceful lines. Notice the two buttresses on the north & south, 'flying' over doorways. Notice the door half-way up the south face of the tower. There is so much to look at. Spend a couple of hours and use your eyes. The musket and pistol ball holes in the roof timbers of the nave are well documented. The battered font is dated at 1449. The bench-end carvings are of the seven deadly sins, and seasons of the year. The 'Jack o' the clock' replaced the hour glass. The holy table and pulpit is Stuart. The 15th c. purbeck tomb of Sir John Hopton, built into the wall, also served as an Easter sepulchre. What is mentioned here is only the tip of the iceberg.

BOULGE

Dedication: St Michael & All Angels
No of Bells: 1
Deanery 1836: Wilford
Hundred: Wilford
Union house: Nacton
Deanery 2000: Woodbridge

2 miles NW of
Woodbridge between
Melton & Debach:
turn south off Scott's Lane.

O.S. grid ref TM 254528
Post Code   IP13 6BS

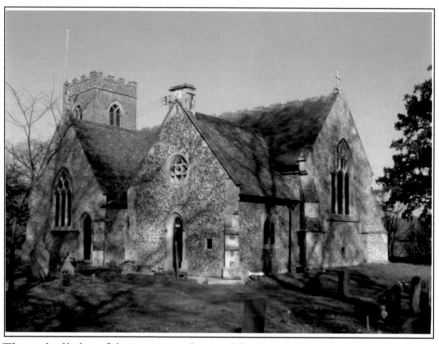

There is little of interest to the architectural historian in this over-restored church. The purbeck font is 13th c. and the base and circular shaft are decorated. A wooden carved set of William III Arms hang on the wall. What is of interest however, especially to the literary historian, is the fact that in this churchyard lies Edward FitzGerald. He became a household name in his day by translating the work of the Persian poet Omar Khayyam. Although born in Bredfield, a mile or two away, he lived at Boulge Hall, and often walked the lanes of the county he loved. He was, through his paternal side, related to Oliver Cromwell and his family were very well-to-do. It was at nearby Wherstead Lodge that he first encountered the mysteries of the East through an Anglo-Indian major who also lived there.

BOYTON

Dedication:	St Andrew	
No of Bells:	1	
Deanery 1836:	Wilford	
Hundred:	Wilford	
Union house:	Nacton	
Deanery 2000:	Woodbridge	

8 miles E of Woodbridge between Hollesley & Butley: turn nth off main street through the village. Church near the almshouses.
O.S. grid ref TM 372471
Post Code   IP12 3LQ

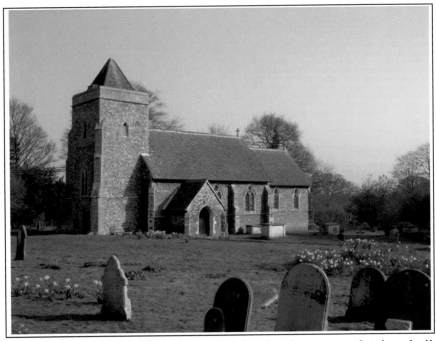

Only the tower is original, the church having been completely rebuilt except the original north-west corner which is attached to the tower. The modern north transept also has 12th c. stonework built into the fabric. The tower is capped with a tiled pyramidal roof. The churchyard, although relatively large for such a small church, has very few memorial stones. Nearby stand the almshouses which were founded in the 17th c. for 12 poor men and 12 poor women on condition they attended church regularly. On the walls of the courtyard are the names of the trustees which include many recognisable names from the 1800s, including the Earl of Stradbroke, Viscount Hereford, Charles Tyrell, Henry Bence, John Revett, Charles Blois, Edward Gooch and others.

BRADWELL

Dedication: St Nicholas
No of Bells: 3
Deanery 1836: Lothingland
Hundred: Mutford & Lothingland
Union house: Oulton
Deanery 2000: Lothingland, Norwich

1 miles W of Gorleston between Gorleston & Burgh Castle: off Green Lane, in Church Walk.

O.S. grid ref TG 502038
Post Code NR31 8QW

Bradwell is one of the many heavily restored churches that offer little to the historian. However there are a few items of interest for the visitor to see. The structure of the church is 14th c. as is the traditional East Anglian font which is in remarkably good condition. Around the octagonal bowl there are carvings of winged angels and other creatures and lions guarding the base. There is a monument to William Vesey who is flanked by his two wives; behind each of them is a child. On a frieze below is a reclining man flanked by what appears to be four more children. Although the woodwork in the church is of good quality it is comparatively modern. The rood loft stairs are still open. There are two piscinas, one 14th c. the other, a cusped Victorian reproduction with matching sedilia.

BRAMFIELD

Dedication:	St Andrew	
No of Bells:	5	
Deanery 1836:	Dunwich	
Hundred:	Blything	
Union house:	Bulcamp	
Deanery 2000:	Halesworth	

3 miles S of Halesworth between Halesworth & Darsham: on the A144 just off The Street, on Walpole Road, behind Queen's Head. O.S. grid ref TM 399737 Post Code IP19 9HT

Bramfield church is unique in that its round tower is detached by 20 feet. Built in the early 13th c. it has walls 3 feet thick, and contains 5 bells which would suggest it was built as a bell tower. The church is thatched and rendered and has been painted cream. Inside the church you will find a fine monument to Arthur Coke and Elizabeth his wife (1629 and 1627 respectively). The 14th c. piscinas have been sympathetically restored. The screen is very impressive with an exceptionally high standard of carving. It is completely original with the exception of the panels, some of which have been restored. Wall paintings which appear in a recess at the north of the nave are also worth examination. There are angels painted on the plasterwork holding chalices and scrolls with Latin proclamations.

BRAMFORD

Dedication:	St Mary	
No of Bells:	6	
Deanery 1836:	Bosmere	
Hundred:	Bosmere & Claydon	
Union house:	Barham	
Deanery 2000:	Bosmere	

3 miles NW of Ipswich
between Sproughton &
Little Blakenham:
via B1067 into The Street
to Church Green.
O.S. grid ref TM 127463
Post Code IP8 4AT

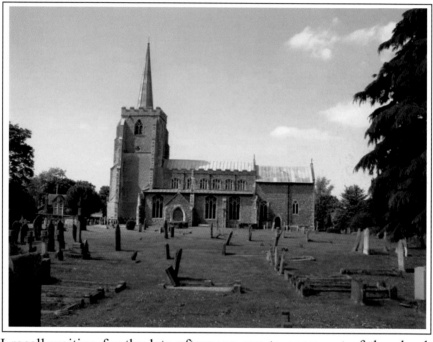

I recall waiting for the late afternoon sun to come out of the clouds and discovered what a peaceful place this is. The main entrance is by the elaborate 15th c. north porch with canopied niches to the buttresses which extend through the parapet as pinnacles. The tower has a zinc-covered spire which is a little out of proportion. Inside, the 15th c. font has a tall panelled and domed 16th c. cover. There are a number of grotesque figures inside and out for you to find. Dowsing, in 1644, destroyed 841 'superstitious pictures', but there is still much to see today: the 15th c. single hammerbeam roof, the Elizabethan pulpit, the famous 14th c. stone screen of three arches, and more. This church is only just short of scoring my 5-star commendation.

BRAMPTON

Dedication:	St Peter	7 miles S of Beccles between Beccles & Blythburgh: on the A145 near the B1124 turn-off.
No of Bells:	5	
Deanery 1836:	Dunwich	
Hundred:	Blything	
Union house:	Bulcamp	O.S. grid ref TM 435815
Deanery 2000:	Beccles & S. Elmham	Post Code NR34 8DS

Brampton church stands on the brow of a hillside surrounded by lime trees. Behind it is Brampton Hall. The tower is 15th c. with pinnacles at each corner. The church is long and narrow and barely differentiates between nave and chancel. There are scratch dials on both jambs of the chancel door. Passing through the 600-year-old door we find only a few items of interest. The casual observer may not notice the absence of a chancel arch, the screen deceiving the eye perhaps. The late 15th c. font has plain panels and an octagonal shaft which is buttressed. The piscina is a simple affair and still has its stone credence shelf. The holy table is dated to the Stuart period and the Royal Arms are those of George III and dated 1797. There is a memorial to Robert Leman, one-time Lord Mayor of London.

BRANDESTON

Dedication:	All Saints	
No of Bells:	6	
Deanery 1836:	Loes	
Hundred:	Loes	
Union house:	Wickham Market	
Deanery 2000:	Loes	

3 miles SW of
Framlingham between
Cretingham & Kettleburgh:
on the Cretingham Road
near Brandeston Hall.
O.S. grid ref TM 247603
Post Code IP13 7AH

A church and churchyard that are well loved and maintained. I was most impressed by the guide book which is very comprehensive. The west door is contemporary with the tower and dates from about 1370. The door itself is decorated in the same manner as the west window. There are 3 scratch dials on buttresses of the nave and chancel. Inside, we see the rood-loft stairs in their original condition and a doorway at the top. Bench ends are interesting being traceried and with animal carvings. The communion rails are unusual in that they are three-sided in the original Laudian manner. The church retains its parish chest, a large but plain object. The typical purbeck font is the oldest thing you will see in the church, being 13th c.. The 17th c. Stuart pulpit is heavily restored.

BRANTHAM

Dedication:	St Michael	
No of Bells:	1	
Deanery 1836:	Samford	
Hundred:	Samford	
Union house:	Tattingstone	
Deanery 2000:	Samford	

8 miles SW of Ipswich between East Bergholt & Stutton:
just off the A137 in Church Lane.
O.S. grid ref TM 111341
Post Code CO11 1PZ

The moment you approach Brantham church you are struck by the lychgate with its shingled roof and carved roses. The church itself is 14th c. but has been much restored and added to, giving it an especial charm. Inside the pulpit has richly carved panels depicting the tree from which the crown of thorns was cut. There are two 14th c. piscinas, one with a detached corner pillar. Some of the glass in the south-east nave window is 15th c. with figures in the tracery lights of a bishop and a figure holding an arrow. The carving at the left lower extreme of the chancel arch also carries an angelic St George slaying a dragon. The church has an original John Constable painting, painted in his early years and presented to the church as an altarpiece in 1804.

BREDFIELD

Dedication: St Andrew
No of Bells: 6
Deanery 1836: Wilford
Hundred: Wilford
Union house: Nacton
Deanery 2000: Woodbridge

3 miles N of Woodbridge
between Wickham Market
& Woodbridge: west off
the A12, situated in The
Street.
O.S. grid ref TM 268530
Post Code IP13 6AX

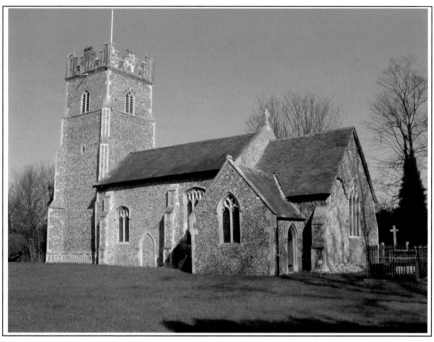

Edward Fitzgerald the poet was born here and is buried a mile or so away at Boulge (see page 31). The square tower has a crenulated parapet in Tudor brickwork which looks slightly out of place. Inside one must look up to see what the church has to offer, a fine hammerbeam and arch-braced collar roof. Strangely, the two furthest bays are decorated as a canopy of honour to the rood; normally it is only one bay that is used for this purpose. Above the upper opening of the rood stairs, the lower opening of which has been blocked off, the keen eye will just make out that at one time it was lavishly painted, but now only a head can be distinguished. The south door is blocked but the stoup remains to the east just inside the doorway. The pulpit is of the Stuart period.

BRIGHTWELL

Dedication:	St John the Baptist	5 miles E of Ipswich
No of Bells:	1	between Newbourne &
Deanery 1836:	Carlford	Martlesham Heath:
Hundred:	Carlford	east off the A12, signposted
Union house:	Nacton	Brightwell. (on a hill)
Deanery 2000:	Colneys	O.S. grid ref TM 249435
		Post Code IP10 0BE

The road by which you approach the 600-year-old church is very much a hollow way, and the path is quite steep. In the spring there are bluebells everywhere. The brick tower was built by benefactor Thomas Essington in 1656. It has corner pinnacles which are repeated as obelisks at each corner of the church and on the east gable. Inside the south porch the door has the original sanctuary ring. The font is 14th c. with a traceried bowl and the shaft is vertically moulded. There are two monuments, one to Thomas Essington who was 5, and another to Anna, a 'gracious' 17-year-old. Both bearing sad inscriptions. Also remembered here is Arthur Barnardiston, who was one-time lord of the manor. Items of Barnardiston family armour are here, consisting of crested helmets, gauntlets, spurs and a sword.

BROMESWELL

Dedication:	St Edmund
No of Bells:	2
Deanery 1836:	Wilford
Hundred:	Wilford
Union house:	Nacton
Deanery 2000:	Woodbridge

2 miles NE of Woodbridge between Rendlesham & Melton: north off the A1152 (Orford Road) in School Lane.
O.S. grid ref TM 302506
Post Code IP12 2PJ

Inside the porch the Norman doorway is quite impressive with its chevron carving. and a scratch dial on the right jamb, indicating that the porch is a more recent addition. The font is a traditional 15th c type. The single hammerbeam and arch-braced collar roof of the nave is quite unusual and 1960's fibreglass angels look down on the congregation. On the west wall the sanctus bell window can still be seen. There are a few poor quality 15th c. poppy-head bench ends. The pulpit is of the Stuart period as is the holy table and altar rails. The former has an extremely slender support post. The main feature of the church is the famous Mechlin bell of 1530, but it is in the belfry and unlikely that it can be seen without special arrangement.

BRUISYARD

Dedication:	St Peter
No of Bells:	1
Deanery 1836:	Orford
Hundred:	Plomesgate
Union house:	Wickham Market
Deanery 2000:	Loes

4 miles NE of Framlingham between Badingham & Rendham: on a narrow country lane, on Church Road.

O.S. grid ref TM 325662

Post Code IP17 2EG

This church sits easily in a very peaceful setting and a reasonably kept graveyard. The tower is of rubble construction, plain and round, being wider at the base and tapering at the height of the eaves giving it a kind of bottle-like appearance. There is no parapet. Some authorities date the tower at 14th c. but others have it 300 years earlier. The north door into the nave is Norman, but the remainder of the church is 15th c.. The chapel is 100 years later. The font is traditional 15th c.. The nave roof has arch braces to the ridge and an unusually high collar. The holy table and rails are Stuart in date. The effigies of the wives of Michael Hare (1611) are quite impressive although his likeness has disappeared. The arms are Hanoverian and very crudely carved.

BRUNDISH

Dedication:	St Lawrence
No of Bells:	3
Deanery 1836:	Hoxne
Hundred:	Hoxne
Union house:	Stradbroke
Deanery 2000:	Hoxne

5 miles N of Framlingham between Dennington & Wilby:
to the east, just off the B1118.
O.S. grid ref TM 271695
Post Code IP13 8AY

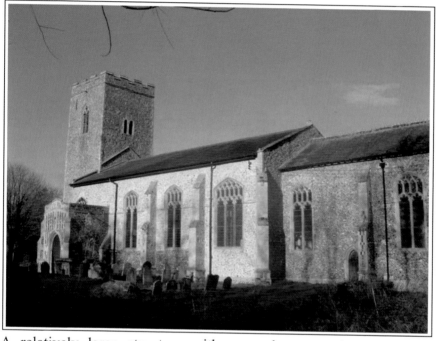

A relatively large structure with a porch to match. The square western tower is 12th c.. The slope of the nave roof has been lessened in the past but remains quite lofty. The porch is of stone with flint flushwork and has a pillar-stoup inside. The ironwork on the south and tower doors is 14th c.. The font is a 14th c. octagonal type. There is an old misericorde, and the back and sounding board to the Stuart pulpit are hanging over the north door. The piscina is a nice 14th c. example. Some of the benches are 15th c. and of quite simple design. There is quite a considerable amount of good 15th c. glass in the window tracery. The Arms are of George III and are dated 1765. The earliest of all church brasses is here dated 1360 and depicts Sir Edmund de Burnedish.

BUNGAY

Dedication:	Holy Trinity	
No of Bells:	1	
Deanery 1836:	Wangford	
Hundred:	Wangford	
Union house:	Shipmeadow	
Deanery 2000:	Beccles & S. Elmham	

6 miles W of Beccles between Beccles & Harleston: from town centre follow one-way into Trinity Street.

O.S. grid ref TM 338897

Post Code NR35 1EY

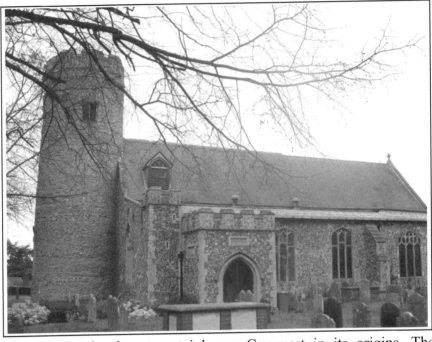

Holy Trinity is almost certainly pre-Conquest in its origins. The tower is certainly Saxon, although the octagonal parapet was added in the first year of the 15th century and has armorial shields on each facet. The north wall of the nave has a very early slit window. The north porch has been rebuilt as a vestry, and the south porch is very late in date. There is a scratch dial on the south east corner of the south aisle. The north-east buttress has an archway built into it because the building is so close to the boundary. Inside there is a Stuart holy table and altar rails; the pulpit was made for 5 shillings in 1558. Originally the churchyard had two other churches but their origins have been long forgotten. Just across the road is St Mary's and the ruins of the convent of 'God and the Holy Cross'. (see over)

44

BUNGAY

Dedication:	St Mary	
No of Bells:	8	
Deanery 1836:	Wangford	
Hundred:	Wangford	
Union house:	Shipmeadow	
Deanery 2000:	Beccles & S. Elmham	

6 miles W of Beccles between Beccles & Harleston: between St Mary's Street and Trinity Street. Easily seen.
O.S. grid ref TM 336897
Post Code NR35 1AX

In the churchyard stand the remains of a much older building, a 13th c. priory. The church was attached to the convent of 'God and the Holy Cross' founded in 1160 by Roger de Granville and Gundreda his wife. The tower is 15th c. with fine pinnacles at each corner. The original church was gutted by fire in the 17th c. but was rebuilt and the event is recorded, carved into a beam in the belfry. Much restoration was carried out by the Victorians and St Mary's is no exception. Work began in the 1860's and continued to 1877. The exterior of the church is highly decorated with tracery and flushwork Inside there is an unusual dole cupboard carved with a Q and a rat, suggesting the word 'curate'. The church was made redundant in 1977 but is always open.

BURGH

Dedication:	St Botolph
No of Bells:	6
Deanery 1836:	Carlford
Hundred:	Carlford
Union house:	Nacton
Deanery 2000:	Woodbridge

4 miles NW of
Woodbridge between
Grundisburgh & Hasketon:
on the B1079 / Drab's Lane
junction.
O.S. grid ref TM 223522
Post Code IP13 6QB

Pronounced Berg not Borough as in the north of the county. Unsighted coming from the Clopton direction, the church is north of the parish it serves. This church sits on the top of a steep bank of a Roman encampment overlooking the valley below. Only 400 yards away is Clopton church in a similar situation. Uncommonly the tower is south of the nave and serves as a porch for the south doorway. The south door has a 13th c. ring on a large boss and as you enter the church the modern wall painting in a niche is very attractive. The carved font bowl is octagonal with matching pillar and base. The pulpit is of the Stuart period and there is also an iron-bound parish chest about 4 feet long. The roofs in the nave and chancel are of an unusual arch and hammerbeam construction.

BUCKLESHAM

Dedication:	St Mary
No of Bells:	1
Deanery 1836:	Colneis
Hundred:	Colneis
Union house:	Nacton
Deanery 2000:	Colneys

6 miles SSE of Ipswich
between Ipswich & Kirton:
at the A12/A45 interchange
follow sign 'Bucklesham'
to Church Road.
O.S. grid ref TM 244420
Post Code IP10 0DY

This church was built in 1878 and only a very small part remains of the former building. The original church was a small and ancient structure and was re-pewed in 1842 but just 35 years later was completely demolished and this 'modern' Victorian church built. It was designed by William Smith and financed by the 'Incorporated Church Building Society'. One of the original doors was saved and incorporated as the north door of the nave and the stoup set into the wall beside it. The single bellcote turret is a wooden structure with a shingled broached spire. The font, which has an octagonal bowl and square base, both with carved figures, is from the original church but all else inside is of a date contemporary with the construction of the building.

BURGH CASTLE

Dedication:	Sts Peter & Paul
No of Bells:	3
Deanery 1836:	Lothingland
Hundred:	Mutford & Lothingland
Union house:	Oulton
Deanery 2000:	Lothingland, Norwich

3 miles W of Gt. Yarmouth between Great Yarmouth & Belton: from the A143 turn north then to Church Road; near the Roman Fort. O.S. grid ref TG 476049 Post Code NR31 9QG

Rough and ready would be the way to describe this little church, which is often ignored by visitors to the nearby Roman fort of Burgh Castle after which the parish is named. The tower especially is built from Roman building materials, bricks, tiles and flint. The castle has been robbed for all kinds of uses including roads, driveways and cottages. Inside the church the windows are modern but worth further investigation. One is to Herbert Laws, killed on Martinique when a volcano erupted. Another is to St Fursey, an obscure saint and evangelist to the castle. King Alfred and Queen Victoria are also represented in glass. The font is the typical octagonal variety with figures around. Some of the wood carving is well executed but there is nothing of exceptional note.

BURSTALL

		5 miles W of Ipswich
Dedication:	St Mary	between Sproughton &
No of Bells:	3	Hintlesham: turn off the
Deanery 1836:	Samford	A1071, on Church Hill.
Hundred:	Samford	
Union house:	Tattingstone	O.S. grid ref TM 097445
Deanery 2000:	Samford	Post Code IP8 3DP

The attractive half timbered porch is 15th c. and some preservation work has been carried out. The tower is a hundred years older and has quatrefoil windows north, west and south and an east sanctus bell window, in the nave. The embattled brickwork on the top is later and adds a neat finish. The outward appearance is neat with rendered walls and tiled roof, and the grounds are well maintained. The hammerbeam roof of the nave has arch-braced collars. Some of the 15th c. rood screen panels remain. The font is plain but is unusually buttressed on shaft and bowl. The north aisle is 14th c. and is quite exceptional and unusual. The main feature is the 14th c. nave arcade. The mouldings and carvings are all original and quite outstanding.

BUTLEY

Dedication:	St John the Baptist	
No of Bells:	1	
Deanery 1836:	Loes	
Hundred:	Loes	
Union house:	Wickham Market	
Deanery 2000:	Woodbridge	

5 miles E of Woodbridge between Chillesford & Boyton: from B1084 (Woodbridge Rd), turn south towards the Priory. O.S. grid ref TM 379501 Post Code IP12 3NT

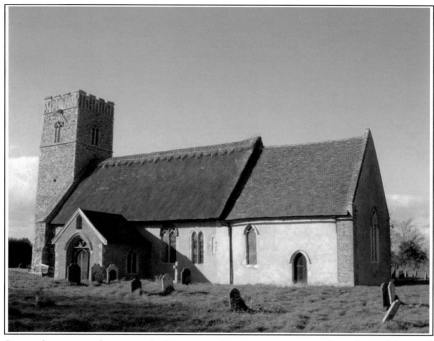

Over the attractive porch doorway is an uncommon hoodmould. Both north and south doors of this little church are 12th c., the south being the more elaborate with an unusual arch mould. There is a scratch dial on the south chancel wall. The tower is without buttresses and has a sanctus bell window. The font is an octagonal traditional type with emblems of the Trinity and Passion accompanied by the usual lions and shields. The rood screen is a simple affair dating from the 15th c.. Butley Priory, which once stood in 20 acres of this quiet English countryside, is close by and the Abbey gatehouse, which has been a private home for 250 years or more, is worth viewing. The flint flushwork is of exceptional quality and superior to that in any church hereabouts.

BUXLOW

Dedication:	St Peter
No of Bells:	2 in 1553
Deanery 1836:	Dunwich
Hundred:	Blything
Union house:	Blything
Deanery 2000:	Saxmundham

2½ miles W of Leiston
between Saxmundham &
Leiston: from the B1119
turn north to Knodishall
Green, 600 yds on the right.
O.S. grid ref TM 413631
Post Code nr IP17 1TH

Buxlow or Buxlee church was demolished in or around 1622 and has since 1722 been part of the parish of Knodishall known as Knodishall Green. The church was very possibly of Saxon origin and originally had a round tower. It was partially dismantled and left ruinous, the remains of which are to be seen as a landscape feature in the back garden of a cottage. Not more than five hundred yards to the north west is Buxlow Manor (once Knodishall Hall) which is worth a visit. The present owner is Guy de Moubray and he will be happy to show you around his home by appointment. In a niche in the central west Gables is a unique carving of a 'Suffolk angel', a ram with wings held in the arms of a saint, possibly rescued from the church when it fell into disrepair.

51

CAMPSEY ASHE

Dedication:	St John the Baptist	
No of Bells:	4	
Deanery 1836:	Loes	
Hundred:	Loes	
Union house:	Wickham Market	
Deanery 2000:	Loes	

5 miles NE of Woodbridge between Wickham Market & Tunstall: from the A12 east onto B1078 (just past Wickham Market station). O.S. grid ref TM 329559 Post Code IP13 0PU

The tower is 14th c. and the internal structure is exposed. A small spirelet sits above the 76 feet tall tower with a weathervane on top. Unfortunately the church was almost completely rebuilt in the 18th c. and very little remains of the original structure and contents, with the obvious exception of the 14th c. font which is octagonal and simply decorated with stylised floral design. There are a few ledger slabs and poppy-head bench ends and the piscina is also original. For some, the interest lies in the wall memorial to Viscount Ullswater who died as recently as 1949. A road in the parish bears the name Ullswater Road. For the architectural student the interest lies at Ashe Abbey, a mile or so south of the church. On the north side a priests bell hangs on a small gantry above the vestry.

CAPEL ST MARY

Dedication:	St Mary	
No of Bells:	5	
Deanery 1836:	Samford	
Hundred:	Samford	
Union house:	Tattingstone	
Deanery 2000:	Samford	

6 miles SW of Ipswich
between   Copdock & East
Bergholt: turn off the A12
at Capel, into The Street
and follow for 1 mile.
O.S. grid ref TM 085382
Post Code   IP9 2EL

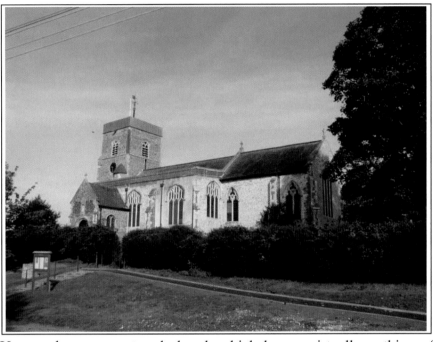

Yet another over-restored church which leaves virtually nothing of interest for the architect or historian. The church sits on the sloping hillside by the side of the main road through the parish. Above the south porch door is a niche with the Madonna and Child. Entering through the studded door one is struck by the colourful modern altar and reredos. The font is a very plain octagonal affair surrounded by wood panelling and a piano sits against the wall of the baptistery. Even the hammerbeam roof is relatively modern and the angels hanging precariously from the timbers of the chancel certainly are. Nevertheless the church is attractive in a modern way and vibrant, far better than a ruinous heap of unloved flint and stone.

CARLTON (with KELSALE)

Dedication:	Sts Peter & Mary	
No of Bells:	4	
Deanery 1836:	Hoxne	
Hundred:	Hoxne (detached)	
Union house:	Bulcamp	
Deanery 2000:	Saxmundham	

1 mile N of Saxmundham between Kelsale & Saxmundham: off Carlton Road, at end of trackway heading south.
O.S. grid ref TM 382640
Post Code IP17 1AT

Parts of this church date back to the 13th c.. It was a detached part of the Hoxne Hundred along with its neighbour, Kelsale. The parish is now consolidated with Kelsale. The brick tower is embattled and has a very old door. The experienced eye will notice a scratch dial on one of the buttresses. Inside, the nave is panelled in oak and among the church treasures are the pulpit and holy table which are unusually dated, 1626 and 1630 respectively. However, the table is actually of an earlier date, as the upper parts are Elizabethan. The builder of the early 14th c. chancel is buried there on the south side. Some of the benches are 15th c. but there is little else of real interest. The approach to the church is across a meadow which would be inadvisable in wet conditions.

CARLTON COLVILLE

Dedication:	St Peter	
No of Bells:	6	
Deanery 1836:	Lothingland	
Hundred:	Mutford & Lothingland	
Union house:	Oulton	
Deanery 2000: Lothingland, Norwich		

2 miles SW of Lowestoft
between Lowestoft &
Mutford: on the B1384
between A146 to the west,
and A1117 to the east.
O.S. grid ref TM 510901
Post Code NR33 8AT

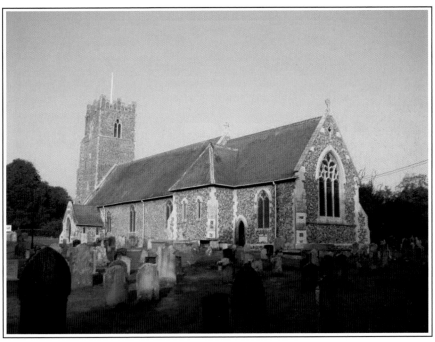

The original fabric of the church is 13th c. but it was virtually rebuilt in 1884 in the Decorated style by Howard Gaye. Some of the original features were incorporated into the design. The church had been heavily buttressed as an early drawing of 1852 illustrates even the porch had succumbed to subsidence. The old roof was replaced with a wagon roof with bosses and moulded ribs. The thatch was replaced with tile. Everything except perhaps the stoup is reproduction from the altar to the font. The only feature which was virtually left untouched was the tower which did receive a new parapet. A scratch dial is still visible on the south side. The churchyard is well maintained, but there is little here to excite the antiquarian. A modern extension has been built over many 19th c. graves on the north side.

CHARSFIELD

		5 miles N of Woodbridge
Dedication:	St Peter	between Wickham Market
No of Bells:	5	& Otley: from the B1078,
Deanery 1836:	Loes	north into the village,
Hundred:	Loes	opposite the school.
Union house:	Nacton	O.S. grid ref TM 254565
Deanery 2000:	Loes	Post Code IP13 7QB

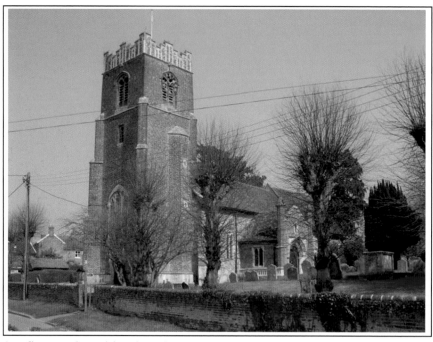

On first seeing this church, the tower and porch are recognisable as Tudor brickwork. However, the stone and flint plinth of both, and the doorways, are of an earlier date. There are signs of Norman work, with a slit window in the north wall of the nave; the south one has been blocked. The font is traditional East Anglian type and bears St Botolph, church in hand. The roof of the nave is hammerbeam type which has been plaster-boarded giving it a strange appearance with only the hammers showing. Against the west wall one of the smaller bells (which is broken) rests on the floor with clapper at its side. Four of the traceried rood screen panels are still in situ but internal modernisation has unfortunately taken its toll on the interior character of this otherwise attractive church.

CHATTISHAM

Dedication: All Saints & St Margaret
No of Bells: 1
Deanery 1836: Samford
Hundred: Samford
Union house: Tattingstone
Deanery 2000: Hadleigh

5 miles SW of Ipswich between Copdock & Hintlesham: in the main street running through the village.
O.S. grid ref TM 092421
Post Code IP8 3QA

Chattisham is a strange-looking church with its stumpy tower rising only six feet or so above the apex of the nave roof. It appears to have two porches but the easternmost is a transept chapel. The churchyard is full of trees which cause the 14th c. fabric of the church to be very damp. Inside there is a poor-box with its original ironwork, carved from a single piece of wood. The octagonal font is Victorian. A small wall brass in the chancel depicts a lady with hat and ruff; she is Mary, the wife of John Revers, whose plaque has long since gone. There are portraits of their three sons and seven daughters carved into the floor and partly hidden by pews. The Royal Arms are those of George II.

CHEDISTON

Dedication:	St Mary	
No of Bells:	6	
Deanery 1836:	Dunwich	
Hundred:	Blything	
Union house:	Bulcamp	
Deanery 2000:	Halesworth	

2 miles W of Halesworth between Wissett & Walpole: from the B1123, in the village centre.

O.S. grid ref TM 358777

Post Code IP19 0AU

Gargoyles and griffins stare down at the visitor to this neatly rendered church. Only the 15th c. tower reveals the flint from which it is built. The tower was begun in the 13th c and not completed until the 15th. The porch and south door both have matching 14th c. arches, suggesting they are contemporary. There is a stoup outside the south door and another matching it inside. There are remains of wall paintings, one being St. Christopher, but they are hardly recognisable. The church has a 14th c. parish chest but I could not find it. Perhaps like many other valuables in churches these days we are deprived sight of them in case someone takes a fancy to them. The font is traditional and has wodewoses around the base between the usual lions.

CHELMONDISTON

Dedication:	St Andrew	
No of Bells:	1	
Deanery 1836:	Samford	
Hundred:	Samford	
Union house:	Tattingstone	
Deanery 2000:	Samford	

5 miles SE of Ipswich between Woolverstone & Shotley: from the B1456 turn north into Church Street.

O.S. grid ref TM 205373

Post Code IP9 1HS

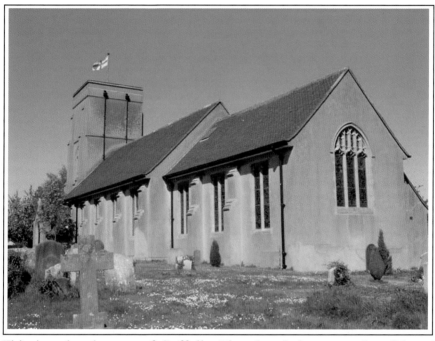

This is a lovely part of Suffolk. The church is very colourful and vibrant inside, but the only item of genuine historical interest is the Elizabethan hourglass which hangs on the wall near the pulpit in the nave. The church was built in the 15th c. but everything has been sterilised with a coat of Portland cement and machine-made tiles on the roof, giving it a hard, stark appearance. Inside everything is neat and square like a doctor's waiting room. The octagonal font supported by eight columns, like everything else, is modern. While you are in the area you will be aware you are quite close to 'Constable Country' with the natural beauty of the river Orwell never far away. On the banks of the Orwell is Pin Mill, only a half-mile away from the church and a much better option.

CHILLESFORD

		7 miles ENE of Woodbridge
Dedication:	St Peter	between Orford & Tunstall:
No of Bells:	1	the church is on the north
Deanery 1836:	Orford	of the B1084 (Orford Road),
Hundred:	Plomesgate	opposite Church Farm.
Union house:	Wickham Market	O.S. grid ref TM 382523
Deanery 2000:	Woodbridge	Post Code IP12 3PX

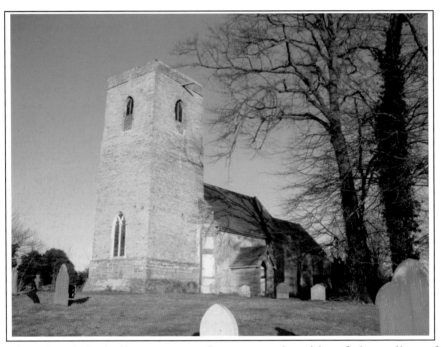

The church is built on a prominence on the side of the valley of Butley river. The tower of Chillesford church is constructed of coralline crag and a church has probably been on this site since before the Conquest. There is evidence of an 11th c. chancel before rebuilding. The tower would have made an ideal watch-tower and that may be why the church is on this site. Unfortunately there is little of interest but it is a beautiful spot to have a picnic. If you venture inside you will see the 13th c. font on its solid octagonal 16th c. shaft. The cinquefoil piscina in the nave still bears its original blue paint. The Royal Arms of Victoria are in plasterwork, which is uncommon, and hangs above the chancel arch. There is a parish chest but it is small and of no great age.

CLAYDON

		5 miles NW of Ipswich
Dedication:	St Peter	between Ipswich & Gt
No of Bells:	1	Blakenham: east of the A14
Deanery 1836:	Claydon	, at Claydon take Church
Hundred:	Bosmere & Claydon	Lane. (near Crown PH).
Union house:	Barham	O.S. grid ref TM 137498
Deanery 2000:	Bosmere	Post Code IP6 0EQ

Made redundant in 1977, this is one of the worst examples of restoration I think I have ever seen. Nothing has been done sympathetically. It has been extensively rebuilt over the centuries but the west end of the nave still reveals the long and short work of the Saxon builders. Inside the south porch is a Norman doorway. The north door, now unused, is 15th c.. The font which stands nearby is unusual in its form, having traceried panels. The 19th c. stone pulpit too is unusual, having pierced traceried sides and front. Other examples of the stone mason's art are scattered throughout the church. The north and south transepts were added in 1862, much to its detriment. The best the church has to offer is a sculpture of Virgin and Child by Henry Moore.

CLOPTON

Dedication:	St Mary the Virgin	
No of Bells:	6	
Deanery 1836:	Carlford	
Hundred:	Carlford	
Union house:	Nacton	
Deanery 2000:	Woodbridge	

4 miles NW of Woodbridge between Otley & Grundisburgh: on the B1079 which runs through the village.

O.S. grid ref TM 221525

Post Code   IP13 6QB

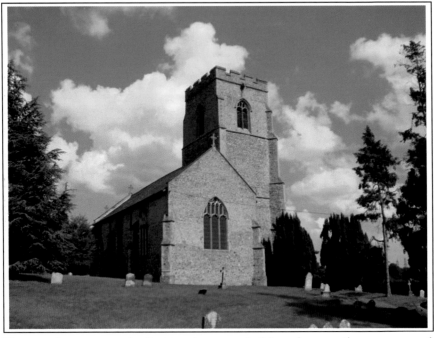

The southern tower is the most unusual thing, here acting as a porch into the church. It is of 13th c. origin but has been over-restored and has lost its antiquarian value. The oldest object to be found is the early 15th c. octagonal font and step base with quatrefoil design. The nave roof is a single hammerbeam, arch-braced with short king-posts. Angels and shields were replaced during the 1883 restoration and the chancel arch was rebuilt with decorated corbels depicting 'the good Samaritan' and 'the good shepherd'. There are nice examples of graffiti on each side of the south porch doorway, one a merchant's mark dated 1570, and the other that of 'John Cooper the adopted childe of Thomas Cooper the archer 1681'.

CODDENHAM

Dedication:	St Mary
No of Bells:	8
Deanery 1836:	Bosmere
Hundred:	Bosmere & Claydon
Union house:	Barham
Deanery 2000:	Bosmere

6 miles N of Ipswich between Needham Market & Ashbocking: on the B1078 which runs through the village.
O.S. grid ref TM 132541
Post Code   IP6 9PZ

Attractive from the west, a mish-mash from the east. When I visited they were pulling out timbers destroyed by death-watch beetle. The damage was quite extensive and will cost thousands to repair. The 14th c. tower is unusually placed at the north west corner of the nave. The church dates back in part, to the Conquest. There are examples of misericordes and some carvings on 15th c. bench ends. The piscina is 13th c. and the sedilia is the usual dropped windowsill type. The treasure of the church is placed high on the wall against the chancel arch. It is a sculptured 15th c. alabaster panel, coloured and gilded with a scene of the crucifixion, probably from a reredos. The nave roof is double hammerbeam with the almost obligatory Victorian angels looking down on the congregation.

COOKLEY

Dedication:	St Michael	
No of Bells:	3	
Deanery 1836:	Dunwich	
Hundred:	Blything	
Union house:	Bulcamp	
Deanery 2000:	Halesworth	

3 miles SW of Halesworth between Halesworth & Heveningham: access is by a lane, between houses north of the main street.
O.S. grid ref TM 349753
Post Code IP19 0LW

Cookley church was one of the last of the Victorian restorations and most of the furnishings, including a fine rood screen, were destroyed. The pulpit, however, was saved and made use of in Chediston church, and is still used today. Somewhat more sympathetic restoration has taken place since and the rescued tracery heads, once part of the rood loft, can be seen on the modern choir stalls. Part of a Stuart period pew has been re-situated in the tower and four traceried and embattled benches have also been saved from the clutches of the Victorian fireplace. The nave roof is single hammerbeam and is greatly restored. The blocked north doorway is Norman with classic chevron pattern over the arch. The font bowl is a typical East Anglian type. The parish was given to Anne of Cleves by Henry VIII.

COPDOCK

Dedication:	St Peter
No of Bells:	6
Deanery 1836:	Samford
Hundred:	Samford
Union house:	Tattingstone
Deanery 2000:	Samford

2 miles SW of Ipswich
between Ipswich & Capel
St Mary: from the old A12,
turn east onto Pound Lane.

O.S. grid ref TM 120415

Post Code IP8 3JZ

Away from the noise and bustle of the A12 this well proportioned church sits in a tranquil setting amid the wild flowers and birdsong of the Suffolk countryside. The tower is flint and dressed stone. We enter the church by the south porch with its crow-stepped gable. The curiously sculpted font is 15th century with a dwarf canopied cover. There is a western gallery on which there are five carved panels, one armorial, another depicting a lady playing a harp and one of Edward VI on horseback. All are of the same period. There is an ancient squint in the north pier of the chancel arch. The north door of the nave is panelled with traceried heads. The roof of the north transept is 15th c. with a central boss. Amalgamated with Washbrook.

CORTON

| | | 3 miles N of Lowestoft |
Dedication: St Bartholomew

No of Bells: 1

Deanery 1836: Lothingland

Hundred: Mutford & Lothingland

Union house: Oulton

Deanery 2000: Lothingland, Norwich

3 miles N of Lowestoft
between Lowestoft & Great
Yarmouth: east of the A12
via Stirrups Lane, north of
the village on Coast Road.
O.S. grid ref TM 538980
Post Code NR32 5HX

Corton is not far from the edge of the North Sea and has remained like this for many years. The tower is 90 feet tall and is a welcome landmark for fishermen returning home to Lowestoft. The tower has fallen into disuse and has the roofless remnants of a collapsed 13th c. nave still attached. The ancient porches and doorways have richly carved mouldings. Some Roman tiles can be seen built into the fabric of the church. Once a fine example of a Suffolk church, it still retains some treasures inside. The chancel contains a 14th c. piscina and sedilia with restored columns and ogee arches. The 14th c. carved stone gable cross is on display, inside the church, because of its uniqueness. Although weatherworn, it shows the crucifixion on one side and the Madonna and Child on the other.

COVEHITHE

Dedication:	St Andrew	
No of Bells:	5	
Deanery 1836:	Dunwich	
Hundred:	Blything	
Union house:	Bulcamp	
Deanery 2000:	Halesworth	

4 miles N of Southwold between Lowestoft & Southwold: off the A12 into Mill Lane, Wrentham and follow to Covehithe.
O.S. grid ref TM 522818
Post Code NR34 7JW

Before 1672 the church was in use, but congregations were becoming ever smaller. Eventually the few that remained could not afford the upkeep of the fabric and it was decided to dismantle it, sell the materials and build a smaller church within the original footprint. They took their example from nearby Walberswick. The tower was preserved intact because it also served as a watchtower. Inside the present church are recorded the names of the church wardens who were responsible for the changes. The 15th c. font remains and depicts angels playing musical instruments. As one might expect. there is little of any age inside; that which is old lies ruinous, but maintains its majestic appearance. With the sea getting ever closer it will one day go the way of the great churches of Dunwich.

CRANSFORD

Dedication:	St Peter	
No of Bells:	3	
Deanery 1836:	Orford	
Hundred:	Plomesgate	
Union house:	Wickham Market	
Deanery 2000:	Loes	

2 miles NE of Framlingham between Framlingham & Rendham: From B1119 turn north to village main street.

O.S. grid ref TM 315647

Post Code IP13 9NZ

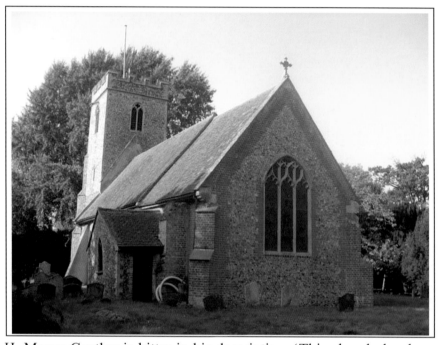

H. Munro Cautley is bitter in his description. 'This church. has been drastically and dreadfully restored and there is nothing of interest except the 15th c. bell inscribed 'HEC FIT SANCTORUM CAMPANA LAUDE BONORUM' (This bell is made in the praise of good saints).' I cannot disagree and although the church is attractive and well maintained it is sad to find such a sterile environment where there should be historical beauty in every corner. The church was completely rebuilt in 1864 by the over-zealous Victorians, but as I have said before, without their restorations we would have many more piles of flint and stone. It does serve the purpose for which it was built and I suppose that is more important than all other considerations.

CRATFIELD

Dedication:	St Mary	
No of Bells:	6 and a clock bell	
Deanery 1836:	Dunwich	
Hundred:	Blything	
Union house:	Bulcamp	
Deanery 2000:	Halesworth	

5 miles SW of Halesworth
between Fressingfield
& Huntingfield:
situated in Church Road,
Cratfield.
O.S. grid ref TM 313748
Post Code   IP19 0BU

Cratfield is renowned for its 15th c. seven sacrament font beautifully carved in stone. It stands on two steps, the upper is quatrefoiled and the main shaft has the four evangelists. The panels of the octagonal bowl are also delicately carved and the whole is quite exceptional. Also quite exceptionally the parish accounts go back to 1490. The fabric of the building dates from the 15th c. and the tower is contemporary with the church although the traceried parapet was added in 1547. The clerestory is also contemporary and has twenty fine windows to illuminate the interior. On the buttress of the nave there is a scratch dial. The west door has a carving of a wodewose on the jamb, more commonly found on fonts. The parish chest is 15th c. and the clock bell dates back to about 1400. Worth a visit.

CREETING

Dedication:	St Mary	
No of Bells:	1	
Deanery 1836:	Bosmere	
Hundred:	Bosmere & Claydon	
Union house:	Barham	
Deanery 2000:	Bosmere	

3 miles SE of Stowmarket between Needham Market & Earl Stonham: between the A14 & A140 on All Saints Rd or Church Lane. O.S. grid ref TM 093567 Post Code IP6 8QA

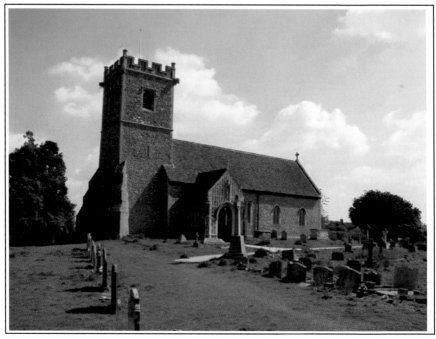

The church has Norman origins and still retains a very much restored Norman south doorway. The main body of the building is 12th c. but the tower is much later and heavily buttressed. The south porch is 15th c. built of flint and stone with a canopied niche complete with St Mary set into the gable above the door. There is a stoup set into the corner of the wall. The fine Norman doorway has engaged columns either side and scallop patterning over the arch. The font is a typical 15th c. East Anglian type which can be seen in so many local churches, but the font cover is particularly fine. The holy table is of an Elizabethan date and is a fine example of 17th c. workmanship with heavy carved legs and rail. The windows contain some interesting memorials from the 19th and 20th centuries.

CRETINGHAM

Dedication:	St Peter
No of Bells:	5
Deanery 1836:	Loes
Hundred:	Loes
Union house:	Wickham Market
Deanery 2000:	Loes

4 miles SW of Framlingham between Framsden & Brandeston: situated in The Street, Cretingham.

O.S. grid ref TM 227605

Post Code IP13 7BG

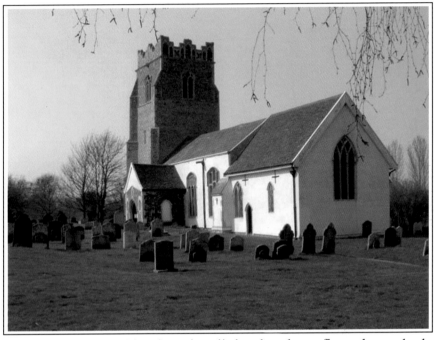

From the outside this charming little church at first glance looks cottage-like. The tower is 14th c. with battlements added by the Tudors, but the church is earlier. Inside, the buttering of the walls is very obvious, particularly at the east end. The hammerbeam roof is a splendid example of 15th c. craftsmanship. The octagonal font with its square base is decorated with roses and lions and is contemporary with the roof. The nave is filled with box pews and there are a few benches with poppy head decoration. The pulpit is a double-decker complete with back and sounding board and dates from Jacobean times as do the three-sided altar rails. A large, late Elizabethan monument to a member of the Cornwallis family dominates the north chancel wall. The Royal Arms are of Charles II .

CROWFIELD

Dedication:	All Saints
No of Bells:	1
Deanery 1836:	Bosmere
Hundred:	Bosmere & Claydon
Union house:	Barham
Deanery 2000:	Bosmere

7 miles N of Ipswich between Pettaugh & Coddenham: from A1120 at Stonham Aspal, turn south to Crowfield.
O.S. grid ref TM 142577
Post Code IP6 9TH

Well away from the village centre you will find this unusual church up a short lane past the edge of a moat. Looking for all the world like a Tudor townhouse, it has been so restored it is difficult to determine what is original and what is not. The construction of the chancel is of oak studwork and more traditional flint for the nave. The timber porch is heavily carved inside, and everywhere else in the church there are other examples of the woodcarver's skill. Very little remains of the 14th c. building except perhaps the hammerbeam roof which has been liberally strewn with carved angels and the like. The benches also bear the mark of the woodcarver with poppy-head bench-ends. There is even a carved Victorian poor box on a turned pillar for your donations as you leave. Different and interesting.

CULPHO

Dedication:	St Botolph	
No of Bells:	1	
Deanery 1836:	Carlford	
Hundred:	Carlford	
Union house:	Nacton	
Deanery 2000:	Woodbridge	

4 miles W of Woodbridge between Tuddenham & Great Bealings: no street names, near Abbey Farm. opposite - 20, Culpho. O.S. grid ref TM 210491 Post Code IP6 9DH

The church is unusual in its configuration as the late 14th c. tower, which is somewhat truncated, also serves as a south porch. The tower has a square pitched roof; inside, the south doorway is early 14th c and has a square moulded label which is curtailed by the arch of the tower showing it to be of a later date. There is a stoup in the eastern jamb of the doorway. Although the church, like many others, was mentioned in Doomsday nothing remains of the Saxon building. The font is 15th c. and still has one of the staples which used to protect the holy water from theft. There are two carved bench ends which date from the 15th c. but these have been mutilated over the years, and a Stuart holy table. There is considerable buttering to the walls of the nave. Usually kept locked.

DALLINGHOO

Dedication:	St Mary	
No of Bells:	4	
Deanery 1836:	Wilford	
Hundred:	Wilford & Loes	
Union house:	Nacton	
Deanery 2000:	Loes	

3 miles N of Woodbridge between Wickham Market & Charsfield: on Church Road in the centre of Dallinghoo.
O.S. grid ref TM 266550
Post Code IP13 0JX

Part of this parish lies in the Loes and part in the Wilford Hundred. On entering the churchyard through the lychgate something looks wrong until you realise the tower of this church is at the east instead of the west and serves as a chancel. This was once a much larger church with a central tower but the chancel collapsed. Instead of rebuilding, the eastern tower arch was blocked with a modern window and the tower modified into a chancel. Inside, the skill of the 17th c. woodcarver is apparent, The pulpit, complete with its back and sounding board, may have elements of earlier work incorporated in it. The reading desk is particularly decorative and would look more at home in one of the great houses, and the holy table, chairs and altar rails are all contemporary.

DARMSDEN

Dedication: St Andrew
No of Bells: 1
Deanery 1836: Bosmere
Hundred: Bosmere & Claydon
Union house: Barham
Deanery 2000: Bosmere

1 mile S of Needham
Market between Needham
Market & Baylham: from
the B1113 turn west opp
Gallows Hill landfill site.
O.S. grid ref TM 094529
Post Code IP6 8RA

White's Directory of 1845 describes the original church as 'a small ancient fabric'. The church, however, was demolished and completely rebuilt in the 1880's. Nothing of the original structure remains, although it is probable it was re-constructed in the same 'footprint'. It cost £1500 to build in the 13th c. Decorated style and was financed by James Kemplay. Being always only a small parish it was long ago consolidated with nearby Barking. There is a small single bell turret at the west end of the gable and the nave and chancel are continuous under the one roof, which is of a very high quality arched collar-braced construction. All the fittings inside are carved in oak including the pulpit, reading desk, bench ends and reredos, which is exceptionally fine and decoratively carved.

DARSHAM

Dedication:	All Saints
No of Bells:	4
Deanery 1836:	Dunwich
Hundred:	Blything
Union house:	Bulcamp
Deanery 2000:	Saxmundham

5 miles NE of Saxmundham between Blythburgh & Yoxford: from the A12 turn east into Darsham Street and follow for ¾ mile.

O.S. grid ref TM 420699

Post Code IP17 3QA

The keen eye will find Roman tiles and brick incorporated in the fabric of the Saxon walls. The Normans modernised the building and the south doorway is still in use. The north door is also Norman in origin. The traditional early 15th c. font is inscribed around the base. The bowl is octagonal with angels and lions and four more lions around the quatrefoil base. Some of the benches are well carved and traceried, dating from the 15th c.. The pulpit and holy table date from the Stuart period. The Bedingfield family once lived in the parish and there is a monument to Sir Thomas Bedingfield who was deeply involved with the Royalists and narrowly escaped execution. He was imprisoned in the Tower and six years later became a judge. After Charles I was executed, he retired here, away from public life.

DEBACH

Dedication:	All Saints	
No of Bells:	1	
Deanery 1836:	Wilford	
Hundred:	Wilford	
Union house:	Nacton	
Deanery 2000:	Loes	

4 miles NW of Woodbridge between   Charsfield & Clopton: from the B1078 turn south to Debach & Boulge. Private Residence. O.S. grid ref TM 242543 Post Code   IP13 8BZ

This church is now a private house. It had been completely rebuilt in 1856 after falling into disrepair in the 1830's and so there is nothing of architectural interest to mention. We look to White's Directory of 1845 and he describes it as 'a small ancient fabric'. Whether that was the church mentioned in Doomsday or a later building I cannot determine. The parish has long been consolidated with Boulge and it was perhaps inevitable that it would become redundant, as the parish became less inhabited during the late Victorian era when many agricultural workers moved into the towns to work in the factories. Many churches have suffered the same fate and have been taken for secular use, but this is better by far than a forgotten heap of rubble in the corner of a field.

DEBENHAM

Dedication:	St Mary	
No of Bells:	8	
Deanery 1836:	Claydon	
Hundred:	Thredling	
Union house:	Barham	
Deanery 2000:	Loes	

8 miles S of Eye, between Framsden & Aspall: on the B1077 in the High Street.

O.S. grid ref TM 174632

Post Code IP14 6QN

A bulky church in appearance. West of the tower is a porch, above which is a chapel. The tower has Saxon foundations and long and short work can be seen in its lower stages. A scratch dial can be seen on the chancel wall. The nave is early15th c. and has alternate hammerbeam and tie-beam construction. Across the chancel arch is a 13th c. beam which was left in situ when the roof was raised for the clerestory. The chancel is still basically 13th c. although it has been restored over the centuries. The font is octagonal without a shaft but standing on an octagonal base of equal diameter. The font cover appears like a hat resting on the ears of the wearer. Although damaged, there is a good tomb monument to Sir Charles Framlingham in armour with his wife lying beside him.

DENHAM

Dedication: St John the Baptist
No of Bells: 1
Deanery 1836: Hoxne
Hundred: Hoxne
Union house: Stradbroke
Deanery 2000: Hoxne

3 m E of Eye between Hoxne & Horham: turn west from the road through the village into Church Road.
O.S. grid ref TM 188747
Post Code IP21 5DE

What a pity that this little church with all its treasures has been so badly neglected. Once there used to be a chapel north of the nave but it was demolished many years ago. The arch is plainly visible. The effigy of a lady, her head supported by angels, was probably moved to its present position at the time. There are six stalls in the chancel which have misericordes. Beneath the altar there is a brass to Anthony Bedingfield (1574), on the reverse is half of a Flemish memorial, the other half of it was discovered in Yealhampton, Devonshire, on a memorial plaque to Isabel Coplestone—1580. The Royal Arms are of Charles I, dated 1637. On the west wall there is a memorial to William de Kirksby, Prior of Norwich from 1280 to 1290. This plaque has been moved from the eastern outside wall.

DENNINGTON *****

Dedication:	St Mary
No of Bells:	6
Deanery 1836:	Hoxne
Hundred:	Hoxne
Union house:	Stradbroke
Deanery 2000:	Loes

3 m N of Framlingham between Badingham & Saxtead: easily recognisable on the A1120 running through the parish. O.S. grid ref TM 281669 Post Code IP13 8AA

Arguably the most interesting church in Suffolk. To try and describe everything there is to see here would take several pages. One thing which is unique is the pyx canopy which, although restored, hangs above the altar. The church is basically 14th c. and in general the restorations have been sympathetic. In the chapel is a memorial tomb to Lord Bardolph and his wife Joan. It dates from around 1450 and is meticulously carved from alabaster. The effigies still carry much of their original colouring. In the nave you will find a sand writing table, 3 parish chests dating from the 14th c., a bier and the old clock mechanism. The roof is of double hammerbeam construction. The font is a modern replacement, and the piscinas and sedilia are somewhat mutilated. The wood-carving is quite exceptional.

DUNWICH

Dedication:	All Saints	
No of Bells:	not known	
Deanery 1836:	Dunwich	
Hundred:	Blything	
Union house:	Bulcamp	
Deanery 2000:	Saxmundham	

3 m N of Framlingham
between Westleton &
Walberswick:
the site of the church is now
beneath the sea.
O.S. grid ref TM 479703
Post Code   -

Dunwich was the original see of Bishop Felix, later Saint Felix, founder of Christianity in East Anglia in 630 AD. All Saints church succumbed to the sea and finally fell over the cliff in 1919. Before it did so a buttress on the left was saved and a portion reconstructed in the grounds of St James churchyard. Dunwich was once very prosperous with six churches, hospitals and monastic houses and was a major port. Despite earlier incursions of the sea there were six churches, All Saints (above, the most westerly), St John, St Leonard, St Martin, St Nicholas and St Peter. All were destroyed by the sea. In 1286 the town was overwhelmed and by 1312 the port was unusable. During the 14th c. the town was totally destroyed and the sandy cliffs still crumble today at high tides.

DUNWICH

Dedication:	St James	
No of Bells:	1	
Deanery 1836:	Dunwich	
Hundred:	Blything	
Union house:	Bulcamp	
Deanery 2000:	Saxmundham	

4 m S of Southwold between Westleton & Walberswick: the main street is St James' Street, follow it west.
O.S. grid ref TM 474705
Post Code IP17 3DX

The church of St James was built in 1820 because all but one of the other churches in the parish had fallen foul of the sea, and All Saints (see previous page) was about to suffer the same fate. The dedication of St James came from the lazar house in whose grounds the church stands. Originally built with a round tower and chiefly of brick. The chancel was enlarged and the round tower encased in a flint and stone square dressing as was the body of the whole edifice. The restructuring was eventually completed about 1881 and financed by the Barne family. The building is finished to a high degree of craftsmanship and cost in excess of £1300 for the chancel alone. For 500 years Dunwich sent MPs to Parliament and Sir George Downing, who gave his name to Downing Street, was born here.

EARL SOHAM
Dedication: St Mary
No of Bells: 6
Deanery 1836: Loes
Hundred: Loes
Union house: Wickham Market
Deanery 2000: Loes

3 m W of Framlingham
between Saxtead &
Ashfield: on the A1120 in
the village centre by the
War Memorial.
O.S. grid ref TM 236632
Post Code IP13 7SE

The tower has three canopied niches on its western face as you approach the church. Above the south porch door there is a stone figure on the gable and a carving of a lion immediately below; and beneath that, an inscription. The church is beautifully kept with a wealth of wood-carving to enjoy. The font is of the traditional East Anglian type with an inscribed base, although unfortunately illegible. The magnificent double hammerbeam roof in the nave is slightly marred by the metal tie-rods which prevent the walls from spreading. The pulpit with back and sounding board is Stuart, as is the holy table. The 15th c. bench ends are carved with grotesques and all are different, some having been restored. The Royal Arms are of King Charles II.

EARL STONHAM

Dedication:	St Mary
No of Bells:	5
Deanery 1836:	Bosmere
Hundred:	Bosmere & Claydon
Union house:	Barham
Deanery 2000:	Bosmere

4 miles E of Stowmarket between Stowupland & Stonham Aspal: north side of the A1120, ¾ m west of the A140 crossroads
O.S. grid ref TM 107588
Post Code IP14 5EE

The site is very ancient and a Roman burial ground exists nearby. The church is mainly 14th c. but signs of an earlier structure remain. It is possible, according to H. Munro Cautley, that the church had a central tower in the 13th c.. The present tower and clerestory are late 15th c.. There is much known about the history of the church and the way it has evolved through the centuries. The roof is one of the finest examples of a single hammerbeam construction to be seen anywhere. Above the chancel arch is a 'doom' preserved from pre-commonwealth times. The octagonal font has a square base on an octagonal plinth and dates to mid-15th c.. It is carved with emblems of the BVM and is somewhat mutilated. The parish chest is 700 years old and quite plain. An interesting church to visit.

EAST BERGHOLT

Dedication:	St Mary	
No of Bells:	5 and a priest's bell	
Deanery 1836:	Samford	
Hundred:	Samford	
Union house:	Tattingstone	
Deanery 2000:	Samford	

9 m SW of Ipswich
between Stratford St Mary
& Brantham: at the
junction of The Street &
Rectory Hill.
O.S. grid ref TM 070344
Post Code CO7 6TE

This is Constable's church, on the beautiful Suffolk-Essex border, but a strange edifice, being so different to most other churches. The unfinished tower was begun in 1525. It has an arched walk-through and vegetation is now growing from the stonework. The mediaeval belfry or bell-house in the churchyard contains the 5 great bells. It is interesting architecturally as well as historically. There are a few mysteries to the purpose of the recesses and some interesting memorials to various famous parishioners. There is a brass in the centre of the nave to Robert Alefounder, 1639. There is also a tomb featuring camels on the chancel wall below a memorial window. The font bowl is old but the base is restored. This is a colourful , interesting church. A guide is usually available to show you round.

EASTON

Dedication:	All Saints	
No of Bells:	6	
Deanery 1836:	Loes	
Hundred:	Loes	
Union house:	Wickham Market	
Deanery 2000:	Loes	

3 m S of Framlingham
between Wickham Market
& Kettleburgh: 600 yards
north of Easton Farm Park,
just off The Street.
O.S. grid ref TM 283587
Post Code   IP13 0ED

The west door in the tower of Easton church serves as a private entrance for the Wingfield family, owners of the adjacent park. The wall was built in the 18th c. and acts as a reminder of how the nobles of the land considered themselves so superior that they could not use the same door as their servants. Inside we find canopied and screened pews on either side of the altar for the same purpose, bearing the Wingfield Arms. The piscina and sedilia are good examples of the late 13th c.. Glass of 100 years later adorns the tracery of the nave windows. The hand-carved Hanoverian Arms are hanging on the wall of the nave. Ancient monuments include John Brook 1426, John Wyngfield 1584 and Radcliff Wingfeld 1601. More recent monuments to the 19th c. Nassau family adorn the nave walls.

ELLOUGH

Dedication:	All Saints	
No of Bells:	3	
Deanery 1836:	Wangford	
Hundred:	Wangford	
Union house:	Shipmeadow	
Deanery 2000:	Beccles & S. Elmham	

3 m SE of Beccles between Beccles & Sotterley: from the A145 at Weston or B1127 near the industrial estate; in Church Road. O.S. grid ref TM 442866 Post Code NR34 7TR

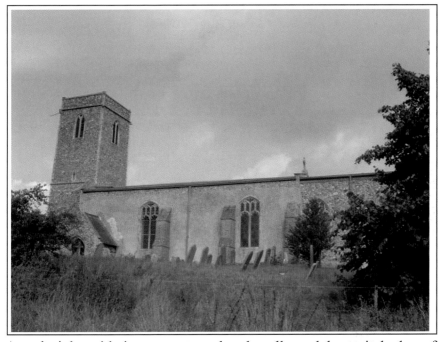

A sad sight with its cement-rendered walls and low pitched roof. After nearby Willingham St Mary was abandoned this church was known as Willingham All Saints. Inside the south door is a stoup and a 15th c. font stands in the nave. The bowl stands on a modern shaft but the plinth is ancient. The roof is cambered tie-beam with braces to the wall posts, allowing the low pitch so evident from the outside. Benches in the chancel have traceried ends and were probably part of an old screen. The piscina has a cusped and crocketted ogee arch and is adjacent to a dropped sill sedilia. The holy table dates from the Stuart period. Interestingly there are three small brasses all to ladies of the parish, the earliest to a nun which is dated 1520, Margaret Chewt 1607 and Anne Gostling 1612. Always locked!

ERWARTON

Dedication:	St Mary	
No of Bells:	1	
Deanery 1836:	Samford	
Hundred:	Samford	
Union house:	Tattingstone	
Deanery 2000:	Samford	

7 m SE of Ipswich
between Shotley &
Harkstead: from the B1456
turn off for Erwarton Hall
and follow to The Street.
O.S. grid ref TM 220346
Post Code IP9 1LJ

From the outside one can recognise the septaria by its brownish colour against the grey of the flint. Unfortunately the south aisle wall is cement-rendered. But it is a pleasant church with a beautiful view of the Stour, with Harwich across the water. Inside the church are some very old monuments, one to a knight, probably Sir Bartholomew D'Avillers who died in 1287. None lie in their original position and the names have been lost during restoration and the restructuring of the church. There is a pathetic monument to the only son of Sir Philip Parker who lived at the nearby Hall. The font is a traditional East Anglian type and the holy table is a poor example of Stuart craftsmanship. While in the area go and see the unique Jacobean gatehouse to the Hall just down the road.

EYKE

Dedication:	All Saints	
No of Bells:	3	
Deanery 1836:	Loes	
Hundred:	Loes	
Union house:	Wickham Market	
Deanery 2000:	Woodbridge	

3 m NE of Woodbridge
between   Rendlesham &
Melton: at the crossroads
as you pass through the
village on the A1152.
O.S. grid ref TM 317517
Post Code   IP12 2QL

It is strange that a church is more renowned for its key than its architecture or treasures. The wards of the key to the original south door form the word 'IKE', the old spelling of Eyke. The key which hangs on the wall of the nave is a replica. The key to the church today is ordinary and is available at the shop opposite. The church used to have a central tower but it fell into disrepair despite the villagers making a protest to the incumbent. Today what remains of the Norman tower can be seen separating the nave from the chancel by its fine arches. The church was restored in 1867, most of the work being concentrated on the western end of the nave. The font is 14th c. as is the nave roof with the original angels revealed during the 1867 restoration.

FALKENHAM

Dedication:	St Ethelbert
No of Bells:	4
Deanery 1836:	Colneis
Hundred:	Colneis
Union house:	Nacton
Deanery 2000:	Colneys

3 m N of Felixstowe
between Kirton & Trimley
St Mary: follow Falkenham
Road from Kirton; very
near the Hall behind a wall.
O.S. grid ref TM 293390
Post Code   IP10 0QY

This 15th c. church is almost hidden behind a high wall and lime and sycamore trees. Above the west door in the tower are the Arms of England, flanked by those of Warwick and 'the Passion'. The font is traditional East Anglian and nothing very special. The roof of the nave is single hammerbeam, arch-braced and collared. A decorative panel of a parish chest from elsewhere has been utilised to create part of the reredos. The chancel has a small apsidal end which was clad with red brick and slate in 1800. Combined with cement rendering on the walls does nothing to enhance the outer appearance of the east end of the church. To the east lies the River Deben and the Felixstowe ferry connecting with Bawdsey on the far bank.

FARNHAM

Dedication:	St Mary
No of Bells:	2
Deanery 1836:	Orford
Hundred:	Plomesgate
Union house:	Wickham Market
Deanery 2000:	Saxmundham

3 m SW of Saxmundham between Benhall & Stratford St Andrew: from the north, turn left off the A12 at the foot of the hill. O.S. grid ref TM 362599 Post Code IP17 1LA

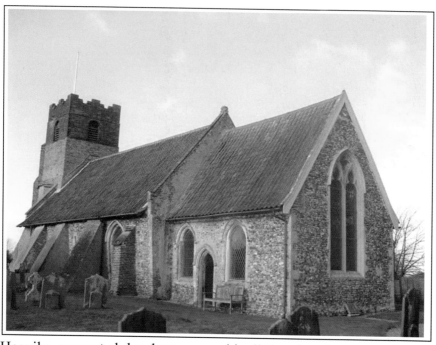

Heavily supported by buttresses this little church retains its slit windows but little else of real architectural interest remains. What remains of the rood screen is well traceried and still retains some traces of the original mediaeval paintwork. The box pews were installed in the early part of the 19th c. and as in most cases ruin the internal appearance of the church. The pulpit was built and installed at the same time and matches the pews as at nearby Benhall. The font is a modern replica of a 13th c. style, probably a copy of the original. The church, although appearing to be well maintained and in good order is now disused and has been declared redundant, as was Stratford St Andrew on the opposite bank of the River Alde which is now a private house. (see page 249).

91

FELIXSTOWE   (Old)

Dedication:	St Andrew	
No of Bells:	1	
Deanery 1836:	Colneis	
Hundred:	Colneis	
Union house:	Nacton	
Deanery 2000:	Colneys	

11 m SE of Ipswich on the coast north of Harwich: take second roundabout; - from Hamilton Road turn east into St Andrew's Road. O.S. grid ref TM 305350 Post Code   IP11 7ED

This modern church has been described as many things. To me it has little appeal. Plans for a church here were mooted in 1898. The land was given by Captain Pretyman and in 1907 a temporary timber and corrugated iron structure was built. It was, however, more attractive than today's concrete edifice. The design for the present church can be attributed to Hilda Mason who worked with H. Munro Cautley. Some of the traditional aspects of church building can be seen in the design, such as the clerestory and the basic Perpendicular style. It was completed in 1931 but lacks the tower that it was originally designed to have. My opinion is that it would have improved the appearance and made it look more like a church and less like a multi-story car park. Best hidden by trees.

FELIXSTOWE

Dedication:	St John the Baptist
No of Bells:	1
Deanery 1836:	Colneis
Hundred:	Colneis
Union house:	Nacton
Deanery 2000:	Colneys

11 m SE of Ipswich
on the coast, north of
Harwich: from Garrison
Lane, east into Orwell
Road.
O.S. grid ref TM 299344
Post Code: IP11 7PL

This is a traditional church by comparison to St Andrew's and was designed by Sir Arthur Blomfield in 1894. It is stark in appearance, being constructed of red brick, but it is well proportioned and has a pleasing façade. The south-west tower is square and pinnacled with a contrasting elegant white stone spire and weathers on the buttressing. The interior is also in red brick and is well complemented by fine woodwork. The nave roof is of tie-beam and scissor frame construction with king-posts. Although everything is early 20th century it is well executed and the workmanship is of very high quality particularly the screen crafted in the mediaeval style. The reredos is elaborately carved from marble and is flanked by murals. I would much rather see this than St Andrew's in Old Felixstowe.

FELIXSTOWE (Old)

Dedication:	Sts Peter & Paul
No of Bells:	1
Deanery 1836:	Colneis
Hundred:	Colneis
Union house:	Nacton
Deanery 2000:	Colneys

11 m SE of Ipswich on the coast, north of Harwich: over two roundabouts into Colneis Road, at ¾ m turn sharp right into Ferry Road. O.S. grid ref TM 314357 Post Code: IP11 9NF

As you enter through the 1914 lych gate the church seems a hotchpotch of buildings. Nothing seems in its proper place, and it isn't until you enter the church that everything seems to make sense. The restoration in the 19th c. was responsible, for it included building north and south transepts which do not sit easily externally. The high peaked timber-lined roofs meet at the crossing and are supported there by great ogee arches. The chancel has a well proportioned apsidal east end. The church is basically Norman with a 14th c. porch. The font is 15th c. but the interest lies in the pulpit or rather that upon which it sits; part of a column, possibly from the old priory. The pulpit itself is Jacobean. There are a few interesting 15th c. bench-ends with grotesques.

FLIXTON

Dedication:	St Andrew	
No of Bells:	?	
Deanery 1836:	Lothingland	
Hundred:	Mutford & Lothingland	
Union house:	Oulton	
Deanery 2000: Lothingland, Norwich		

2½ m NW of Lowestoft
between Blundeston &
Lowestoft: from the B1074
turn east into Old Hall
driveway.
O.S. grid ref TM 518955
Post Code: on private land

What is there to say about a heap of flints intermingled with trees and briars in the corner of a field? Parts of the walls are still standing and the footprint of the building can be easily distinguished. The church had its roof taken off by the hurricane of 1703, the congregation was small and it was left to fall into ruin. The parish was soon combined with nearby Blundeston which still contains Flixton's altar in the north aisle, and is still occasionally used. The Flixton font can be found outside the south priests' door in Blundeston churchyard. St Andrew is better remembered than many ruined Suffolk churches because of the above-ground ruins and the fact the landowner has treated them with respect rather than ploughing them into the ground as happened at Linstead Magna. (see page 171)

95

FLIXTON

Dedication:	St Mary	
No of Bells:	1 now, at one time 3	
Deanery 1836:	South Elmham	
Hundred:	Wangford	
Union house:	Shipmeadow	
Deanery 2000:	Beccles & S. Elmham	

3 m SW of Bungay
between Bungay &
Harleston: from the B1062
at Flixton turn south on a
bend near the village sign.
O.S. grid ref TM 312867
Post Code: NR35 1NX

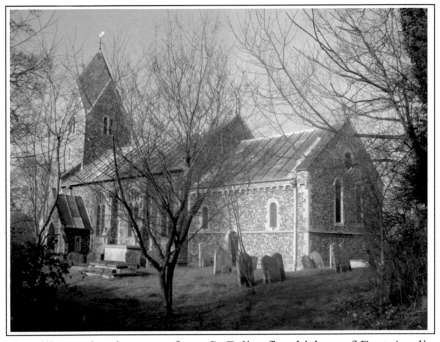

The village takes its name from St Felix, first bishop of East Anglia. The 13th c. church had a Saxon tower with its 'German Helm' roof but in 1835 the tower fell. Almost the whole church was demolished and completely re-built in the same style in 1856. The chancel was added in 1893. What is seen today is a rare copy of Saxon workmanship. There is an apsidal memorial chapel at the western end of the nave dedicated to Theodosia, Lady Waveney, who died in 1871 and she is sculpted by John Bell, life-size, from marble, kneeling on a cushion. The fan-vaulted ceiling and clustered columns make it one of the best I have seen. It was erected by her husband Sir Hugh Adair whose family were great benefactors to the church. The rest of the church is of little interest to the historian.

FLOWTON

		5 miles NW of Ipswich
Dedication:	St Mary	between Bramford &
No of Bells:	1	Elmsett: if you can find
Deanery 1836:	Bosmere	Flowton you will find the
Hundred:	Bosmere & Claydon	church near the centre.
Union house:	Barham	O.S. grid ref TM 081468
Deanery 2000:	Bosmere	Post Code: IP8 4LL

On finding the site you are greeted by an accumulation of notices and signs outside the lych gate welcoming you to Flowton church. From the south side one's eye is immediately drawn to the cross on the chancel roof, picked out in a lighter coloured tile. There are very faint scratch dials on each of the nave buttresses. The tower is a square, squat affair without battlements and has a pyramidal tiled low-pitched roof. The font is a fairly plain example of a 13th c. form. The cover is a simple carved octagonal ogee frame on an octagonal base-board.   The rood stair turret is of an early Tudor design and is exceptionally large. The roof of the nave is of tie-beam and king-post construction and dates from the 13th c. Some poppy-head bench ends are nicely carved but are not of any real age.

FOXHALL

Dedication:	All Saints	
No of Bells:	?	
Deanery 1836:	Carlford	
Hundred:	Carlford	
Union house:	Nacton	
Deanery 2000:	Colneys	

4 m E of Ipswich
between Ipswich &
Martlesham: just off the
A12 east of Ipswich at
Foxhall Hall. Private land.
O.S. grid ref TM 230437
Post Code: IP10 0AQ

Foxhall is unrecognisable as anything other than a flint wall.
At one time, however, this was part of the church. The church was described as being 'much decayed' in 1530. Henry Davy drew what was left of it in 1849. Today what remains is as you see it here, the single outside north wall of a barn in the grounds of Foxhall Hall. Even this wall has been partly rebuilt, and the rest of the barn certainly has, using materials from the ruined church. It is very popular with visitors and there is a clearly marked public pathway leading past the site (this view can be clearly seen). Foxhall was a perpetual curacy until well into the 19th c. and ministers were appointed accordingly, however, many tears ago it was consolidated with Brightwell. (see page 40)

FRAMLINGHAM *****

Dedication:	St Michael	
No of Bells:	8	
Deanery 1836:	Loes	
Hundred:	Loes	
Union house:	Wickham Market	
Deanery 2000:	Loes	

13 m NE of Ipswich between Saxtead & Rendham: situated in Church Street, just south of the castle.

O.S. grid ref TM 285635

Post Code: IP13 9AZ

Framlingham is one of the most magnificent churches in the county. Most of it, as it stands today, is 15th c. building. Some remnants of the 12th c. church remain in the piers of the chancel and elsewhere. The nave roof is hammerbeam and arch-braced construction which is disguised by the vaulting. The font is a traditional East Anglian type. The monuments are quite exceptional and large and must have cost a fortune to erect. They include the tombs of Sir Robert Hitcham, the great benefactor to the town and the church; Thomas Howard, 3rd Duke of Norfolk (1554); Henry Fitzroy, Duke of Richmond and bastard son of Henry VIII (1536). Probably the best tomb is that of Henry Howard, Earl of Surrey (1547). A 13th c. iron bound parish chest, Royal Arms of Charles II dated 1661 are also to be seen.

FRAMSDEN

Dedication:	St Mary	
No of Bells:	8	
Deanery 1836:	Claydon	
Hundred:	Thredling	
Union house:	Barham	
Deanery 2000:	Loes	

9 m E of Stowmarket
between Pettaugh &
Cretingham: from the
A1120 follow signs to
Framsden, in The Street.
O.S. grid ref TM 200597
Post Code: IP14 6HS

Framsden is a pleasant little church of cement-rendered flint and stone construction. The elaborate flushwork panelling on the south porch is quite exceptional and pleasing with its three niches, all unfortunately empty. There is a scratch dial on the chancel buttress. Inside we find the font is a traditional East Anglian type and the piscina is 14th c. with a cusped ogee arch. An upward glance will reveal the double hammerbeam roof of the nave. There are inscribed dates of 1620 and 1676 on the timbers. There are six misericorde stalls with very fine carving and old bench-ends which were once part of the stalls, two of which are finely traceried. The somewhat unusual holy table is of the Stuart period and is dated 1628. The nave is well lit by the twelve-window clerestory.

FRESSINGFIELD *****

Dedication:	Sts Peter & Paul
No of Bells:	8
Deanery 1836:	Hoxne
Hundred:	Hoxne
Union house:	Stradbroke
Deanery 2000:	Hoxne

9 m W of Halesworth
between Harleston in
Norfolk & Laxfield: follow
the B1116 into the village,
situated in Church Street.
O.S. grid ref TM 261774
Post Code: IP21 5PB

This is the birth and resting place of William Sancroft, 1693,
Archbishop of Canterbury. His tomb is on the south side of the
church. This is a fine example of a church built on the strength of the
wool trade. The porch has beautifully executed flushwork with eight
niches set into the walls and a parvise above. At the east end of the
nave roof is the finest example of a sanctus bell turret in the county.
Inside, the nave roof is single hammerbeam and the chancel is arch-
braced. The guild chapel north of the chancel is dedicated to St
Margaret of Antioch. Her effigy is carved in the corner post of the
old Guild Hall (now the Fox and Goose Inn). There is a large iron-
bound parish chest and the richly carved benches in the nave are well
worth closer investigation.

FRESTON

Dedication:	St Peter
No of Bells:	1
Deanery 1836:	Samford
Hundred:	Samford
Union house:	Tattingstone
Deanery 2000:	Samford

4 m S of Ipswich
between Ipswich &
Holbrook: from the B1080
turn west. Just north of the
village on a narrow road.
O.S. grid ref TM 170395
Post Code: IP9 1AH

Be careful, that when looking for Freston church, you don't confuse the Freston Tower with the church tower. Freston Tower is a Tudor folly six stories high. The church tower is half the height. In the churchyard you cannot help but notice the peace or war memorial which is a beautiful figure of Peace carved from solid oak. The church has been over-restored and nothing of any great interest remains. The tower is 14th c. and the nave and chancel are under one single barn-type roof separated only by a great carved beam. The piscina remains as does the sedilia but both are simple and uninteresting. There are a number of memorials to the Latymer family. The churchyard is probably one of the nicest kept and it is pleasing to wander amongst the interesting mixture of memorials.

FRISTON

Dedication:	St Mary
No of Bells:	3
Deanery 1836:	Orford
Hundred:	Plomesgate
Union house:	Wickham Market
Deanery 2000:	Saxmundham

3 m SE of Saxmundham
between Saxmundham &
Aldeburgh: from A1094,
north 1½ m east of Snape,
on B1121 look for signpost.
O.S. grid ref TM 413604
Post Code: IP17 1PX

The tower is unusual in that it has a niche above the weathering of each of the buttresses and a further three on the west face. All are empty. The tower was rebuilt about 1900 using the original materials and in the same 14th c style. The roof is a single barn type and outwardly makes no distinction between the nave and the chancel. The south doorway is 12th c. and has engaged columns to the jambs with consecration crosses either side. The original font is still in use as a base for the more modern one. The nave roof is of the arch-braced type and the holy table and pulpit are both of the Stuart period. The Royal Arms are of James I and are carved from five-inch thick timber. The church is also in possession of a 16th c. Bible bound with leather and brass-work.

FRITTON
Dedication: St Edmund King & Martyr
No of Bells: 1
Deanery 1836: Lothingland
Hundred: Mutford & Lothingland
Union house: Oulton
Deanery 2000: Lothingland, Norwich

7 m NW of Lowestoft
between Haddiscoe &
Great Yarmouth Nfk: from
the A143 take Church Lane;
northern end of Fritton.
O.S. grid ref TG 473001
Post Code: NR32 5PE

This lovely little thatched church has a number of interesting points
to attract the visitor. The tower has a Saxon base with Roman tiles
built into the fabric. The top is 14th c. and tapers considerably east/
west. Inside there are more examples of Saxon work: in the pilaster
buttresses of the chancel and in the lower part of the tower, which is
open and projects into the nave. The thickness of the walls can be
seen by the reveals of the lancet windows. The best feature is the
little 12 ft. wide apsidal Norman chancel which is not central to the
nave and suggests that there was an earlier nave altar. This could
have been dedicated to St John as he is painted on the nearby window
frame. There is a large 15th c. painting of St Christopher, and other
13th c. scroll painting is still present around the chancel arch.

FROSTENDEN

Dedication:	All saints
No of Bells:	3
Deanery 1836:	Dunwich
Hundred:	Blything
Union house:	Bulcamp
Deanery 2000:	Halesworth

4 m NW of Southwold between Lowestoft & Blythburgh: to the west of the A12, well signposted, 'Frostenden Church'.
O.S. grid ref TM 479817
Post Code: NR34 7HS

A thousand years ago Frostenden was a sea port. Not that the sea has receded - the estuary has silted up. Much of the Church is 13th c. but the nave and tower is Norman. Closer inspection will reveal two quern-stone rims built into the tower wall. Over the porch door is a sundial which has been telling the time on sunny days for almost 300 years. Inside, the 14th c. font has eight engaged columns and a simple bowl; the cover is carved and is probably contemporary. There are two very nice traceried bench ends with poppyheads. The piscina is 13th c. with unusual dogtooth decoration in the arch and the sedilia is of the same date. Both the old wheeled bier and the hand bier are still preserved in the church. There is a wall monument to Sir William Glover, who died aged 42 in 1660.

GISLEHAM

Dedication: Holy Trinity
No of Bells: 2
Deanery 1836: Lothingland
Hundred: Mutford & Lothingland
Union house: Oulton
Deanery 2000: Lothingland, Norwich

3 m S of Lowestoft
between Lowestoft &
Henstead: in the centre of
the village, on Church Road
at a three-cross-ways.
O.S. grid ref TM 514885
Post Code: NR33 8DT

The tower of this attractive flint and tile church has a Saxon base
with a 15th c. octagonal embattled belfry. The north door, although
blocked, is 12th c. with engaged columns. A scratch dial can be seen
on the buttress. Inside the south porch there is a stoup. Within the
nave the Saxon work in the tower arch can be clearly seen. A stave
locker is built into the tower wall. The bell ropes are hung directly to
the clappers. The font is a traditional East Anglian type with lions
round the base and emblems round the bowl. The piscina is 14th c.
and the contemporary sedilia is a drop sill type with an early purbeck
marble coffin lid as the seat. There is an early memorial dated 1593
to Adam Bland esquire of London and servant to Queen Elizabeth.
There are some mediaeval wall paintings in the window reveals.

GORLESTON

Dedication: St Andrew
No of Bells: 8
Deanery 1836:   Lothingland
Hundred: Mutford & Lothingland
Union house: Oulton
Deanery 2000: Lothingland, Norwich

5 m N of Lowestoft
between   Great Yarmouth
& Lowestoft: near the
roundabout of the B1370 in
Church Road. Hard to miss.
O.S. grid ref TG 524043
Post Code: NR31 6LS

This church started its life as a small church established by the Bishop of Dunwich in the 7th c. and grew with the parish. Once standing in the middle of the countryside, the town of Gorleston has grown around it. A brass memorial to Sir John Bacon (1320) is in the chancel. The font is somewhat defaced but still depicts the seven sacraments. The Arms of Charles I are dated 1644. Two 17th c. paintings of Moses and Aaron flank the tower. There are two piscinas, one 13th c. in the chancel with cusped arch and another in the chapel. The sedilia is a triple stepped dropped sill design. The fine parish chest is iron-bound and dates from the 14th c.. The tower was restored last century as a memorial to the lifeboatmen of the parish, some of whom took part in the evacuation at Dunkirk.

GOSBECK

Dedication:	St Mary	6 miles N of Ipswich
No of Bells:	1	between Needham Market
Deanery 1836:	Bosmere	& Helmingham: situated
Hundred:	Bosmere & Claydon	west of the village in
Union house:	Barham	Church Road.
Deanery 2000:	Bosmere	O.S. grid ref TM 150556
		Post Code: IP6 9SL

Not the usual configuration when you approach the church from the road. You are greeted by the beautiful 14th c. grey flint tower which serves also as a south porch. The niche above the door is sadly empty and at the time of visiting a window had recently been smashed. I found it an attractive and colourful church but sadly lacking any real treasures. The benches are all modern except the stalls in the chancel, the pulpit is Victorian, as is the lectern. There is long and short work at the east end of the nave but whether it is original Saxon work is debatable. The old bier serves as a memorial to those who fell in The Great War. In the roof you will find angels and shields of various designs, and there are five interesting panels which were salvaged from the rood screen when it was dismantled.

GREAT BEALINGS

Dedication:	St Mary	
No of Bells:	4	
Deanery 1836:	Carlford	
Hundred:	Carlford	
Union house:	Nacton	
Deanery 2000:	Woodbridge	

3 m W of Woodbridge
between Woodbridge &
Grundisburg: on the main
street which runs through
the village.
O.S. grid ref TM 230488
Post Code: IP13 6NL

The striking brick and stone north porch dates from the reformation and bears the Seckford family arms. Note, as you enter, that the centre stile of the finely traceried door is not divided but is part of the right door creating a narrower entrance than expected. The font is 13th c. with shallow arcading on the bowl. The treat in this pleasant little church are the bench ends with poppyheads and grotesques, some of which are original 15th c. and are so varied and interesting that an hour can easily be spent comparing them. The Stuart pulpit retains the very fine back and sounding board. There is an angle piscina and a dropped sill sedilia both of late 13th c. date. There are a number of memorials to the Seckford family with good translations from the Latin, which is always useful (other churches please note).

GREAT BLAKENHAM

Dedication:	St Mary	
No of Bells:	2	
Deanery 1836:	Bosmere	
Hundred:	Bosmere & Claydon	
Union house:	Barham	
Deanery 2000:	Bosmere	

4 miles NW of Ipswich between Baylham & Claydon: on the B1113 Stowmarket Road.

O.S. grid ref TM 118508
Post Code: IP6 0LR

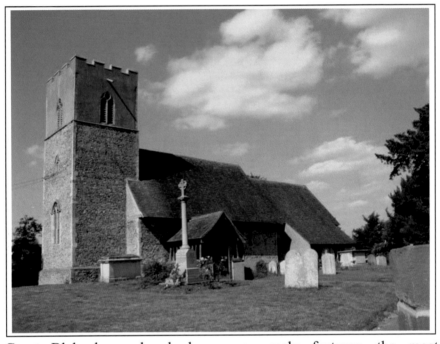

Great Blakenham church has many early features, the most exceptional being the late 12th c. chancel with deep splayed reveals to the windows. The piscina has the typical Norman rounded arch to confirm the period. The arch-braced roofs have obviously gone through changes but the walls are original; outside, a very early scratch dial exists on the south east corner. There are three later dials for comparison on the nave wall. The 15th c. half-timbered porch protects the Norman south doorway while the north remains exposed. Contemporary slit windows remain unblocked and in use. The early 15th c. font bowl and the buttressed shaft are unusual in that they are both heavily carved with details of the Passion and other figures. The lovely Stuart pulpit still retains the back and sounding board.

GREAT BRICETT

Dedication:	Sts Mary & Lawrence	5 miles S of Stowmarket between Wattisham &
No of Bells:	2	Barking: on The Street, just
Deanery 1836:	Bosmere	south east of Wattisham
Hundred:	Bosmere & Claydon	airfield.
Union house:	Barham	O.S. grid ref TM 038506
Deanery 2000:	Bosmere	Post Code: IP7 7DN

Great Bricett or Bricett Magna church was originally a priory church of Augustinian canons at nearby St Leonard's Priory, which was founded in 1114. The chancel had at one time two transepts. Many other changes not always so obvious, have also taken place since it was built by the Normans. The scratch dial is probably Saxon and specially carved in the round. The Norman south door has the word Leonardus engraved in one of the jambs. The blocked north door is of the same date, as is the tower arch . The tower no longer exists. The font is late 12th c. square bowl with arcaded decoration. The nave roof is arch-braced with kingposts. There is a nice example of rood loft stairs which still retain their exit. The pulpit and holy table are interesting and well carved.

GREAT GLEMHAM

		3 m SW of Saxmundham
Dedication:	All Saints	between Parham &
No of Bells:	5	Sweffling: near the junction
Deanery 1836:	Orford	of Chapel Lane & New
Hundred:	Plomesgate	Road.
Union house:	Wickham Market	O.S. grid ref TM 340616
Deanery 2000:	Saxmundham	Post Code: IP17 2DA

The 13th c. church sits very close to the road overlooking the countryside below, dominated by the 15th c. tower. Just inside the north porch is a stoup with a cusped arch. The nave roof is arch-braced and has the usual angels looking down. The central bosses have comical faces carved into them. The stairs to what was the rood loft has floral decoration over the archway still showing the original colouring. The piscina is very plain and is adjacent to the dropped sill sedilia. The seven sacrament font is the real treasure of this church. It has angels round the corbel of the bowl, the seven sacraments depicted in panels, and pots of lilies on the shaft between the buttresses. Two other similar fonts are known at Canterbury and Granborough in Buckinghamshire.

GREAT WENHAM

Dedication:	St John
No of Bells:	3
Deanery 1836:	Samford
Hundred:	Samford
Union house:	Tattingstone
Deanery 2000:	Samford

8 m SW of Ipswich between Capel St Mary & Raydon: approach from Capel St Mary or Holton, situated fairly centrally.
O.S. grid ref TM 070381
Post Code: CO7 6PR

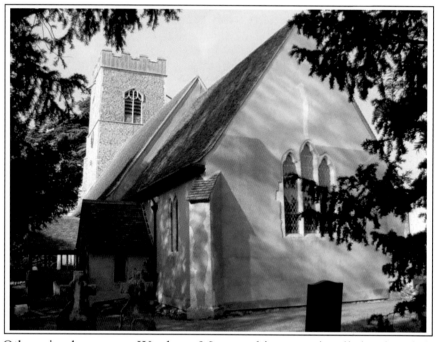

Otherwise known as Wenham Magna, this attractive little church is surrounded by trees and sits comfortably in the well-kept churchyard. The embattled tower with an old clock-face still shows the flint construction, but the body of the church is unfortunately cement-rendered. The lovely half-timbered south porch protects the ancient doorway. Inside there is regrettably little of real interest but there are 15th c. patterned tiles on the floor of the sacrarium which are unglazed. The East family arms are quite impressive, with sword and helmet surmounted by the horse of the family crest. The bench ends are also quite special: one particularly good example has been removed to the Victoria and Albert museum in London.

GRUNDISBURGH

		3 m NW of Woodbridge
Dedication:	St Mary	between Woodbridge &
No of Bells:	12	Swilland: situated on The
Deanery 1836:	Carlford	Green on the north side of
Hundred:	Carlford	the parish.
Union house:	Nacton	O.S. grid ref TM 223510
Deanery 2000:	Woodbridge	Post Code: IP13 6NF

This is a church with two distinct faces. The south one facing the road has all the attractive decoration but the north is very drab in comparison. The south-west tower was rebuilt in brick in the 18th c. but looks very modern with sundial, clock-face and dark quarrelled windows. The church itself is a pleasing mixture of 13th to 16th c. architecture. The interior is well lit by the clerestory, and the 14th c. screen is a beautifully bright example of the wood-carver's art. The font is 15th c. traditional type standing on a three-tier plinth, the upper two being decorated with quatrefoils. The roof is a false double hammerbeam with kingposts. The 13th c. piscina has dogtooth decoration to the arch and hood-mould. The south aisle memorial chapel is to Thomas and Alicia Walle.

114

GUNTON
Dedication: St Peter
No of Bells: none
Deanery 1836:   Lothingland
Hundred: Mutford & Lothingland
Union house: Oulton
Deanery 2000: Lothingland, Norwich

1 m N of Lowestoft
between Lowestoft &
Hopton St Margaret: turn
off the A12 into Gunton
Church Lane and follow.
O.S. grid ref TM 542957
Post Code: NR32 4LQ

As you enter the churchyard, on the left is a small bronze statuette of a young girl holding a bird bath. Dorothy Riley was one of the first victims of the motor car in Gunton. This is a very sterilised church with little to interest the architect or the historian. The nave and chancel are under one roof in what is known as a barn-type church. The round tower is Norman, as are the north and south doorways of the nave. There is also a narrow slit window of the same period. After 'restoration' in the 18th c. and yet more at the turn of the 1900's little else remains of any age or note. It was from the clay of Gunton that the famous Lowestoft china was made. However much of the wealth it created was, it would seem, unfortunately spent on virtually remodelling the church.

HACHESTON

Dedication:	All Saints
No of Bells:	4
Deanery 1836:	Loes
Hundred:	Loes
Union house:	Wickham Market
Deanery 2000:	Loes

3 m SE of Framlingham between Easton & Marlesford: situated south of the village on the B1116. Difficult parking.
O.S. grid ref TM 312585
Post Code: IP13 0DN

The 14th c. tower has niches in the buttresses and gargoyles for decoration. The lower stages may be as early as 12th c.. The west doorway has deep slots in the jambs for a slip-bar, obviously built-in as the tower was constructed. The font is the traditional East Anglian type with wodewoses and lions on the base of the shaft. The pulpit, holy table and font cover are all of the Stuart period. The roof of the nave is 15th c. single hammerbeam construction, alternating with arch-braced collar beams. The rood-beam is still in position, the screen having been removed to the west wall and preserved. Although mutilated, the apostles are still recognisable. The bench-ends are all worth a closer look, being beautifully carved. The piscina and adjacent dropped sill sedilia are both 13th c..

HALESWORTH

Dedication:	St Mary
No of Bells:	8 plus clock bell
Deanery 1836:	Dunwich
Hundred:	Blything
Union house:	Bulcamp
Deanery 2000:	Halesworth

9 m SW of Beccles
between Holton &
Chediston: on the B1123
easily found in the town
centre.
O.S. grid ref TM 386773
Post Code: IP19 8BA

Although traces of a Saxon church on this site have been found, there is not very much of interest to see today (although it does depend on your viewpoint). The church has aisles both north and south of the nave. The piscina has a quatrefoil arch and hood-mould. The font is a traditional East Anglian type with faces round the corbel of the bowl, good deep carving showing the emblems and figures to perfection. The Victorians marred the character of the church by insensitive enlargement of the nave, and more recent renovations have not improved the situation. It is a living church and for that we must be grateful, but I do feel it is lacking the spiritual feeling one should get when entering a building such as this. Compare the feeling with Huntingfield just five miles away. (see page 139)

HARKSTEAD

Dedication:	St Mary
No of Bells:	6
Deanery 1836:	Samford
Hundred:	Samford
Union house:	Tattingstone
Deanery 2000:	Samford

6 m S of Ipswich between Holbrook & Erwarton: north-west of the parish near Harkstead Hall Farm.
O.S. grid ref TM 194352
Post Code: IP9 1DD

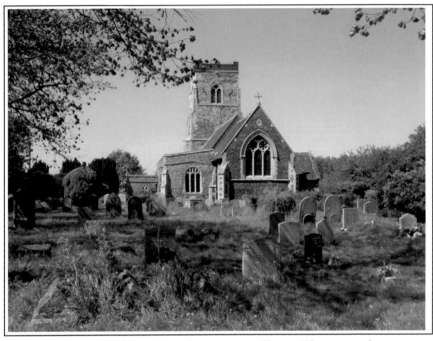

Such a pretty church in attractive surroundings. The tower has a stone panelled base with tracery within. The church is of Norman origins and has a fairly plain north doorway and two Norman windows on the north wall of the nave. The 15th c. font is traditional East Anglian design with the apostles represented around the bowl. Mutilated during the Puritan period, it was re-cut in 1875. The piscina and sedilia are also Victorian restorations. The nave roof is arch-braced whereas the chancel has a single hammerbeam roof. Set into the north wall of the chancel is the very fine 14th c. Easter sepulchre, flanked by ornate pinnacles and central finial. Look closely at the fine detail. There has been much Victorian restoration in this church and it has been exceptionally well executed.

HASKETON

Dedication:	St Andrew
No of Bells:	6
Deanery 1836:	Carlford
Hundred:	Carlford
Union house:	Nacton
Deanery 2000:	Woodbridge

2 m NW of Woodbridge
between Woodbridge &
Grundisburgh: from A12 at
Woodbridge turn west then
north to Church Road.
O.S. grid ref TM 250504
Post Code: IP13 6HA

A rather plain church but with a long history dating back to before the Conquest. The tower is Norman as far as it is circular and the upper octagonal belfry was added in the early 14th c.. The parapet was restored in red brick in the 18th c.. We enter the oldest part of the church (the nave) by the south porch. The nave and chancel have panelled wagon roofs. The font is early 15th c. with shields carrying the Brewes family arms and is in excellent condition, having been protected by plaster during the Commonwealth period. In the base of the tower a Norman pillar piscina is stored: this was discovered in the rockery in the rectory garden. The pulpit and most other fittings are Victorian in origin; some small fragments of 15th c. glass remain in various windows.

HELMINGHAM

		9 m N of Ipswich
Dedication:	St Mary	between Ashbocking &
No of Bells:	8	Framsden: at the northern
Deanery 1836:	Claydon	junction of the B1077 &
Hundred:	Bosmere & Claydon	B1079, east of The Hall.
Union house:	Barham	O.S. grid ref TM 190576
Deanery 2000:	Loes	Post Code: IP14 6EQ

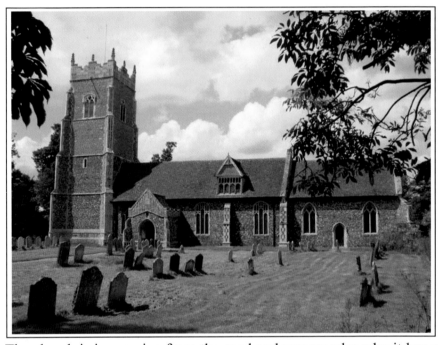

The church is impressive from the road and you wonder why it has a gable window in the roof. Inside you will find the answer. The 16th c. tower was probably funded by Lionel Tollemache, High Sheriff of Norfolk and Suffolk, Helmingham being the ancestral home. There is a scratch dial on the chancel buttress. You enter the church by the 16th c. porch and the early 13th c. south doorway. The doors are 16th c.. The font is 15th c. and has angels and lions around the bowl; four more lions sit round the shaft. The church has many memorials to various members of the Tollemarche family and the largest is the reason for the gable window. The roof is 16th c. arch-braced construction with the braces joining the wall-posts and split with a pendant at the collar. Note the lovely carvings.

HEMINGSTONE

Dedication:	St Gregory
No of Bells:	3
Deanery 1836:	Bosmere
Hundred:	Bosmere & Claydon
Union house:	Barham
Deanery 2000:	Bosmere

7 m N of Ipswich
between Coddenham &
Ashbocking: south of the
B1078 east of Coddenham
on Church Lane.
O.S. grid ref TM 285423
Post Code: IP6 9RE

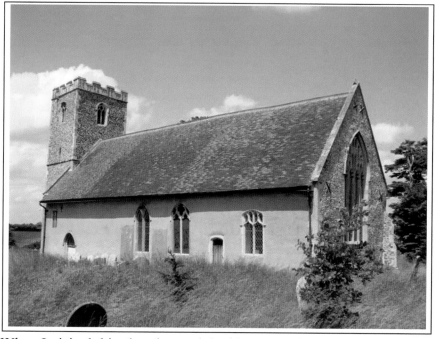

When I visited this church a path had been cut through the deep grass which covered most of the headstones and an artist sat at the gate painting the tranquil scene. The church proudly boasts Saxon long and short work on the corner of the nave. A church has probably stood on this promontory since 7th c.. Inside the north porch stands an enormous pair of organ bellows, now redundant. The door to the tower is 14th c. and completely iron-bound. The 14th c. font is unusually carved with tracery and canopies; the upper part of the cover is 100 years later, the lower part restored. Ralph Cantrell, a Catholic, made his mark by having built a room on the side of the church. His conscience would not allow him to attend church when the law said that one must. Called 'Ralph's hole', it is now a vestry.

HEMLEY		4 m S of Woodbridge
Dedication:	All Saints	between Waldringfield &
No of Bells:	1	Kirton: unmissable as you
Deanery 1836:	Colneis	reach the end of the road
Hundred:	Colneis	near Church Farm.
Union house:	Nacton	O.S. grid ref TM 285423
Deanery 2000:	Colneys	Post Code: IP12 4QE

Hemley is a tiny village on the banks of the river Deben with Ramsholt on the opposite bank. Time hasn't passed it by, it is a thriving community. The tower of the church appears at first glance to be quite modern but it is not. The body of the church is 13th c. and is entered by the half-timbered porch through a south doorway with a cusped arch. Inside there is little distinction between the nave and the chancel, only the style of the roof really sets them apart. The 13th c. font is very mutilated and has a large square bowl supported by a heavy central pillar and four smaller ones at each corner. The base is rather crudely mounded. The reredos is beautifully carved from mahogany, but what it originally was escapes me; a bed-head perhaps!

HENLEY

Dedication:	St Peter	
No of Bells:	8	
Deanery 1836:	Claydon	
Hundred:	Bosmere & Claydon	
Union house:	Barham	
Deanery 2000:	Bosmere	

5 m N of Ipswich
between   Claydon &
Ashbocking: at the junction
of Ashbocking Road &
Church Lane, in the village.
O.S. grid ref TM 159513
Post Code: IP6 0RH

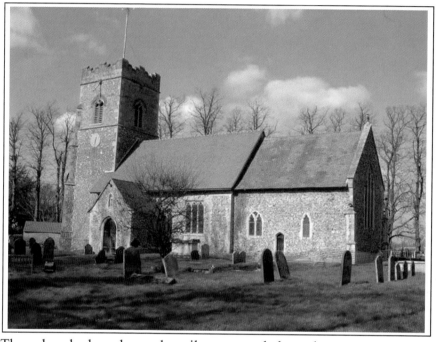

The church has been heavily restored but the restorers were sympathetic and most periods are still well represented. Outside there are two scratch dials on quoin stones of the nave and porch. The 15th c. tower has St Peter's crossed keys on the spandrel of the doorway. The south doorway is 12th c. with a pointed arch and chevron moulding. In the chancel the piscina is contentious as it appears to be a conglomerate of 12th and 13th c. pillar-piscina and stoup respectively. It is flanked by the usual dropped sill sedilia with cusped arches above and nicely merged into the window frame. Above the western door of the tower is an inscription requesting us to sing for Thomas Seckford and his wife Margaret. He died in 1505, and is not to be confused with Sir Thomas Seckford of Woodbridge.

HENSTEAD

		5 m SE of Beccles between
Dedication:	St Mary	Beccles & Kessingland: on
No of Bells:	1	the B1127 at a crossroads
Deanery 1836:	Dunwich	near Henstead Hall. Good
Hundred:	Blything	parking opposite.
Union house:	Bulcamp	O.S. grid ref TM 488860
Deanery 2000:	Halesworth	Post Code: NR34 7LB

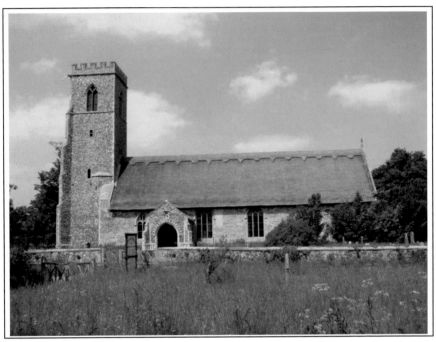

This pretty little thatched church has a treat awaiting you just inside the porch: a Norman doorway with three engaged shafts to the jambs, and a richly moulded arch that wouldn't look out of place in a much grander church. The north doorway is also Norman but not quite so grand, and while you admire the doorway notice the stratification of the flints in this early example of rubble walling. Inside there is a photograph of how the church looked about 1900 although it isn't dated. The old tortoise stove and the sounding board over the pulpit both have disappeared along with the uncomfortable-looking stalls. At about the time of the Great Fire of London (1666) the chancel was destroyed and later rebuilt. Memorials to the Sparrow and Bence families are plentiful.

HERRINGFLEET
Dedication: St Margaret
No of Bells: 2
Deanery 1836:   Lothingland
Hundred: Mutford & Lothingland
Union house: Oulton
Deanery 2000: Lothingland, Norwich

6 m NW of Lowestoft
between   Blundeston & St
Olaves, Norfolk:
unmissable by the side of
the B1074.
O.S. grid ref TM 476978
Post Code: NR32 5QS

Quite a pretty little part thatched church that has plenty of history. Very much associated with St. Olave's Priory in the 11th and 12th centuries. Today only the nave and porch remain thatched. The early Norman tower is a fine example with baluster windows. The tower arch has billet ornamentation around the jambs and head. The south doorway is Norman with 2 engaged columns and a chevron-moulded arch. The old organ in the gallery still has the original handle for pumping the bellows in the event of electrical failure. Some of the glass in the windows originated in a monastery in Cologne and was brought here for safe keeping at the time of the French Revolution. Although the church is usually kept locked the key is readily available at Manor Farm , 400 metres towards Lowestoft.

HEVENINGHAM

Dedication:	St Margaret
No of Bells:	5
Deanery 1836:	Dunwich
Hundred:	Blything
Union house:	Bulcamp
Deanery 2000:	Halesworth

3 m SW of Halesworth between   Laxfield & Walpole: situated in Church Road on the B1117 as is passes through the village. O.S. grid ref TM 333725 Post Code: IP19 0EA

Everyone has heard of Heveningham Hall. The church is less well known, but visitable. It is built on the brow of a hill just south of the river Blyth. Visit here in the early spring and you will find a carpet of daffodils to greet you. The clerestory with its double hammerbeam roof is a 16th c. addition to allow more light into the nave. Close inspection will reveal the apostles in the wall posts. In fact most of the work in the church is of a similar date; almost everything you see is 17th c.. There is a unique carved wooden effigy, said to be that of Sir John Heveningham 1452, but is probably at least 50 years earlier (ref. H. Munro Cautley). It is badly damaged and was rescued from a bonfire which destroyed the effigy of his wife that once lay beside him.

HIGHAM

Dedication:	St Mary
No of Bells:	6
Deanery 1836:	Samford
Hundred:	Samford
Union house:	Tattingstone
Deanery 2000:	Hadleigh

4½ m S of Hadleigh
between Stoke by Nayland
& East Bergholt: south of
the B 1068 down a track
south of Heigham Road.
O.S. grid ref TM 035352
Post Code: CO7 6JY

There are two Highams in Suffolk, the other being in the far west of the county. Neither, unfortunately have much to offer architecturally. St Mary's was over-restored and much of the history and interest have been lost. The 15th c. embattled tower is showing its age and has three distinct stages of building. The church is entered through the north porch which is half-timbered but of no great age. The octagonal font is a very plain affair with quatrefoil decoration. The only real point of interest is the beautiful pier arcade between the nave and the north aisle. The columns have well carved capitals with vine leaves and Tudor rose decoration. There are faces to look for on the wall brackets and two canopied wood-carved figures on the chancel arch. The fine carving on the benches is relatively recent.

HINTLESHAM

Dedication:	St Nicholas	
No of Bells:	6	
Deanery 1836:	Samford	
Hundred:	Samford	
Union house:	Tattingstone	
Deanery 2000:	Hadleigh	

4 m E of Hadleigh between Hadleigh & Sproughton: on the A1071 in George's Street opposite the playing field.
O.S. grid ref TM 087434
Post Code: IP8 3NH

The 15th c. flint embattled tower appears short and stumpy, with only three stages and the clerestory adding to the illusion. The south porch is half-timbered and open to the weather. The church is cement-rendered and the walls look shabby. Inside it is bright and the St Christopher painting takes your attention. The 13th c. pier arcades with moulded capitals are the chief feature of the church. On the south wall of the chancel is a slate monument of 1558 to members of the Timpley or Timperley family. Another is carved in alabaster. The altar rails are late 17th c. with twisted balusters. Behind the Stuart holy table the remains of the rood loft can be seen. The beam across the chancel arch rests upon heads of men. Havelock Ellis, author of 'The Psychology of Sex', died here in 1939.

128

HOLBROOK

Dedication:	All Saints
No of Bells:	6
Deanery 1836:	Samford
Hundred:	Samford
Union house:	Tattingstone
Deanery 2000:	Samford

5 m S of Ipswich
between Stutton & Freston:
on the B1080 (Church
Road) as it passes through
the parish.
O.S. grid ref TM 170361
Post Code: IP9 2PQ

The tower is actually on the south side of the church and acts as a porch; however, the large south aisle makes it appear as at the west. Above the door there is a considerable amount of septaria which was commonly used as building material. There is a scratch dial on the jamb of the south door. The church was constructed in the 14th c. but later extensions have destroyed or hidden much of the original. There is a small piscina in the nave and a 13th c. double piscina in the chancel, flanked by the sedilia. All have cusped arches. The south aisle contains a monument to John Clench, who died in 1607, and whose effigy lies beside his wife. Their 15 children are also represented in a smaller scale. Note the consecration crosses in the walls, which take the form of a stone disc 12 inches in diameter.

HOLLESLEY

Dedication:	All Saints
No of Bells:	8
Deanery 1836:	Wilford
Hundred:	Wilford
Union house:	Nacton
Deanery 2000:	Woodbridge

6 m SE of Woodbridge between Shottisham & Boyton: just east off the main road (Fox Hill) as it passes through the parish. O.S. grid ref TM 353443 Post Code: IP12 3RE

A handsome church by any standards, dating from the 15th c. with neatly slated roof. In the buttress of the tower we notice what appears to be a broken stoup, (H. Munro Cautley claims it is not). The small octagonal 14th c. font decorated with roses and shields is badly mutilated and stands on a single shaft. The finely carved pulpit and holy table are of the Stuart period. A poor example of the Royal Arms of Charles II hangs in the church. The piscina has been re-slabbed and is merely a corner shelf. The real interest for me was the variety of carvings of grotesques and other animals on the bench ends. Although relatively modern they are fascinating, one of them being a sciapus with his huge feet shading his body from the sun.

130

HOLTON

Dedication:	St Mary	
No of Bells:	3	
Deanery 1836:	Samford	
Hundred:	Samford	
Union house:	Tattingstone	
Deanery 2000:	Hadleigh	

5 m SE of Hadleigh between Stratford St Mary & Capel St Mary: just off the A12 on the south side of the B1070.

O.S. grid ref TM 059367

Post Code: CO7 6NP

There are two parishes with the name Holton, the other being near Halesworth. (p. 132) The tower of Holton church has an enormous girth but now lacks height since it became unsafe. What is left is about one third of the original height. The font is 15th c. with quatrefoil design around the bowl and stands on a 13th c. base which still retains the sockets for eight detached columns. The piscina is a simple affair with a cinquefoil cusped arch from engaged columns and is flanked by an even more simple dropped sill sedilia. There are remains of carved Stuart pews in the vestry. The roof is a good example of a barrel vault roof with tie-beams and king-posts. Although I do not ordinarily mention windows because their detail is so specialised, these here are very colourful and interesting.

HOLTON

Dedication: St Peter
No of Bells: 1
Deanery 1836: Dunwich
Hundred: Blything
Union house: Bulcamp
Deanery 2000: Halesworth

1 m E of Halesworth
between Halesworth &
Brampton: on the B1124
(Beccles Road) on the north
side of the road.
O.S. grid ref TM 402778
Post Code: IP19 8NG

If you want to see a fine Norman round tower, look no further. The crenulations and louvered windows are a later addition but most of what you see is how the builders left it. Closer inspection of the tower's east face will reveal the line of an earlier thatched roof. This is not uncommon but is unmistakable here. The south doorway is also Norman and has an engaged shaft to the jamb. Above the door is a contemporary carving of a dragon. Inside, there are two distinct roof styles, a simple arch-braced roof and a scissor-beam roof. The 15th c. font has a traceried design on the bowl and the central shaft has eight small engaged columns. The holy table is of the Stuart period and the Royal Arms that hang above the tower arch are those of George III. (see page 131 for Holton St Mary).

HOMERSFIELD

Dedication:	St Mary	
No of Bells:	3	
Deanery 1836:	South Elmham	
Hundred:	Wangford	
Union house:	Shipmeadow	
Deanery 2000:	Beccles & S. Elmham	

4 m SW of Bungay between Bungay & Harleston, Nfk: from the B1062 turn into the village, Church Lane is on the left.

O.S. grid ref TM 285854

Post Code: IP20 0EU

It is unfortunate that access to the tower is restricted because there is no better view of the Waveney valley than from here. This is a lovely little 13th c. church in a beautiful setting, surrounded by the flora of the season and birdsong, standing on a promontory above the parish it serves. It has not been well restored, but interest remains, notably the Norman slit window in the south wall of the nave, and above it the 14th c. gable cross. The chancel door is unusually elaborate for a small church, having five orders of moulding. Inside there is, in the chancel a 13th c. double drained piscina with a central column and double moulded arch and although it has been restored some original stonework remains. The best access to the church is from the street opposite the thatched cottages.

HOO

Dedication:	St Andrew & Eustachius	
No of Bells:	1	
Deanery 1836:	Loes	
Hundred:	Loes	
Union house:	Wickham Market	
Deanery 2000:	Loes	

4 m SW of Framlingham between Kettleburgh & Charsfield: north on four-crossways, in Church Lane, near The Hall.

O.S. grid ref TM 256592

Post Code: IP13 7QT

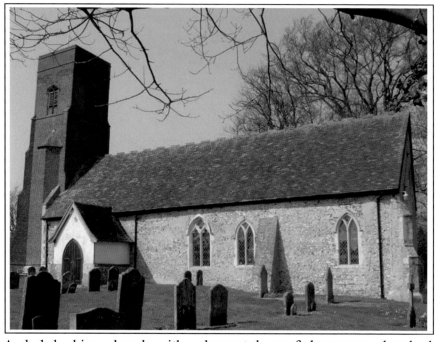

A drab-looking church with a barn-style roof, buttresses that look like a pile of bricks leaning against the wall, and a tower and porch that both lack any interesting features. Having said that, the tower is Tudor with the turret staircase to the belfry clearly visible on the outside. Inside we find a much mutilated font of typical East Anglian style. The most interesting object is probably the parish chest which dates from around 1300 and is iron-bound with what appear to be various bits of scrap metal. The holy table is late Stuart and the altar rails are triangular with square balusters supporting them. The most interesting thing about this church is the unusual dedication of St. Eustachius, a rather obscure 2nd c. Roman saint. The church was featured in Sir Peter Hall's film 'Akenfield'.

HOPTON

Dedication: St Margaret
No of Bells: 2
Deanery 1836: Lothingland
Hundred: Mutford & Lothingland
Union house: Oulton
Deanery 2000: Lothingland, Norwich

4 m N of Lowestoft
between Lowestoft & Gt.
Yarmouth, Norfolk. Just off
the A12. East then north
onto the old road, (on left).
O.S. grid ref TG 524000
Post Code: NR31 9AH

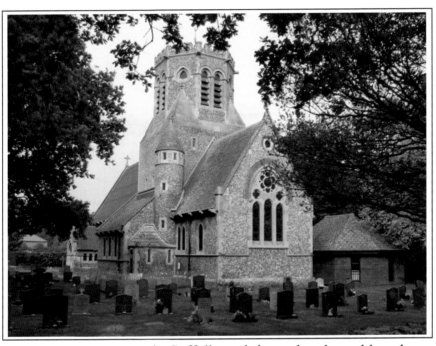

There are two Hoptons in Suffolk, and three churches, although one is a ruin. The other is near Garboldisham. This church is modern and was built in 1865/ 66 and replaces the mediaeval church which was destroyed by fire (see page 136). It was designed by S.S.Teulon and built by Brown & Bailey of Norwich. The design is revolutionary and has a central square tower which becomes octagonal above the roof-line. The belfry is accessed by the turret staircase with the conical roof. The interior is mainly red and white brick dressing with stonework around the windows. Everything in the church is modern and nothing was retrieved from the old church. St. Margaret's has been acclaimed as 'a fine example of a Victorian church in which everything is boldly executed'.

HOPTON with BROTHERTON

Dedication: St Margaret
No of Bells: 2
Deanery 1836:   Lothingland
Hundred: Mutford & Lothingland
Union house: Oulton
Deanery 2000: Lothingland, Norwich

4 m N of Lowestoft
between Lowestoft & Gt.
Yarmouth, Nfk: turn off the
A12 then follow east and
into Coast Road.
O.S. grid ref TM 530999
Post Code: NR31 9BT

This ruin was created when the church burned down (the heating stove went out of control) on a cold January 2nd 1865. The church and tower is 14th c. and the east window shows typical tracery for that period. The roof was thatched, which obviously contributed to the ferocity of the fire. Although the tower still stands at its full height the structure is covered in ivy and detail cannot be seen. The nave was served by a north door without a porch. The west tower is offset to the south corner of the nave allowing an unobstructed west nave window. The font was described as 'curiously sculptured' it would be nice to know where it is today, if it survived. The hamlet of Brotherton, which was to the west of Hopton, was consolidated with Hopton many years ago.

HORHAM

Dedication:	St Mary
No of Bells:	8
Deanery 1836:	Hoxne
Hundred:	Hoxne
Union house:	Stradbroke
Deanery 2000:	Hoxne

5 m E of Eye between Eye & Stradbroke unmissable on the B1117, Stradbroke to Eye road as it passes through the village.
O.S. grid ref TM 210724
Post Code: IP21 5DY

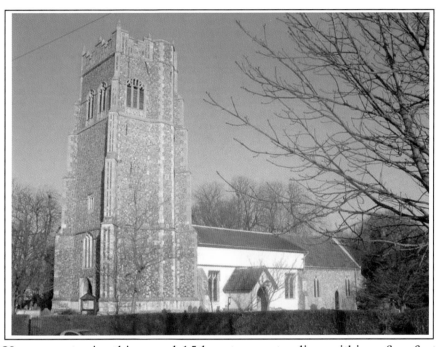

You cannot miss this grand 15th c. tower standing within a few feet of the road. Here is a Norman church with Norman doorways north and south, the latter having two engaged columns to the jambs with a double-order arch with chevrons. Beneath the tower is stored the old two metre long iron-bound parish chest. A few old poppy-head benches remain in use. The Stuart period is represented by the holy table and pulpit. The font is the traditional East Anglian type and has an old conical crocketted cover. The piscina in the chancel is 14th c. cut into the window reveal with a corner column, next to the dropped sill sedilia. It is worth mentioning that in a chancel window there is a quite rare 13th c. grisaille and 14th c. glasswork depicting shields.

HOXNE

		4 m NE of Eye between
Dedication:	St Peter & St Paul	Stradbroke & Scole, Nfk:
No of Bells:	5	on the B1118 next to The
Deanery 1836:	Hoxne	Vicarage near a 90° bend,
Hundred:	Hoxne	use the Vicarage driveway.
Union house:	Stradbroke	O.S. grid ref TM 181775
Deanery 2000:	Hoxne	Post Code: IP21 5BE

Surrounded by a sea of grass and weeds, this copper-roofed church is well worth a visit. A much older church once stood here and the remains can be seen at the west end of the nave where the quoins terminate. There is a scratch dial on one of the buttresses. The nave roof is arch-braced with tie beams with a very low pitch; the chancel is single hammerbeam. The font is octagonal East Anglian style with a tall cover of three tiers. You cannot miss the late 14th c. parish chest which is iron-bound for all of its 8 feet and the matching iron bound cupboard sits next to it. There are eight old bench-ends with carvings on each. The wall paintings above the nave arches are particularly interesting. There is a finely carved memorial to Thomas Maynard and much, much more to see.

HUNTINGFIELD

Dedication:	St Mary
No of Bells:	5
Deanery 1836:	Dunwich
Hundred:	Blything
Union house:	Bulcamp
Deanery 2000:	Halesworth

5 m SW of Halesworth between Linstead Parva & Heveningham: in the centre of the parish turn east onto the Walpole road.
O.S. grid ref TM 336743
Post Code: IP19 0PR

This is a church that once visited is never forgotten. It started life as a Norman church but has been so restored that very little of the original remains. The north wall of the nave (although pierced for the north aisle) with the 12th c. window is original. Some carved stones, apparently discovered buried in the chapel field, have been incorporated into the internal wall of the tower. The south porch is well panelled and two scratch dials are visible, one on the jamb of the 13th c. south door. The font is traditional East Anglian but the very tall elaborate cover is a memorial to Mildred Keyworth Holland, the rector's wife, whose work you see on the ceilings of the nave and chancel. H. Munro Cautley described the work as bedizened, but to me it is restoration at its best.

IKEN

Dedication:	St Botolph
No of Bells:	4
Deanery 1836:	Orford
Hundred:	Plomesgate
Union house:	Wickham Market
Deanery 2000:	Woodbridge

6 m SE of Saxmundham
between Snape &
Sudbourne: once in the
village turn north towards
'The Anchorage'. (signed)
O.S. grid ref TM 412566
Post Code: IP12 2ES

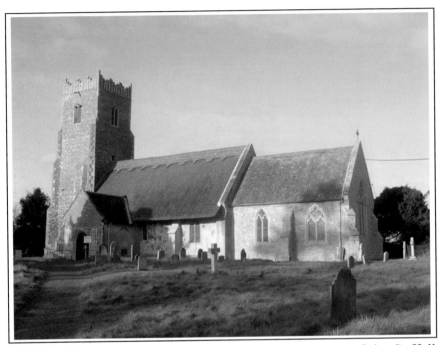

What a beautiful spot to place a church. The richness of the Suffolk countryside all around and Iken Bay as a backdrop. A lovely spot to stop for a picnic. This well cared-for church is part-thatched and part tiled. The 15th c. tower with the embattled parapet is nicely proportioned. There is a scratch dial to find on the door jamb as you enter the windowless porch. This leads us through the south doorway into the nave with its brand new timber-lined roof (the old one caught fire in 1968). The chancel is 19th c. consequently there is no piscina or sedilia. The 14th c. font is the usual traditional East Anglian shape with quite unusual carvings in panels round the bowl. A rare Saxon cross shaft, or upright, which had been built into the base of the tower, has now been placed on display in the nave.

140

ILKETSHALL ST ANDREW

Dedication:	St Andrew	
No of Bells:	4	
Deanery 1836:	Wangford	
Hundred:	Wangford	
Union house:	Shipmeadow	
Deanery 2000:	Beccles & S.Elmham	

4 m SE of Bungay between Halesworth & Bungay: from A144 east into Top Road. follow 1 m then left onto Gt Common. (signed). O.S. grid ref TM 379872 Post Code: NR34 8HX

Situated between the expanse of the huge commons, this church is unusually long. The tower is Norman with a round lower half and an octagonal top. Although the recently discovered wall paintings have aroused a lot of publicity due to their age, for quality the ones at North Cove are far better. Outside is a scratch dial, and the porch, which has a parvise, contains a stoup. The south door is Norman with engaged column and a chevron-moulded arch. The north door, also Norman, is bricked up but there is a slit window in the north nave wall. The font is early 15th c.. The roof of the nave is arch-braced with carved arch braces between the wall posts. The chancel roof is more modern with ten angels depicted in prayer. The tomb in the chancel was once very fine but is now badly mutilated.

ILKETSHALL ST JOHN

Dedication:	St John	
No of Bells:	1	
Deanery 1836:	Wangford	
Hundred:	Wangford	
Union house:	Shipmeadow	
Deanery 2000:	Beccles & S.Elmham	

1½ m SE of Bungay
between Beccles &
Halesworth: south from
Bungay, at the first road
junction on the left.
O.S. grid ref TM 360875
Post Code: NR34 8JJ

The present church dates back to the 14th c.. The square tower has no buttresses and appears very elegant with its fine crenulations. There is a scratch dial on the jamb of the south doorway. The nave and chancel are under a single roof outwardly, but inside the distinction is more apparent. There is cusped ornamentation which follows the line of principal which separates the nave from the chancel. This probably was something to do with a canopy of honour to the rood which has been long since removed. In the south pier of the tower arch is a recess which may at some time have been a banner stave locker. The Royal Arms are those of William IV but are a rather poor example. The stonework of the east window was a gift of Edward VII when he was Prince of Wales.

ILKETSHALL ST LAWRENCE

Dedication:	St Lawrence	4 m SE of Bungay
No of Bells:	2 / 1	between Bungay &
Deanery 1836:	Wangford	Halesworth: unmissable on
Hundred:	Wangford	the east side, in Top Road.
Union house:	Shipmeadow	2½ m north of the school.
Deanery 2000:	Beccles & S.Elmham	O.S. grid ref TM 367863
		Post Code: NR34 8NL

The middle 12th c. church stands on a former Roman camp or way-station, along what is still known as Stone Street.   Scotch pines outline the site, which is entered by a thatched lych-gate. Within the fabric of the walls are Roman tile and brick 2000 years old. It is by no means unattractive from the south, but from the north it is very uninteresting and looks very sorry for itself. Inside, the font is a very plain 15th c. example of its kind. One of the bells dated 1619 has been removed from the belfry because it cracked and is stored below where it once hung. Set into the north wall of the chancel is a small Easter sepulchre with plain arches.   The Royal Arms are those of George II and are dated 1760. Among other memorials is a slate tablet to Anthony Style who died in 1739.

ILKETSHALL ST MARGARET

Dedication:	St Margaret	
No of Bells:	3	
Deanery 1836:	Wangford	
Hundred:	Wangford	
Union house:	Shipmeadow	
Deanery 2000:	Beccles & S.Elmham	

3 m S of Bungay between Bungay & Rumburgh: from near St Lawrence church turn west and follow 1¾ m to village. (on the left). O.S. grid ref TM 350852 Post Code: NR35 1QZ

A pleasant little church set at a bend in the road. The round crenulated tower is Saxon at the base at least and the rest Norman at the latest. The present flint and rubble walls are built on Norman foundations. The nave and chancel are under one roof, raised in the 15th c.. Inside, the chancel has a barrel roof while the nave roof is plastered over. The 500-year-old font is octagonal with blank shields and Tudor roses around the bowl. This is a very plain and austere church which would have suited the Puritans down to the ground. The altar rails are from the Stuart period and the Royal Arms are those of Queen Anne and dated 1704. Beneath the altar are memorial slabs to Thomas Hunne who died in 1689 and various other members of his family, (some earlier some later).

IPSWICH

		South-east of the town
Dedication:	Holy Trinity	centre at the junction of
No of Bells:	1	Fore Hamlet & Back
Deanery 1836:	Ipswich	Hamlet: (Fore Hamlet being
Hundred:	Borough of Ipswich	the Felixtowe Road).
Union house:	Wherstead Rd, Ipswich	O.S. grid ref TM 171440
Deanery 2000:	Ipswich	Post Code: IP3 8AJ

The mediaeval Holy Trinity church was demolished in the reign of William IV and re-built in 1835 from scratch on the same site, the first new church in Ipswich since the Reformation. It was completely re-designed by Frederick Harvey and then extended 60 years later by E. F. Bisshopp. Harvey designed a simple rectangular church with a small chancel at the east and the tower at the west, later to be converted for use as a baptistery. Bisshopp enlarged the chancel with a high aisle to the north, and an organ chamber and vestry was added to the south. Great semi-circular arches were added by piercing the east wall, and two similar arches formed a chancel arcade. The wood-carving was the work of John Groom at a cost of £2000.

IPSWICH

		South east of the town
Dedication:	St Clement	centre between Long Street
No of Bells:	6	& Back Hamlet: near
Deanery 1836:	Ipswich	University College Suffolk,
Hundred:	Borough of Ipswich	Grimwade Street.
Union house: Wherstead Rd, Ipswich		O.S. grid ref TM 168442
Deanery 2000:	Ipswich	Post Code: IP4 1JH

A stone's throw from Holy Trinity, this church is now disused, at least as a church. As a rubbish dump it is thriving. Such a shame that one of the nicest looking churches in Ipswich, a town that prides itself in its number of churches, can allow this to happen. H. Munro Cautley says that it contains a traditional East Anglian font and a very fine set of Charles II Arms dated 1661. I cannot argue as I was unable to gain access. The chancel and vestry were apparently renewed in 1860 and more modernisation done twenty years later with the removal of the side galleries. The clerestory walls have been refaced with knapped flint and stonework replaced over time. The stone tracery in the windows is worth viewing for the number of variations of style and type.

IPSWICH

Dedication:	St Helen
No of Bells:	2
Deanery 1836:	Ipswich
Hundred:	Borough of Ipswich
Union house: Wherstead Rd, Ipswich	
Deanery 2000:	Ipswich

Directly east of the town centre in St. Helen's Street (via Spring Road) left off the A1214. Right beside the road.

O.S. grid ref TM 170445

Post Code: IP4 2LS

Standing beside the road named after the church, this comparatively small church is a hotch-potch of add-ons squeezed between other buildings. The 19th c. tower, built in flint with Bath stone dressings surmounted by the zinc-covered spire, is similar in appearance to Great Finborough but on a much smaller scale. Built in the Perpendicular style, the restorations have faithfully followed suit and the overall appearance is, despite everything, reasonably pleasing. Inside you will find two old bells removed from the belfry and placed in the nave. One is 15th c. mediaeval, the other dated 1621. Inside it has been modernised to accommodate the 21st century style of worship with seats in a semicircle around a holy table giving it the general appearance of a music hall.

147

IPSWICH

Dedication: St Lawrence
No of Bells: 5
Deanery 1836: Ipswich
Hundred: Borough of Ipswich
Union house: Wherstead Rd, Ipswich
Deanery 2000: Ipswich

Within the confines of the town centre in St. Lawrence Street: between the Buttermarket & Tavern Street.
O.S. grid ref TM 163445
Post Code: IP1 1DL

This is another of the town's churches that is squeezed between other buildings with little room to breathe. The church is basically 15th c. although the east wall and window were replaced in 1858. The tower was demolished and rebuilt to 97 feet in 1881/2. It is very extravagant, with flushwork and much decorative stonework with quatrefoil banding, topped battlements and four delicate pinnacles. The belfry openings are large and elaborate. Inside the church very little remains of any historical interest except perhaps a Stuart holy table. There is one notable memorial, to John Baldwin and his wife Joane: it is outside, below the east window, and begs that their souls be prayed for along with the souls of all Christians.

148

IPSWICH

Dedication: St Margaret
No of Bells: 8
Deanery 1836: Ipswich
Hundred: Borough of Ipswich
Union house: Wherstead Rd, Ipswich
Deanery 2000: Ipswich

Within the town centre on St. Margaret's Green, just north of St. Margaret's Road southern inner relief road.
O.S. grid ref TM 166448
Post Code: IP4 2BX

This is the only church within the town that is not crammed in by houses, shops or offices; and rightly so. It is a handsome church in grey flint and stone with a sturdy square tower, beautifully decorated. The 15th c. porch has three canopied niches. The lovely clerestory is doubly embattled with pinnacles. Inside the church the 15th c. double hammerbeam roof of the nave is quite outstanding, the wall-posts having canopied niches with seated figures. The font is of the same date and has engraved panels. The Arms of Charles II hang on the west wall. The organ occupies the south transept which was formerly a Lady chapel. Here there is a canopied altar tomb to Sir William Roskin (1512) flanked by a piscina and aumbry. There is much to see and admire in and around this lovely church.

IPSWICH

		Within the town centre
Dedication:	St Mary at Elms	in Elm Street, eastwards off
No of Bells:	5	Civic Drive near the Police
Deanery 1836:	Ipswich	Station.
Hundred:	Borough of Ipswich	
Union house: Wherstead Rd, Ipswich		O.S. grid ref TM 160445
Deanery 2000:	Ipswich	Post Code: IP1 2AA

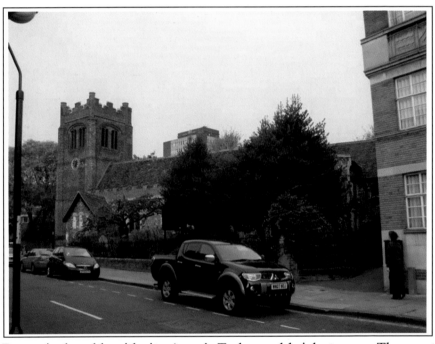

Deceptively old with its 'new' Tudor red-brick tower. The neat crenulations, octagonal corner-posts, and double belfry openings make it quite attractive and comfortable in the modern office-block surroundings. The porch and walls seem ancient but have been deliberately aged by facing with knapped flint by the Victorians. The church has Norman origins, as the south doorway will bear out, with an engaged shaft to each jamb. Even the ironwork may be contemporary. Much has been altered on the inside. The chancel was added in 1883 and the north aisle lengthened, and at the same time the fine hammerbeam roof was constructed. The west gallery was removed and the fittings replaced with new. All this modernisation took place while the building stood in open ground.

IPSWICH

Dedication: St Mary at Quay
No of Bells: 6
Deanery 1836: Ipswich
Hundred: Borough of Ipswich
Union house: Wherstead Rd, Ipswich
Deanery 2000: Ipswich

South of the town centre between College Street & Key Street off Star Lane in Foundation Street.

O.S. grid ref TM 165440
Post Code: IP4 1BN

Is it Quay or Key, who knows? Both are used for the church and street names. There is however, a large key on the weather vane. The church was made redundant and is cared for by the Churches Conservation Trust. It is an Arts Centre but retains the atmosphere of a church. The fine double hammerbeam roof and clerestory offer plenty of space and light. The traditional East Anglian-type font is very defaced but an eagle, cow and lion can just be discerned among the heraldic angels, and round the shaft are the usual four lions. In the north aisle there is a blackened monument to Henry Tooley (1551) who was an important local benefactor. A short distance away, in Foundation Street, his alms houses are still standing. A bell stands by the south door, having been removed from the belfry.

IPSWICH

Dedication:	St Mary at Stoke
No of Bells:	2
Deanery 1836:	Ipswich
Hundred:	Borough of Ipswich
Union house:	Wherstead Rd, Ipswich
Deanery 2000:	Ipswich

South of the town centre in Stoke, between Stoke Street & Burrell Road on Belstead Road.

O.S. grid ref TM 162438
Post Code: IP2 8DA

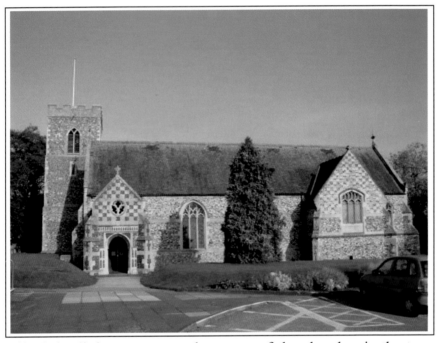

Afforded a little more space than most of the churches in the town but still under stress from nearby buildings and roads. Unrecognisable from the drawing that Davy made in 1839 when the west tower stood central to the nave. The present tower, only two-thirds of the height of the former appears to stand further north, but it was in fact the nave that was extended southwards, building over the top of some of the graves. Nothing seems to have changed in that respect! The brick porch with the parvise and fine south face it once had was demolished and a flint and stone one built in its place. The roof, too, has lost the dormer window that once allowed light onto the rood, but no clerestory was never added. The Arms displayed in the church are those of the Dean and Chapter of Ely.

IPSWICH

Dedication:	St Mary le Tower	
No of Bells:	12	
Deanery 1836:	Ipswich	
Hundred:	Borough of Ipswich	
Union house: Wherstead Rd, Ipswich		
Deanery 2000:	Ipswich	

Within the town centre near the Tower Ramparts Bus Station reachable from Tower Street or Northgate Street. Park the car & walk. O.S. grid ref TM 164446 Post Code: IP1 3BN

Because this building is so enclosed by surrounding buildings it is impossible to photograph in its full glory. I have used this black and white I discovered on a postcard. My grateful thanks to the photographer, because no-one will ever be able to see that view again. Shame on you, Ipswich! This beautiful church has been restored and rebuilt over the centuries and the result is this elegant Victorian edifice. The spire rises to 176, feet, and the present church is the result of work carried out between 1830 and 1880 by various architects and builders. Originally the intention was to restore the building, but there were so many 'encumbrances and disfigurements of the last two centuries' that the whole lot was demolished and work started afresh. Hardly restoration, but the result speaks for itself.

IPSWICH

Dedication:	St Matthew	
No of Bells:	6	
Deanery 1836:	Ipswich	
Hundred:	Borough of Ipswich	
Union house:	Wherstead Rd, Ipswich	
Deanery 2000:	Ipswich	

Within the town centre on the west side of Civic Drive, near the underground car park.

O.S. grid ref TM 158447
Post Code: IP1 2AX

A church with unusually pierced battlements on the tower should make it easily recognisable. However, it is often missed by drivers and passengers. It is a much restored church, but, if you can, pull into the car park and have a look at the gloriously unique 15th c. font. It has an octagonal bowl and is richly carved with double canopies of fine tracery and figures of 'The Virgin' at various stages of her life. The shaft is also carved, with evangelistic figures. In the north aisle the screen incorporates six early 16th c. panels from the old rood screen. Before restorations there was, like St Mary Stoke and St Nicholas, a dormer window in the roof to light the rood; but this was probably letting in water and therefore was not replaced when the roof was renewed.

IPSWICH

Dedication: St Nicholas
No of Bells: 5
Deanery 1836:   Ipswich
Hundred: Borough of Ipswich
Union house: Wherstead Rd, Ipswich
Deanery 2000:   Ipswich

Within the town centre
in Franciscan Way between
Cromwell Square & Cutler
Street.

O.S. grid ref TM 161442
Post Code: IP1 1LG

This little church is almost dwarfed beside the great edifices of commerce that are its neighbours. Built into the parapet of the tower are four niches, occupied by four male figures. The north aisle contains carvings dated to the 11th c., one inscribed 'HER SANCTUS MICHAEL FEHT WID DANE GRAGON'. The 14th c. nave and aisles are also interesting in that the pier arcade is particularly well carved with moulded capitals and arguably the finest in Suffolk. All the windows in the aisle have sills wide enough for members of the congregation to sit upon. The roof still retains the 15th c. dormer windows which give light to the rood. The pulpit and altar rails are Stuart. There has been some restoration of this church but more of the original retained than in any of the others in the town.

IPSWICH

Dedication:	St Peter	
No of Bells:	6	
Deanery 1836:	Ipswich	
Hundred:	Borough of Ipswich	
Union house:	Wherstead Rd, Ipswich	
Deanery 2000:	Ipswich	

South of the town centre at the western junction of College Street & Star Lane, next to a roundabout.

O.S. grid ref TM 163441

Post Code: IP4 1LB

Standing guard over a roundabout near the docks and within a stones-throw of St Mary at Quay the 15th c. tower has six tiers. The lower tier accommodating the western doorway has two canopied niches, each side large enough for life-size images. The upper portion of the tower was rebuilt in 1881. The 12th c. font is famous, for it is one of the Tournai group, with a 42" square bowl. These fonts were carved from black marble imported from Tournai in Belgium and there are only 7 in England. The 13th c. piscina is situated beside the rood loft stairs. There is a brass to John Knapp (1604) and his wife in the south chapel. It is currently undergoing restoration and I look forward to seeing the result. Beside the church and leading to the east end are Wolsey's Gates.

IPSWICH

Dedication:	St Stephen	Within the town centre in St. Stephen's Lane.
No of Bells:	3	Now the Tourist Office!
Deanery 1836:	Ipswich	Just follow the 'tourist
Hundred:	Borough of Ipswich	information' signs.
Union house:	Wherstead Rd, Ipswich	O.S. grid ref TM 164444
Deanery 2000:	Ipswich	Post Code: IP1 1DR

Now utilised as a tourist information centre, access is through a doorway beneath the west tower, (to the right is a large niche). The roof is 16th c. braced tie-beam with king and queen posts. There are large carvings of flowers at the intersections of the purlin and principal. The chancel roof is single hammerbeam construction of the same period. Various stages of restoration and modernisation have taken place over the centuries but the building retains its charm, despite the hubbub within. There is a memorial in the chancel to Robert Leman and his wife Mary who both died the same day in 1637. *"The same sun that closed her eyes in the morning shutting up his in the evening."* The Royal Arms of Charles II are very fine and hang high above the heads of the visitors.

157

KELSALE (with Carlton)
Dedication: Sts Mary & Peter
No of Bells: 8
Deanery 1836: Hoxne (detached)
Hundred: Hoxne
Union house: Bulcamp
Deanery 2000: Saxmundham

1 m N of Saxmundham
between Saxmundham &
Yoxford: on the A1121 (old
A12) east by the playing
field and into Church Lane.
O.S. grid ref TM 387651
Post Code: IP17 2NZ

Kelsale is probably better known for E.S. Prior's lychgate than the
church. It was built by the Rector of the time as a tribute to his wife,
but it would be more at home in Asia than in a Suffolk churchyard.
The imposing 14th c. crenulated tower sits at the west of the south
aisle. To the north there is a Norman doorway with two engaged
columns and a four-order arch with chevron and billet ornamentation.
Another original Norman doorway has been moved and rebuilt into
the south aisle chancel. It has undergone a good deal of restoration
and change but in general has been well carried out. The porch is
15th c. complete with scratch dial. The font is unusually wide with
deep, bold carving on the panels with four lions around the shaft. The
pulpit is early 17th c. and takes an unusual form.

KENTON

Dedication:	All Saints	6 m SE of Eye, between Debenham &
No of Bells:	2	Worlingworth: in the centre
Deanery 1836:	Loes	of the village opposite
Hundred:	Loes	Church Farm.
Union house:	Wickham Market	O.S. grid ref TM 191659
Deanery 2000:	Loes	Post Code: IP14 6JW

Kenton church has a Norman pedigree and some Norman work can still be seen; the south doorway for instance is 12th c. complete with two scratch dials. The east chancel wall is heavily buttressed but offers no support north or south. The tower with its neat crenulations is 14th c. and the nave 100 years later. The porch with its attractive doorway abuts the small south aisle of early Tudor construction. Inside we find the 13th c. font while the square parish chest is a century later. There are eight old but simple bench-ends and the holy table is Tudor. The stairs to the rood loft remain open although they lead nowhere. In an oak frame on the wall are portraits of John Garney (1524) and his wife Elizabeth, with their 15 offspring immortalised in brass.

KESGRAVE

Dedication:	All Saints
No of Bells:	1
Deanery 1836:	Carlford
Hundred:	Carlford
Union house:	Nacton
Deanery 2000:	Ipswich

4 m E of Ipswich
between Ipswich &
Martlesham: on the A1214
near The Bell Inn, PH,
(behind a low wall).
O.S. grid ref TM 218457
Post Code: IP5 1NN

Although a church was recorded in the Domesday Book there is no evidence to suggest it was this church, or any part of it. Today it is a sorry sight to behold, with a carbuncle of a community centre on its backside. No doubt some graves, which people had paid for, had to be moved to dig the footings. The cement rendering on the walls of the nave and chancel, although sound, add to the drabness of the building. It is one of the most disappointing churches I have seen and although the graveyard is well kept I was saddened by what has happened to what was at one time a beautiful little country church. The tower is of red brick and of no great age. The 14th c. north porch has lovely floral decoration on the hood-mould. The piscina is early 14th c. and the Royal Arms are those of George III.

KESSINGLAND

		4 m S of Lowestoft
Dedication:	St Edmund	between Lowestoft &
No of Bells:	6	Wrentham: turn off the A12
Deanery 1836:	Lothingland	at roundabout; signed as
Hundred:	Mutford & Lothingland	Kessingland Beach (B1437)
Union house:	Oulton	O.S. grid ref TM 527862
Deanery 2000: Lothingland, Norwich		Post Code: NR33 7SQ

The 15th c., 29 metres tall tower is a landmark for miles around, but the church that once stood to the east has long since gone. The west window in the tower is flanked by striking niches and corbels. A board high on the wall of the nave tells us that the old church was 'put out' and rebuilt in 1694 / 95. Part of what was the south wall is still standing to the south of the church. The octagonal 14th c. font is exceptionally well carved and arguably the finest in the county. Unfortunately the figures, of which there are many, have been mutilated and it is not easy to recognise who they represent. But Kings, Bishops and Apostles they certainly are. Throughout the church there are memorials to those who have risked and often lost their lives at sea.

KETTLEBURGH

Dedication: St Andrew
No of Bells: 6
Deanery 1836: Loes
Hundred: Loes
Union house: Wickham Market
Deanery 2000: Loes

3 m SW of Framlingham between Earl Soham & Wickham Market: situated just north of the village in Church Road.
O.S. grid ref TM 264606
Post Code: IP13 7LF

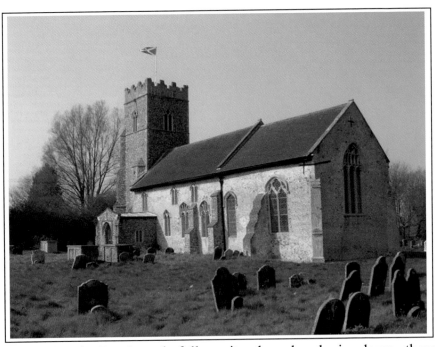

Find Church Road and follow it, the church is down there somewhere. It is a pleasure to come upon, with the 14th c. tower with its embattled parapet and flag of St. Andrew at the top of the pole. The chancel is obviously in trouble, as metal straps and enormous buttresses are all that is keeping it vertical. On the north side is the redundant piscina of a long dismantled chapel. The porch is a low affair with an empty niche in the gable. As you enter through the ancient doorway you are surrounded by old Elizabethan and Jacobean woodwork and carving of varying degrees of skill. The 15th c. font is typical East Anglian style but the support columns are missing. There is an old brass in the sanctuary to Arthur Pennyng (1593) and his two wives.

KIRKLEY (or South Lowestoft)
Dedication: St John
No of Bells: 1
Deanery 1836:   Lothingland
Hundred: Mutford & Lothingland
Union house: Oulton
Deanery 2000: Lothingland, Norwich

200 yds S of Lowestoft
bridge: on the junction of
Belvedere Road & London
Road South; Levington
Court was built on the site.
O.S. grid ref TM 546925
Post Code: NR33 0PH

Built by Sir Morton Peto to serve those living on the south side of the
bridge in 1853 it served for just over 100 years as the parish church
for north Kirkley or as it is more commonly known, South Lowestoft.
The weathercock, which was the first thing on the east coast to greet
the sun for almost a century, was rescued from the steeple and is in
the Lowestoft museum. It was designed by J. L. Clemence in
transitional Decorated style. The tower was unusually situated at the
east of the south transept. An aisle was added in 1881 but continual
flooding in the 20th c. began to undermine the foundations and it was
demolished in 1977. Nothing remains from the inside of this fine
church and the dedication is now combined with that of St. Peter's,
Kirkley.

KIRKLEY

Dedication: St Peter & St John
No of Bells: 1
Deanery 1836: Lothingland
Hundred: Mutford & Lothingland
Union house: Oulton
Deanery 2000: Lothingland, Norwich

½ m S of Lowestoft bridge between Lowestoft & Pakefield: junction of St Peter's Road and Rectory Road.
O.S. grid ref TM 540915
Post Code: NR33 0ED

This church, which until the 1970's was dedicated solely to St. Peter, has undergone so many changes over the centuries. If it was not for the uniqueness of the pinnacles on the 22-metre tower it would be totally unrecognisable to its builders. In the early history of the structure the tower stood at the north west corner of the nave and it was surrounded by open countryside. As the nave was widened northwards it became more central to the footprint of the building. So much rebuilding has taken place that little of the original nave and chancel remain. The present church interior is thoroughly modern and uninteresting to the historian. It has an apsidal baptistery at the west end of the nave. The church does possess an Elizabethan cup, and a mediaeval bell still hangs in the belfry.

KIRTON

Dedication:	Sts Mary & Martin	
No of Bells:	1	
Deanery 1836:	Colneis	
Hundred:	Colneis	
Union house:	Nacton	
Deanery 2000:	Colneys	

8 m SE of Ipswich
between   Bucklesham &
Felixstowe: from the
Falkenham Road turn north
into Church Road.
O.S. grid ref TM 281397
Post Code: IP10 0PT

As you approach the church you will notice how brown the tower appears. This is because septaria was largely used in its construction. It seems to blend in nicely with the colour of the roofs. The church was mentioned in Domesday but no sign of the Saxon building remains today. Today's church is mainly 15th c. with the tower being added half a century later. The roof of the nave has the appearance of an inverted hull of a ship. The 14th c. piscina is flanked by a dropped sill sedilia. The font is a strange one; it is of 13th c. square design with a supporting column at each corner, but lacks the usual decorations apart from flowers around the base of the bowl. The 18th c. rector's daughter was the writer Clara Reeve. She is buried in St. Stephen's churchyard in Ipswich.

KNODISHALL
Dedication: St Lawrence
No of Bells: 1
Deanery 1836: Dunwich
Hundred: Blything
Union house: Bulcamp
Deanery 2000: Saxmundham

3 m SE of Saxmundham
between Saxmundham &
Leiston: from the B1119
turn south near Leiston
House Farm.
O.S. grid ref TM 425619
Post Code: IP17 1TP

Knodishall includes the old parish of Buxlow or Buxlee, now Knodishall Green. The church sits on a prominence and the 15th c. tower can be seen some distance away. The tower is without battlements and would look rather plain if it were not for the flushwork and armorial shields on the parapet, and there is a scratch dial on the south doorway. There is a west doorway in the tower. There are still signs of the Norman builder's achievements if you look hard enough. The purbeck font is typical 13th c. example with shallow carving on the bowl. It has a central shaft and eight detached columns. The pulpit is of Stuart origins and there are three traceried panels of a 16th c. screen. There is an old brass on the nave wall dated 1460 of John Jenny and his wife.

LAXFIELD

Dedication:	All Saints	
No of Bells:	6	
Deanery 1836:	Hoxne	
Hundred:	Hoxne	
Union house:	Stradbroke	
Deanery 2000:	Hoxne	

6 m N of Framlingham
between Stradbroke &
Heveningham: on the
B1117 in the village centre,
next to The Royal Oak PH.
O.S. grid ref TM 296724
Post Code: IP13 8DH

This is an imposing looking 15th c. church with a fine embattled tower surmounted by elegant pinnacles. The porch, with niches either side of the doorway, was once much grander with a parvise above. Just inside the door is a poor-box on a simple turned leg, dated 1664. The nave is 36 feet wide and is a large span for a timbered roof . The 15th c. benches are beautifully carved on the ends and backs, with various stylised poppyheads. The 15th c. font is very elaborate and stands on a pedestal which in turn stands on a Maltese cross on an octagonal foot on an octagonal plinth. It is carved with the seven sacraments around the bowl and decorated at all levels with geometric patterns and foliage. The pulpit is Stuart and the prayer desk is Elizabethan. William Dowsing was born here.

LEISTON

Dedication:	St Margaret
No of Bells:	8
Deanery 1836:	Dunwich
Hundred:	Blything
Union house:	Bulcamp
Deanery 2000:	Saxmundham

4 m E of Saxmundham
between Saxmundham &
the coast: on the B1119
(Waterloo Avenue) turn
south into Church Road
O.S. grid ref TM 438624
Post Code: IP16 4HG

The only thing of any age here is the 15th c. tower. All that stands around it is mid 19th c. and modern in comparison. It was privately funded by a small grant, and the parishioners paid only for restoration of the tower. It is a cruciform church with the tower retained at the west end, designed by Edward Lamb and built in 1853. All around the church there are bands of Caen stone about 3 feet apart, dividing the flint infill, somewhat less noticeable now than when new. Inside, the nave has a double hammerbeam roof but it is the technical achievement of the crossing that is most impressive. The church has retained the original circular 13th c. font and 17th c. oak cover. The parish chest is a strange affair with a pyramidal lid. There is a bust of Richard Garrett.

LETHERINGHAM

Dedication:	St Mary
No of Bells:	1
Deanery 1836:	Loes
Hundred:	Loes
Union house:	Wickham Market
Deanery 2000:	Loes

4 m S of Framlingham
between Wickham Market
& Kettleburgh: just west of
Easton Farm Park, head to
Abbey Farm near bridge.
O.S. grid ref TM 268585
Post Code: IP13 7QU

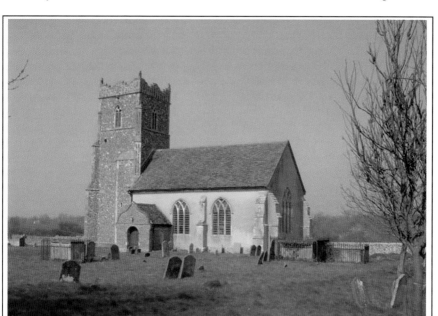

This is a very small church and is noticeably without a chancel at the east end. It is nevertheless an attractive church sitting comfortably on the banks of the river Deben. Today it seems more of a museum than a church, with displayed ancient artefacts in glass cases. Outside there is a sundial dated 1608. The builders were Norman and there is much of their work still visible. The nave was originally the priory church. The priory was founded by William de Boville in 1194 and lasted until 1537 when it was dissolved. There were many great monuments to members of the Wingfield family but only one remains, to Sir John de Wyngefeld (1389). The 'church wardens' in 1789 demolished the chancel, and the monuments were used to repair the roads thereabouts. Worth a visit for curiosity alone.

LEVINGTON

Dedication:	St Peter	
No of Bells:	3	
Deanery 1836:	Colneis	
Hundred:	Colneis	
Union house:	Nacton	
Deanery 2000:	Colneys	

4 m SE of Ipswich
between Nacton & the
Trimleys: once in the
village centre, follow
Church Road, southwards.
O.S. grid ref TM 234390
Post Code: IP10 0LQ

Although the 17th c. tower is somewhat truncated it has a beautiful view of the Orwell from the northern bank on a sunny day. The porch is as quaint as the rest of the church, half timbered with a brick base and strangely curved roof. We can see from the outside that the windows are all different. and as we enter the church through the askew doorway we find the walls are leaning outwards to a greater extent than we are used to. All that stops the roof falling outwards is the arch-braced collar roof. The font is 15th c. and has heraldic panels around the bowl. The pulpit is a nice example of Stuart workmanship. Just down the road are the ruins of Stratton St Peter which fell into disrepair and was abandoned 500 years ago. The parish has been part of Trimley St Martin ever since.

LINSTEAD MAGNA

Dedication:	St Peter
No of Bells:	1
Deanery 1836:	Dunwich
Hundred:	Blything
Union house:	Bulcamp
Deanery 2000:	Halesworth

4 m WSW of Halesworth between Fressingfield & Halesworth: Nothing remains of this church and is on private farmland.
O.S. grid ref TM 317763
Post Code: -

This photograph, which I think is the only photograph in existence of Linstead Magna was taken in 1922. It illustrates very well the manner in which a church can fall into decay. It stood in this state until, in 1964, it was bulldozed by the farmer and the material used to make roadways on the farm. Hardly a pathway to heaven! The headstones from the churchyard were unceremoniously flung into a nearby ditch. Some of those later rescued can be seen leaning against the wall of Linstead Parva. (see over) I am pleased to say that the 13th c. font was also rescued, along with the single mediaeval bell. Both were installed at St Augustine's church in Ipswich, which was built in 1926 and designed by H. Munro Cautley. The site and the church at Linstead Magna were obliterated and nothing remains above ground.

LINSTEAD PARVA

Dedication: St Margaret of Antioch
No of Bells: 1
Deanery 1836: Dunwich
Hundred: Blything
Union house: Bulcamp
Deanery 2000: Halesworth

3 m W of Halesworth
between Halesworth &
Metfield: on the B1123
(Halesworth Road) at an
offset crossroads.
O.S. grid ref TM 337777
Post Code: IP19 0AE

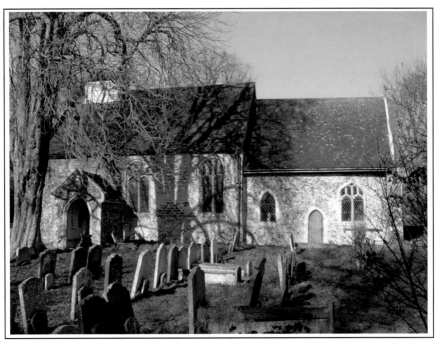

This small church was probably built in the 12th c. by William de Huntingfield who founded Mendham priory. Then in the 15th c. some changes and modernisation took place. Some windows were enlarged and the nave was re-roofed. The traditional octagonal East Anglian font is virtually unscathed and the carving is quite fine. The benches with their poppyhead carved ends came from Linstead Magna before its demise. In 1553 there were two bells in the belfry, but since 1789 there has been only one. The small wooden belfry can be seen on the west end of the nave roof. Leaning against the west wall are about 10 or 12 headstones which were rescued from the drainage ditch at Linstead Magna where the farmer tossed them (see previous page). A lovely little church, best visited in spring.

LITTLE BEALINGS

Dedication:	All Saints	
No of Bells:	2	
Deanery 1836:	Carlford	
Hundred:	Carlford	
Union house:	Nacton	
Deanery 2000:	Woodbridge	

3 m SW of Woodbridge between Woodbridge & Culpho: north of the Railway line at north end of The Street.
O.S. grid ref TM 229479
Post Code: IP13 6LJ

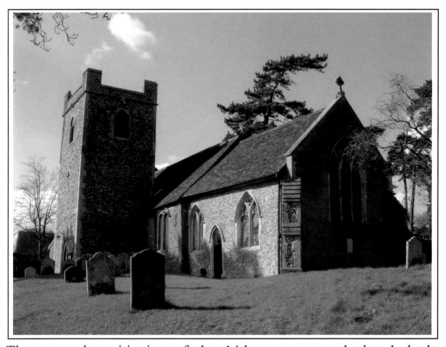

The unusual positioning of the 14th c. tower and church looks awkward but it was probably due to the contours of the ground on which the church sits which brought about this configuration. The tower serves as south porch and the bells are rung from here. As we enter the nave it is bright and welcoming. The poor font has suffered as badly as any I have seen. Attacked with an axe by Dowsing and his thugs, only two of the eight panels are still recognisable. The roof of the nave and north aisle have been plastered but the nave still has the embattled cornice. The pulpit is Stuart in date. On the wall of the chancel is a memorial to members of the Colvin family: Maria, James, her husband, and John and Edward two of their sons. The first of the Rectors of the parish was Giles Dodingesles in 1296.

173

LITTLE BLAKENHAM

Dedication:	St Mary
No of Bells:	2
Deanery 1836:	Bosmere
Hundred:	Bosmere & Claydon
Union house:	Barham
Deanery 2000:	Bosmere

4 m NW of Ipswich between   Somersham & Claydon: once in the village centre, turn north into Valley Road.
O.S. grid ref TM 104488
Post Code: IP8 4LS

This mediaeval church stands with its un-buttressed tower and south porch overlooking the Gipping valley in a very pleasant part of the county. A niche above the door arch has a small statue of Madonna and Child. There was an old scratch dial on the wall but I believe it has been rendered over. The chancel is 750 years old and adorned with frescoes. In a window reveal are some of the best preserved wall paintings I have seen, although small. The piscina has a moulded arch but the sedilia has disappeared. Although the restorations have not been as mindful as they might have been, it is still a pleasant little church. Probably the most valuable possession is the very good set of Royal Arms of James I dated 1685.

LITTLE GLEMHAM

Dedication:	St Andrew	
No of Bells:	5	
Deanery 1836:	Orford	
Hundred:	Plomesgate	
Union house:	Wickham Market	
Deanery 2000:	Saxmundham	

5 m SW of Saxmundham between Marlesford & Stratford St Andrew: turn east into Church Road near village sign, & follow ¼ m.
O.S. grid ref TM 346587
Post Code: IP13 0BH

If you visit this church you must get a key to go inside if it isn't open already. When you enter you will realise, as I did, why it is kept locked. As you approach the15th c. tower notice the niche and statue above the door; turn left, and have a look at the Norman north door with engaged column and billeted decoration to the arch. As you enter the nave you will notice the early 18th c. painting of the Ten Commandments. The font is 13th c. with shallow arcading. In the south chancel, a somewhat mutilated carved stone trinity has been integrated into the window reveal. But the reason you came here is in the north transept mausoleum. Seated in a chair is the life-size white-marble figure of Dudley North. The Glemham family is also well represented in wall plaques dating from 1535.

LITTLE WENHAM

Dedication:	All Saints	
No of Bells:	1	
Deanery 1836:	Samford	
Hundred:	Samford	
Union house:	Tattingstone	
Deanery 2000:	Samford	

8 m SW of Ipswich
between Capel St Mary &
Hadleigh: east of Capel,
follow Gypsy Lane near
Queen's Head. for ¾ mile.
O.S. grid ref TM 080391
Post Code: CO7 6PU

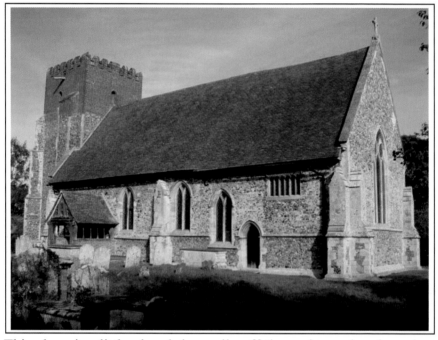

This charming little church is a mile off the main road and receives very few visitors (I could not find a keyholder). Nevertheless the windows are clear and I draw on H. Munro Cautley and Arthur Mee for the following information. The church with the exception of the 15th c. tower is 13th c. and little has changed. No drastic restorations to destroy the ancient dignity. There are scratch dials on the buttress nearest the porch. The porch itself is half-timbered and has three niches in the gable. The octagonal font is early 14th c. but has been restored. There are ancient wall paintings in the nave and in the south wall is an altar tomb in a recess. The chancel has, on the north wall, an elaborate Easter sepulchre. Among others, Gilbert de Debenham, Joseph Thurston, Sir John and Thomas Brewse are remembered here.

LOUND

Dedication: St John the Baptist
No of Bells: 3
Deanery 1836: Lothingland
Hundred: Mutford & Lothingland
Union house: Oulton
Deanery 2000: Lothingland, Norwich

4½ m NW of Lowestoft
between Somerleyton &
Hopton St Margaret: from
A12 west into Jay Lane and
follow, for just over 1 mile.
O.S. grid ref TM 506989
Post Code: NR32 5LL

Lound is one of our round-tower churches and is of uncertain date. The porch is 15th c. with lions guarding the door. Before entering, look through the peephole in the west wall of the nave on the north side of the tower. The purpose is uncertain, but one possible explanation is that it was to comply with the law when it was compulsory to attend worship. Catholics or non-believers could do so without entering the church. The church has been over-restored and very little remains of the original. The font is traditional East Anglian type and has a cover that is gaudy and almost vulgar. The 15th c. screen has had the same treatment and while I admit that this is how churches were once decorated, I can also sympathise with the puritanical regime of the 17th century.

LOWESTOFT

Dedication:	Christchurch
No of Bells:	6
Deanery 1836:	Lothingland
Hundred:	Mutford & Lothingland
Union house:	Oulton

Deanery 2000: Lothingland, Norwich

6 m S of Gt. Yarmouth, Norfolk, between Great Yarmouth, & Southwold: in Battery Green, on the eastern side of the town. O.S. grid ref TM 552934 Post Code: NR32 1UH

Lowestoft Christchurch is the most easterly church in the British Isles. It was built as a parish church for the 2,500 fishermen and beach-men and their families who lived in the Beach Village. The church was opened on February 12th 1869 and cost £1,400 to build. The whole area, including the church, suffered from frequent flooding. In 1953 the whole area flooded again and properties were damaged to such an extent that Beach Village was demolished and is now an industrial complex. The design of the church follows the Early English style; an aisle for the organ was added in 1879. The nave arcade is composed of five arches supported on cast iron columns. The nave roof is open to the timbers but the chancel roof is panelled. The church office is just to the left, and has a key.

LOWESTOFT
Dedication: St Margaret
No of Bells: 8
Deanery 1836:   Lothingland
Hundred: Mutford & Lothingland
Union house: Oulton
Deanery 2000: Lothingland, Norwich

6 m S of Great Yarmouth
between Gt. Yarmouth, and
Southwold, in St Margaret's
Road/ Hollingsworth Road
north of the town.
O.S. grid ref TM 541941
Post Code: NR32 4BW

This church is outstanding, being 60 yds long by 20 yds wide. It is a
pity that it cannot be admired in its entirety, as trees block the view.
The body of the church is 15th c., the tower a century earlier, the
spire covered in copper since about 1950. There is a grand porch with
three niches and statues; above it is a parvise which is known as 'The
Maid's Chamber'. The east window is the church's proudest boast.
The brass eagle lectern is dated 1504, and there is a Jacobean parish
chest. Above you will see the fine roof which gets progressively
more elaborate towards the east. It is supported on a glorious pier
arcade with aisles both north and south. The octagonal font on the
octagonal shaft is 14th c. and is quite mutilated, but the 15-inch
figures can still be recognised in most cases.

LOWESTOFT

Dedication: St Peter
No of Bells: 1
Deanery 1836:   Lothingland
Hundred: Mutford & Lothingland
Union house: Oulton
Deanery 2000: Lothingland, Norwich

6 m S of Great Yarmouth
between Great Yarmouth,
Norfolk & Southwold:
at the eastern end of St.
Peter's Street. (see text)
O.S. grid ref TM 549936
Post Code: NR32 1PQ

St Peter's church is looked upon with much affection in the town. It was built in the 1830's to a design by John Brown of Norwich. There never was a tower and it was completely brick-built with a single bellcote amidships. Even when new, it never was an attractive building, but it is fondly remembered. In 1903 a chancel was added, designed by E. P. Warren who also designed the reredos. The roof was wooden tunnel-vaulted construction. After the Second World War the congregation began to fall in numbers, and although the church never fell into disrepair it was made redundant in 1974 and demolished in the late 1970's. A block of old people's flats called Runnymead Court was built on the site (a similar fate to that of St John's in Kirkley). (see page 163)

MARLESFORD

Dedication:	St Andrew
No of Bells:	6
Deanery 1836:	Loes
Hundred:	Loes
Union house:	Wickham Market
Deanery 2000:	Loes

4 m SE of Framlingham
between Wickham Market
& Stratford St Andrew:
from A12 into Bell Lane, -
Hall Road, - Church Road.
O.S. grid ref TM 323583
Post Code: IP13 0AL

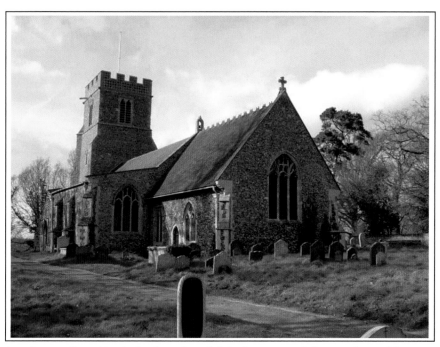

A pleasantly situated church which has stood here since Norman times. The porch, which has been horribly botched with brick repairs instead of flint, has 15th c. stone and flint flushwork panelling. There is an empty niche in the gable and carved spandrils over the door; the gable apex is also decoratively carved in stone. Over the nave at the east end is a stone sanctus bellcote. The roof of the nave is arch-braced still showing patches of colour to the careful observer. The south pier arcade is Norman with round columns and divides the nave from the south aisle. The font is plain 15th c. and unimpressive. The pulpit, however, is octagonal with carved panels of the Stuart period. Two of the bells are 15th c. Brasyer bells, both of which are inscribed.

MARTLESHAM

Dedication:	St Mary
No of Bells:	3
Deanery 1836:	Carlford
Hundred:	Carlford
Union house:	Nacton
Deanery 2000:	Colneys

2 m SW of Woodbridge between Ipswich & Woodbridge: off A12 at round about, onto Main Street, left to School Lane, to Church Lane.
O.S. grid ref TM 262469
Post Code: IP12 4PQ

Approached from the west through a mass of spring flowers this most attractive church is best visited early in the year. You will notice the flint panelling around the parapet, base and plinth of the tower. On the north wall of the nave is an almost unrecognisable painting of St. Christopher, below which, in a recess, is the round-top parish chest. Some of the 15th c. tracery carved bench-ends have animals on them although some have been mutilated. The Stuart pulpit, complete with door, is dated 1614. The font is traditional 15th c. East Anglian style and is in good repair; even the lions around the shaft are virtually complete. The elaborately carved piscina with shelf and double sedilia were restored 1836 and show the craftsmanship of the stone-carver . The Royal Arms are those of Charles II.

182

MELTON (Old Church)

Dedication:	St Andrew
No of Bells:	3
Deanery 1836:	Wilford
Hundred:	Wilford
Union house:	Nacton
Deanery 2000:	Woodbridge

1 m NE of Woodbridge between Woodbridge & Ufford: 1 m NE of Melton new church, off B1438 between Melton & Ufford. O.S. grid ref TM 295513 Post Code: IP13 6DH

Melton old church is some way from the centre of Melton and that proved its downfall. It was made redundant by the building of the new church just off the high street in 1868. The churchyard remained as the primary burial ground and the church became a mortuary chapel during that time. The west window above the door in the tower is 14th c. and contemporary with the tower. The embattled parapet is later. In the nave there is a simple arch-braced roof and in the floor a brass with three figures of a lady, a man and a priest. Who they were is not known but they are getting on for 600 years old. The rare seven sacrament font was moved to the modern church: confusingly, both are dedicated to St Andrew. The church is now owned by the Melton Old Church Society.

MELTON

Dedication:	St Andrew	
No of Bells:	3	
Deanery 1836:	Wilford	
Hundred:	Wilford	
Union house:	Nacton	
Deanery 2000:	Woodbridge	

1 m NE of Woodbridge between Woodbridge & Ufford: from the B1438 (The Street) turn east into Station Road.
O.S. grid ref TM 283506
Post Code: IP12 1PZ

This is Melton New Church obscured by trees and screened by other buildings. (I prefer a country church with plenty of space around it). This church was started in 1866 and consecrated in 1868 and cost £3,400. How prices have changed! It was decided to build it in Early English Gothic (12th / 13th c.) style with geometric tracery. The effect is most pleasing for a modern church.. The material used was Kentish rag with dressings of Caen stone. The roof is arch-braced with the braces being supported on hammerbeams. A number of memorials of various dignitaries and benefactors are incorporated in the modern window designs. The font was removed from Melton Old Church (see previous page) and is a rare and well preserved seven sacrament font; the eighth panel has the martyrdom of St Andrew.

MENDHAM		6 m SW of Bungay between
Dedication:	All Saints	Harleston, Norfolk &
No of Bells:	6	Homersfield: in The Street,
Deanery 1836:	Hoxne	50 yds from the River
Hundred:	Hoxne	Waveney Bridge.
Union house:	Stradbroke	O.S. grid ref TM 269829
Deanery 2000:	Hoxne	Post Code: IP20 0NH

This 14th c. church has been heavily restored over the centuries, particularly by the Victorians after it fell into disrepair. The clerestory is 15th c. but the roofs were virtually replaced in 1868 after they partially collapsed. The tower was repaired at the same time and crenulations restored. The rebuilt chancel and arch are most notable, being constructed in wood as part of the chancel roof. The corbels and other carved figures were the work of local artisan Mr. Godbold of Harleston in Norfolk. There are portrait brasses dating back to the 17th c. of Cecily and two Richards of the Freston family. The trefoil piscina is restored and is flanked by a single seat sedilia. There was a priory in the parish founded by William de Huntingfield in 1140. The Arms are of George III but are housed in the Rectory.

METFIELD		8 m NW of Halesworth
Dedication:	St John the Baptist	between Harleston, Norfolk
No of Bells:	4	& Halesworth: unmissable
Deanery 1836:	Hoxne	in the village centre on the
Hundred:	Hoxne	B1123. Easy parking.
Union house:	Stradbroke	O.S. grid ref TM 294803
Deanery 2000:	Hoxne	Post Code: IP20 0LA

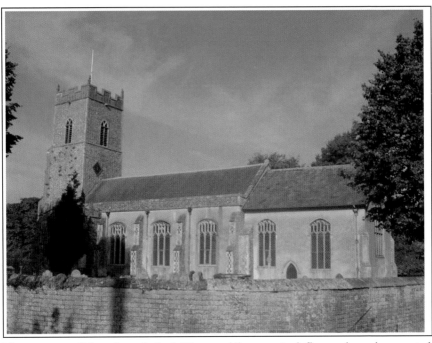

The tower of the church is 14th c. with a seated figure keeping watch at each corner above the crenulated parapet. The clock, unusually, is placed above the apex of the nave roof facing the street to the east. The porch is 15th c. with stone panels and Lierne-vault ceiling and a parvise above. Both nave and chancel roofs are arch-braced, but the chancel is boarded in and has the Metfield imp on one of the bosses. The font is 15th c. octagonal typical East Anglian type on a square base, and still bears traces of paint. The western gallery houses the organ, the latest of which was installed in 1953. The rood stairs are still open but lead nowhere. The lower panels of the rood screen are now at the west end of the nave. The piscina is early 14th c.. In the base of the tower is housed the 1719 clock mechanism. Interesting.

METTINGHAM

Dedication:	All Saints
No of Bells:	4 now all removed
Deanery 1836:	Wangford
Hundred:	Wangford
Union house:	Shipmeadow
Deanery 2000:	Beccles & S. Elmham

1 m E of Bungay between Bungay & Beccles: immediately off the B1062 on the Beccles side of The Tally-Ho PH. Steep drive. O.S. grid ref TM 362899 Post Code: NR35 1TL

This is a Norman round-tower church. The north door with its two engaged columns, three-order arch, and chevron and billet carvings bear this out. Although it is probable that a church stood here for many years before the Normans arrived, the large glacial erratics built into the north west corner are a Saxon practice. (also to be seen at Barsham, nearby). Recent (2007) renovations to the tower have revealed an east-facing doorway half-way up the tower suggesting it may, at one time, have been a Saxon defensible stronghold. Inside the nave there is a traditional Tudor East Anglian font; note the unusual women in frilled head-dress on the base and the curious mini-font within. In the chancel is a 14th c. canopied tomb to John de Norwich who built the gateway and fortified the nearby Mettingham castle.

MICKFIELD

Dedication:	St Andrew
No of Bells:	1 sanctus
Deanery 1836:	Bosmere
Hundred:	Bosmere & Claydon
Union house:	Barham
Deanery 2000:	Bosmere

6 m NE of Stowmarket between Little Stonham & Debenham: about 1 mile off the A140, signed Mickfield. Driveway up to Church.
O.S. grid ref TM 134617
Post Code: IP14 5LF

Mickfield church has a south tower, beneath which is the porch into the nave. Built in the early 14th c. it was declared redundant in 1977 after a crack was found in the tower. The 3 bells were removed in 1982. Today the church is privately owned by The Anglian Church Trust and run as a Christian Centre. Saxon foundations still support the walls in places. The nave roof is supported by corbels with carved grotesques. There is a stoup in the porch and inside the church the simple piscina is flanked by a dropped window sill sedilia. The rood screen has been recently restored and now separates the chancel from the nave. The nave is used for other purposes but the chancel remains a place of worship. There are portrait brasses to Peter Preston and his wife. You will always get a warm welcome here.

MIDDLETON (cum Fordley)
Dedication: Holy Trinity
No of Bells: 5
Deanery 1836:   Dunwich
Hundred: Blything
Union house: Bulcamp
Deanery 2000:   Saxmundham

4 m NE of Saxmundham
between   Yoxford &
Leiston: from either B1122
or B1125 follow sign to the
'Bell Inn' Public House.
O.S. grid ref TM 430677
Post Code: IP17 3NW

Fordley church stood not 50 yards away from Middleton Church and
in 1620 a complaint was made that the services interfered with each
other. The result was that Fordley was eventually made redundant
and has since been completely demolished. The nave and chancel of
the present church were thatched, but in 1955, after a disastrous fire
during renovations, they were re-roofed with tile. The tower has an
elegant zinc spire. Much of the church is Norman: the south door
with two engaged columns; the north west window; south window;
even the piscina has two 12th c. shafts and capitals, although the arch
is later. The lovely traditional East Anglian font has wodewoses and
lions round the shaft. Around the base is an old English verse. The
Royal Arms are of George III.

MONEWDEN

Dedication:	St Mary	
No of Bells:	6	
Deanery 1836:	Loes	
Hundred:	Loes	
Union house:	Wickham Market	
Deanery 2000:	Loes	

4 m SW of Framlingham between Otley & Kettleburgh: on a road junction as you pass through the village.

O.S. grid ref TM 238585

Post Code: IP13 7DA

A Norman church which has been 'restored' almost beyond recognition. The slit windows are 12th c. but have had their arches replaced with later pointed ones. The 15th c. font is unremarkably simple. The holy table and pulpit are Stuart in date and are again simple. The stairs to the rood loft are still open but the rood and screen have long since gone. There is some nice carving of canopies on the spring of the chancel arch just above the corbel. The roofs are timbered barrel-style and on the north wall hangs an hour-glass holder. Some of the benches have some nicely carved poppy-heads. There is an impressively large brass on the east wall of the chancel to Thomas Reve (1595), one-time rector. The east window bears an interesting shield relating to the Black Prince.

MONK SOHAM

Dedication:	St Peter
No of Bells:	5
Deanery 1836:	Hoxne
Hundred:	Hoxne
Union house:	Stradbroke
Deanery 2000:	Hoxne

4 m WNW of Framlingham between Worlingworth & Ashfield: near The Hall, up a narrow lane off School Road.

O.S. grid ref TM 213650

Post Code: IP13 7EN

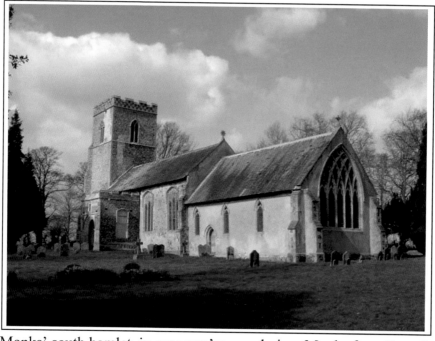

Monks' south hamlet, in case you're wondering. Monks from Bury St Edmunds quartered here and did penance. The church is 13th c. and built upon glacial erratic boulders. The porch is embattled with a wooden roof but otherwise dull. The nave with a hammerbeam roof is 100 years later than the chancel. There are two piscinas: one is a simple one recessed into the south wall, and above it in the window reveal is a niche for a saint. The other was at one time very decorative but all decoration has been hacked off to be flush with the wall. The treasure is the 15th c. seven sacrament font which is deeply carved and although it has suffered some mutilation is a beauty. Between the benches at the west end is the 14th c. parish chest, one of the largest I have seen at 8 feet long and iron-bound.

MUTFORD

Dedication: St Andrew
No of Bells: 3
Deanery 1836: Lothingland
Hundred: Mutford & Lothingland
Union house: Oulton
Deanery 2000: Lothingland, Norwich

5 m SW of Lowestoft
between North Cove &
Kessingland: at the junction
of Chapel Road & Church
Road, north of Mill Lane.
O.S. grid ref TM 485885
Post Code: NR34 7UZ

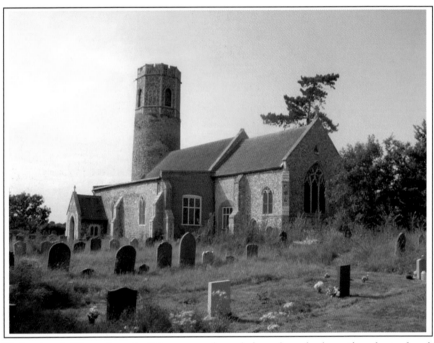

This should be a lovely Norman church in a lovely location but alas it has been horribly neglected over the centuries. It is the only church in Suffolk with a 14th c. Galilee porch at the western side of the round Norman tower. The octagonal top was added in the 14th c.. In the early 20th c. the Galilee porch was restored but now it is just used as a shed with locked iron gates. At the east end of the south aisle is what looks like a scullery window but the brickwork is Tudor. There is also a mysterious bricked-up arch in the south wall. The roof of the south aisle has arch-braced principles and traceried spandrils. The 14th c. piscina is elaborate with a nice ogee arch with pinnacles and foliage. The canopied background is panelled and traceried. The typical East Anglian font is stripped of its panel carvings.

NACTON

Dedication: St Martin
No of Bells: 2
Deanery 1836: Colneis
Hundred: Colneis
Union house: Nacton
Deanery 2000: Colneys

5 m SE of Ipswich
between Ipswich &
Levington: lying south of
the village in Church Road.

O.S. grid ref TM 217396
Post Code: IP10 0ER

The church is 15th c. although it has been so restored that there is very little of the original to see. The walls have been rendered with cement and all character erased. The height of the tower is less than twice its girth giving it a stunted appearance. The dormer window was to allow light onto the rood, but that too has gone. The 15th c. traditional font has wodewoses and lions around the base of the shaft. Nacton is more famous for its inhabitants than the church. Margaret Catchpole lived here but is buried in Australia where she was deported for horse stealing. Admiral Vernon of Porto Bello fame is buried here, as is Sir Philip Broke who commanded the 'Shannon' at Boston in 1813. His brother Sir Charles Broke, who was at Waterloo, is here too. The ruins of Alnesbourne Priory are not far away.

NEEDHAM MARKET

Dedication:	St John the Baptist	
No of Bells:	1	
Deanery 1836:	Bosmere	
Hundred:	Bosmere & Claydon	
Union house:	Barham	
Deanery 2000:	Bosmere	

8 m NW of Ipswich between Stowmarket & Claydon. on the B1113 (High Street) in the town centre.
O.S. grid ref TM 087551
Post Code: IP6 8DG

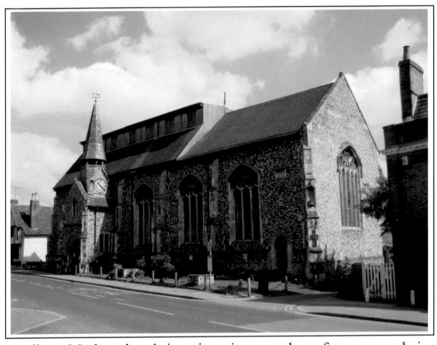

Needham Market church is unique in a number of ways, one being that it is not aligned east/west, being much nearer north/south. Some of the buttresses on the road side have canopied niches, and the spire complete with clock sits on top of the porch. There is no tower. The timbered clerestory above the nave has the appearance of motel windows. The access to the rood loft was from the outside, but this is now blocked. The nave is like a grand hall with a roof that spans 30 ft; it is also unique. The hammerbeams project far into the nave and support a post into which is set an arch-braced beam. It is a triumph of carpentry and should be admired. Angels, added in 1892, abound from the ends of beams. More are carved into the cornice, some playing horns, others reading, praying and holding depictive shields.

NETTLESTEAD

		5 m NW of Ipswich
Dedication:	St Mary	between Offten & Great
No of Bells:	1	Blakenham: on a narrow
Deanery 1836:	Bosmere	lane (Hall Road) north of
Hundred:	Bosmere & Claydon	Somersham.
Union house:	Barham	O.S. grid ref TM 088494
Deanery 2000:	Bosmere	Post Code: IP8 4QS

Nettlestead 15th c. church is easily missed. It is behind a tall hedge in a narrow country road. Approaching the church you are immediately struck by the Tudor porch with an unusual round brick gable with Arms over the door. The tower is free of buttresses and the tracery in the windows has been destroyed. There is a Norman slit window in the north wall of the nave revealing an earlier phase of building. The 15th c. font is interesting, in that the octagonal bowl is richly carved with evangelistic emblems. There are two orders of corbelling and the shaft has pinnacled buttresses as well as the usual four crowned lions. The roofs of both nave and chancel are of braced tie-beam construction. The pulpit and holy table are Stuart. On the wall of the chancel is an alabaster memorial to Samuel and Thomasine Sayer.

195

NEWBOURN(E)

Dedication: St Mary
No of Bells: 1
Deanery 1836: Carlford
Hundred: Carlford
Union house: Bacton
Deanery 2000: Colneys

4 m S of Woodbridge
between Martlesham &
Kirton: on Ipswich Road
near the junction of The
Street & Mill Road.
O.S. grid ref TM 272430
Post Code: IP12 4NS

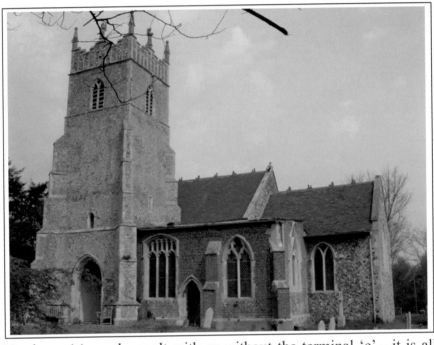

Newbourn(e) can be spelt with or without the terminal 'e' - it is all the same place. Sitting high above the road, it is a strange-looking church. The heavily buttressed tower with pinnacles and four stone angels facing the cardinal points also serves as a south porch. The church dates from the 13th and 14th centuries and the nave has a single hammerbeam roof with arch-braced collar. The fine 15th c. font is traditional East Anglian type and beautifully carved. The shaft is supported by four lions and wodewoses. The carved wooden font cover is a relatively simple tracery framework with pinnacles. The stairs to the rood loft are open but are blocked at the top. The 16th c. rood screen is a poor example. The south chapel contains a 13th c. piscina with shafts and a cusped arch, sadly mutilated.

NORTH COVE

Dedication:	St Botolph	
No of Bells:	3	
Deanery 1836:	Wangford	
Hundred:	Wangford	
Union house:	Shipmeadow	
Deanery 2000:	Beccles & S. Elmham	

3 m E of Beccles, between Beccles & Lowestoft: just off the A146 on the old Lowestoft Road near the Three Horse Shoes PH.
O.S. grid ref TM 461893
Post Code: NR34 7PH

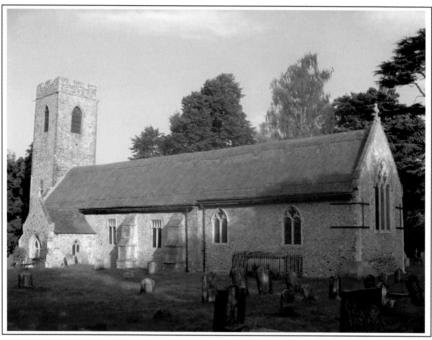

The fine thatched roof only just distinguishes the nave from the chancel. The 15th c. tower was built using Roman bricks in window reveals and at the corners instead of quoin stones. There are two magnificent Norman doorways, north and south, the latter having columns and three orders of carving to the arch. The nave roof has been plastered over. The corbels have carved heads of kings. The 14th c. wall paintings are some of the best in the area. It has been suggested that these have been repainted, but certainly not in the last 400 years. Circular plaques with 17th c. texts also feature among the paintings. The early 15th c. octagonal font is well preserved, with crisply carved heads of men and women around the corbel, and has eight engaged columns around the shaft.

OFFTON

Dedication:	St Mary
No of Bells:	8
Deanery 1836:	Bosmere
Hundred:	Bosmere & Claydon
Union house:	Barham
Deanery 2000:	Bosmere

7 m NW of Ipswich
between Barking &
Somersham: on Bildeston
Road as it passes through
the village.
O.S. grid ref TM 066496
Post Code: IP8 4RG

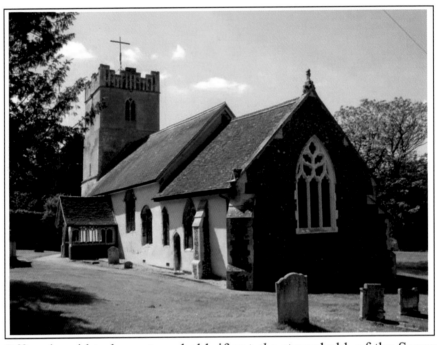

Offton is said to be a stronghold, if not *the* stronghold, of the Saxon King Offa (757 - 796). So the church may well have deeper roots than can be seen today. The present building has Norman origins. Before you venture inside, take a look at the monument opposite the door to Sarah (and John) Wyatt with the superb carving. Through the 14th c. half-timbered porch is the 12th c. south door. The tower also dates from the 14th c. and has a later crenulated parapet. The roof to the nave has braced tie-beams and king-posts to the roof. There is some rare 15th c. glass in the south-east nave window. The 14th c. font is a traditional type and among other floral decoration is a depiction of St Edmund's crown, pierced with arrows. The pulpit and holy table are both of the Stuart period.

ORFORD

ORFORD		9 m E of Woodbridge
Dedication:	St Bartholomew	between Woodbridge &
No of Bells:	5	the Coast: at the top of
Deanery 1836:	Orford	Church Road, at junction of
Hundred:	Plomesgate	Market Hill & High Street.
Union house:	Wickham Market	O.S. grid ref TM 422499
Deanery 2000:	Woodbridge	Post Code: IP12 2LN

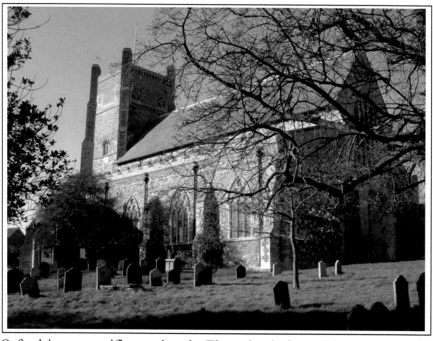

Orford is a magnificent church. The ruined chancel has some of the finest Norman architecture to be seen anywhere in the county. Unfortunately it was built for beauty rather than strength. But take a moment to admire the outstanding Norman stonework before you go inside. Part of the old nave is now the chancel. The upper tower was rebuilt after it collapsed in 1830 but the exceptional 14th c. doorways are original. Most of what you see is 14th c.. The exceptions are the brasses, of which there are many late 15th c. onwards; the unusual parclose screen which is 16th c. and the parish chest, dated 1634. The font is actually dated 1400 and is an early traditional East Anglian type with wodewoses and lions around the base, double corbel beneath the bowl, and rich carving round it.

199

OTLEY

Dedication:	St Mary	
No of Bells:	6	
Deanery 1836:	Carlford	
Hundred:	Carlford	
Union house:	Nacton	
Deanery 2000:	Woodbridge	

6 m NW of Woodbridge between Helmingham & Grundisburgh: on the B1079 (Church Road), narrow drive up to church. O.S. grid ref TM 204549 Post Code: IP6 9NP

There is a scratch dial on the buttress of the chancel. The church was built around the latter part of the 14th c. with a clerestory being added towards the end of the 15th c.. The door beneath the western end of the tower has tracery carvings and three figures on the central and both outer panels. The nave roof is single hammerbeam and arch-braced construction. The typical East Anglian font is of standard design with shields and lions at the base. The rood loft stairs are enclosed by the original door. The pulpit is richly carved and the holy table has six legs with an unusual reed-like design. Both are of the Stuart period. Some of the benches are 15th c. and have nicely carved ends. One of the later 17th c. bench ends has the Arms of the Gosnold family. Samuel Rogers was rector here for 87 years.

OULTON

Dedication: St Michael
No of Bells: 5
Deanery 1836: Lothingland
Hundred: Mutford & Lothingland
Union house: Oulton
Deanery 2000: Lothingland, Norwich

2 m W of Lowestoft
between Lowestoft &
Blundeston: from the
A1117 take Sands Lane and
follow, left into Church Rd.
O.S. grid ref TM 510935
Post Code: NR32 3JN

Not mentioned in Domesday but probably built just after as a cruciform church with a central tower. It still has the Norman doorways north and south, and the tower arch which faces the nave is moulded with chevrons. The chapel, which was south of the tower, was removed last century, the north transept being long gone. Alterations were made to the chancel in the 14th c. and to the nave 100 years later. The font is traditional East Anglian style and quite ordinary. Access to the tower is from a door at the height of the tower arch which would suggest that originally it was accessed from the rood-loft. The Royal Arms are of James II and are believed to have come from St Margaret's, Westminster. Memorial brasses which were once stolen have since been replaced. (Always locked).

PAKEFIELD
Dedication: All Saints & St Margaret
No of Bells: 8
Deanery 1836: Lothingland
Hundred: Mutford & Lothingland
Union house: Oulton
Deanery 2000: Lothingland, Norwich

1½ m S of Lowestoft
between Lowestoft &
Kessingland: at the Tram-
way Hotel take Pakefield
Street - right into Causeway
O.S. grid ref TM 538904
Post Code: NR33 7BS

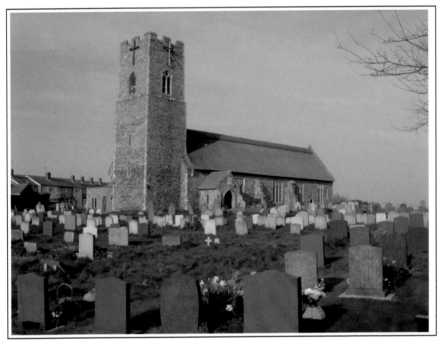

This is a unique church, being two churches in one. The two aisles were at one time completely separate, one being All Saints the other St Margaret, and woe betide anyone who crossed the line. They each had their own vicar at one time. After 1743 they were united as one. The full history is available in the church. The central pier arcade dates from the 14th c. and was originally bricked up. The church still has some hints of Norman workmanship but later work is more prevalent. The font is also of the 14th c. and supporting the bowl is a floral decorated 6-inch wide band. There are brasses to John Bowf (1417) and his wife Agnes, and another to Richard Folkard (1751). The Royal Arms are those of Charles II and are dated 1681. There is a rare example of a Lenten veil pulley still in situ in the north wall.

PARHAM

Dedication:	St Mary	
No of Bells:	3	
Deanery 1836:	Orford	
Hundred:	Plomesgate	
Union house:	Wickham Market	
Deanery 2000:	Loes	

2 m SE of Framlingham between Framlingham & Wickham Market: in the village, at the junction of Hall Road & The Street.
O.S. grid ref TM 309605
Post Code: IP13 9LS

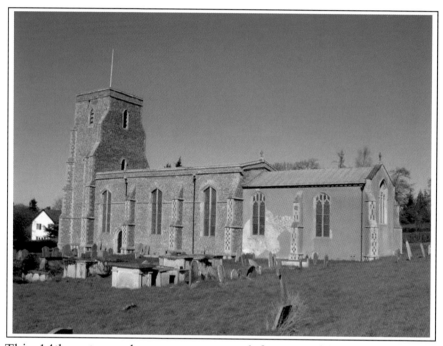

This 14th c. tower has a very unusual feature midway up the west wall, namely a large canopied niche with cusped arch. Although it has suffered from the effects of rain and frost it is still quite impressive. On the south side is a neat scratch dial with numerals. Access to the nave is through the north porch. The church structure is basically 15th c. but restoration and modernisation have destroyed the character. The font has delicate tracery in its panels and is dated early 15th c.. The piscina in the south wall is fairly plain and the one in the chancel is of a similar simple style, with a dropped sill sedilia flanking it. There is one old bench to look for with a nicely carved angel on the arm-rest. Also to be seen is a wig peg with R.H. 1716 inscribed, and an enormous padlock on the north door.

PEASENHALL

Dedication:	St Michael
No of Bells:	6
Deanery 1836:	Dunwich
Hundred:	Blything
Union house:	Bulcamp
Deanery 2000:	Saxmundham

4 m NW of Saxmundham between Dennington & Yoxford: just off the A1120 (The Street), south into Church Road.

O.S. grid ref TM 355692

Post Code: IP17 2HL

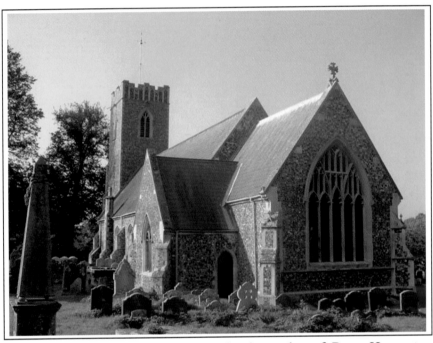

Peasenhall is renown for the unsolved murder of Rose Harsant, a young servant girl murdered in 1902. The church is so rebuilt and over-restored that it would probably not be recognised by those who built it. The north side faces the road and consequently the porch is on that side. It is a not unattractive church but sits uneasily in a small churchyard filled with headstones and monuments, many of which are very old. The porch has stone panelling with dressed flint flushwork and matches the buttresses and parapet on the 15th c. tower. Inside the church there is a sketch by Henry Davy dated 1845 showing the church as it was with a lower pitch on the roof. The font is late 12th c. with the undecorated bowl sitting on four engaged columns around a circular central column.

PETTAUGH

Dedication: St Catherine
No of Bells: 1
Deanery 1836: Claydon
Hundred: Thredling
Union house: Barham
Deanery 2000: Loes

10 m N of Ipswich between Stonham Aspal & Earl Soham: north up a short drive off the A1120 (The Street); drive easily missed. O.S. grid ref TM 167596 Post Code: IP14 6JB

Pettaugh's 14th c. church stands on a prominence on the east side of the parish, overlooking a small tributary of the River Deben. The tower is the same date as the church but the battlemented parapet and solitary gargoyle was added a century later. The chancel is quite unaltered internally and retains the old south door. Unfortunately the exterior has been cement-rendered. There are two piscinas but neither is exceptional. The font is of the traditional East Anglian variety and is contemporary with the church. During restoration work last century some small brasses were discovered, probably memorials to the Fastolfe family who lived at Pettaugh Hall in the 16th and 17th centuries. The prayer desk is made partly of Stuart bench ends with interesting carvings. The holy table is similarly dated.

PETTISTREE

Dedication:	Sts Peter & Paul
No of Bells:	6
Deanery 1836:	Wilford
Hundred:	Wilford
Union house:	Nacton
Deanery 2000:	Loes

4 m N of Woodbridge between Wickham Market & Ufford: just off The Street in Walnut Lane near The Greyhound PH.
O.S. grid ref TM 298549
Post Code: IP13 0HP

The massive tower on the 15th c. church is mainly due to the massive buttresses on the eastern corners. They extend the full width of the nave and more, giving the impression of a pyramid when viewed from the east. The flushwork extends up the buttresses on to a wide band just below the embattled parapet. Although the body of the church has been heavily restored the contents may hold your interest. Carvings on the bench ends, particularly the poppyheads, are worth a look. There is a font base dating back to the 13th c. and the 16th c. font has a pelican feeding its young among the carvings. There are three piscinas in all; the oldest in the chancel is 14th c. with a detached column flanking the dropped sill sedilia. Don't miss the 13th c. grisaille glass in the south chancel window.

PLAYFORD

		4 m NE of Ipswich
Dedication:	St Mary	between Grundisburgh &
No of Bells:	2	Kesgrave: in Church Road,
Deanery 1836:	Carlford	north-east of the village.
Hundred:	Carlford	
Union house:	Nacton	O.S. grid ref TM 217480
Deanery 2000:	Woodbridge	Post Code: IP6 9DS

Standing proudly above the parish it serves, the 14th c. tower also acts as a south porch. Over the decorated door arch there is a canopied niche, complete with St. Mary. Before you enter, glance left and you will see a granite obelisk . The name it bears is Thomas Clarkson, (friend of the slave) who is buried to the right; near the chancel door. Inside, a wall memorial gives a fuller story. Another name of note is Sir George Airy, Astronomer Royal who died 1892. Playford is very proud of them both and rightly so. The bench end carvings are different from the usual but have no great age. You may hear Playford's claim to fame but I doubt that you will see them; they are 2 bells that have hung in the belfry since Tudor times. There is a nice wall brass in the chancel to Sir George Felbrigg (1400).

RAMSHOLT		5 m SE of Ipswich, between
Dedication:	All Saints	Sutton & Bawdsey: ¾ mile
No of Bells:	1	west along unmade road,
Deanery 1836:	Wilford	north of the road to The
Hundred:	Wilford	Ramsholt Arms, signposted.
Union house:	Nacton	O.S. grid ref TM 306420
Deanery 2000:	Woodbridge	Post Code: IP12 3AE

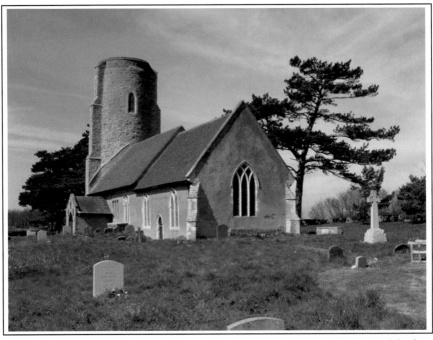

Far away from the road and overlooking the River Deben, this is a lovely peaceful location. The church has a Norman round tower which was buttressed at a later date. There is only one other similar, at Beyton. In all probability it was originally built as a Saxon early warning system against the Vikings . The earliest datable work in the construction of the church is 13th c. which is the north wall of the nave, the rest having been restored or rebuilt. It is apparent from the old curved roof-line that the building was, at one time, thatched. There is little to see in the church beyond a stone coffin, dug up during the mid 19th c. The 15th c. octagonal font with quatrefoil decoration is supported by what is possibly a Norman shaft. The late 14th c. piscina is flanked by a dropped sill sedilia.

RAYDON

Dedication:	St Mary
No of Bells:	1 (tenor)
Deanery 1836:	Samford
Hundred:	Samford
Union house:	Tattingstone
Deanery 2000:	Hadleigh

3 m SE of Hadleigh between Hadleigh & East Bergholt: on the B1070 (The Street) up a driveway near the War Memorial.
O.S. grid ref TM 049386
Post Code: IP7 5LW

As you approach this towerless church you cannot help but notice the carved pinnacles and crocketted finials on the buttresses at the east end. All the buttresses are unusual, some being triangular. Between these on the north wall is a projection, the purpose of which will only become clear from the inside. It is a canopied tomb of the type used as an Easter sepulchre. The chancel is early 14th c. with some notable windows. The modern font is a strange one with a waisted octagonal shaft supported by an octagonal cushion, otherwise quite plain. Just above the springing of the chancel arch are two protruding wooden brackets, at one time used to support the rood beam. The 13th c. traceried piscina has a central column and double drain. Originally there was a tower and 3 bells but it collapsed in the 18th c..

REDISHAM MAGNA

		4 m S of Beccles, between
Dedication:	St Peter	Beccles & Ilketshall St
No of Bells:	1	Lawrence: just west of the
Deanery 1836:	Wangford	Brampton turn-off on the
Hundred:	Wangford	Halesworth Road.
Union house:	Shipmeadow	O.S. grid ref TM 408843
Deanery 2000:	Beccles & S. Elmham	Post Code: NR34 8NE

From outward appearances this church could be a barn. There is no tower, but a wooden bell-cote sits atop the west nave roof. From the evidence of the style of construction it is very early pre-Conquest. The Norman south doorway is exceptional for such a small edifice; it even has an early scratch dial from before the porch was added. But it doesn't stop there: pop round the back and look at the north doorway. Now bricked up and partly hidden by a shed is another, perhaps not quite so grand but outstanding nevertheless. The font is octagonal and has Tudor rose decoration and angel heads on the corbelling of the bowl. The pulpit has a bracketed book-board which is dated 1619. The Royal Arms bear the skinniest lion and unicorn I have ever seen and are inscribed G. R.

RENDHAM

Dedication:	St Michael
No of Bells:	8
Deanery 1836:	Orford
Hundred:	Plomesgate
Union house:	Wickham Market
Deanery 2000:	Saxmundham

3 m NW of Saxmundham between, Framlingham & Saxmundham: on a right-angle bend in the B1119 opposite the 'White Horse'. O.S. grid ref TM 394644 Post Code: IP17 2AZ

The 15th c. tower dominates the skyline and the church itself which is younger by a century. There is a scratch dial near the window of the chancel, of little use today, as trees block out the sun. The church is to the south of the road which means the north door is the one we use to gain entrance. The nave roof is of simple arch-braced type. The chancel has a dropped window sill sedilia. and little else. The main object of interest is the excellent Stuart pulpit which still retains its back and sounding board. It is clearly inscribed 1632 W.P.. In the floor of the nave is a brass inscribed with a chalice and the name Thomas King (1523). The Royal Arms are of Charles II, and instead of the Royal motto are the words, 'God save the King'. Just in case history were to repeat itself, perhaps.

RENDLESHAM

Dedication:	St Gregory the Great	4 m E of Woodbridge between Snape &
No of Bells:	3	Woodbridge: just off the
Deanery 1836:	Loes	A1152, west of the village,
Hundred:	Loes	in Ash Road.
Union house:	Wickham Market	O.S. grid ref TM 325528
Deanery 2000:	Woodbridge	Post Code: IP12 2QY

Resting in the Deben valley this fine church reminds me of Pettistree with its enormous eastern buttresses on the 14th c. embattled tower. The porch is 15th c. and has a small room above. The roof of the nave is a simple arch-braced type which at one time had angels looking down. Originally the nave was much narrower, as can be seen from the weathering on the tower above the present roof. Interestingly, the buttresses have never been enlarged. The font is 15th c. and in very good condition. Set into the wall of the chancel is a fine tomb with a stone ogee arched canopy with pinnacles, and a full-size figure beneath. The cusped piscina in the chancel is contemporary 14th c. and has roses decorating the stonework. The chancel also contains 19th c. monuments to the Thellusson family.

REYDON		2 m NW of Southwold
Dedication:	St Margaret	between Blythburgh &
No of Bells:	6	Southwold: on the B1126
Deanery 1836:	Dunwich	west of the parish. Nice
Hundred:	Blything	large car park.
Union house:	Bulcamp	O.S. grid ref TM 490781
Deanery 2000:	Halesworth	Post Code: IP18 6PB

This lovely little church sits in an enormous churchyard with a beautiful bronze monument by Paul Montford. It is inscribed 'To Fanny my beloved wife vivet in æternum amor'. In fact the monuments are more interesting than the church. The font is of no great age and very simple. One of the piscinas has had a door added and is now an aumbry. The other is a very simple affair. There are nice traceried recesses in some of the window reveals which once housed various Saints. There seem to be recesses or niches in every available spot. The rood loft stairs are open, but bricked-up at the top. The Royal Arms are those of Queen Anne and are dated 1713. The one 15th c. bell in the belfry is inscribed in Latin, 'In this chamber, Gabriel, now sound sweetly'.

RINGSFIELD		2 m NW of Southwold
Dedication:	All Saints	between Beccles &
No of Bells:	4	Bungay: 1 mile north of the
Deanery 1836:	Wangford	village on the Barsham
Hundred:	Wangford	Road, nr The Manor House.
Union house:	Shipmeadow	O.S. grid ref TM 403884
Deanery 2000:	Beccles & S. Elmham	Post Code: NR34 8JU

A tall tower with pinnacles at each corner and not a buttress in sight, despite this being built not 50 yards from a fast-flowing stream, liable to flooding. The church is damp, mainly because it is kept locked. Against the north nave wall is the tomb of Princess Caroline Murat, who lived at Redisham Hall. The church is still completely thatched. The nave and tower date from the 15th c. On the south wall is an elaborate brass monument to Nicholas Garnys (circa 1600) and Anne, his wife; above is a bare-breasted mermaid in a niche. The traditional East Anglian font is very simple. There is a considerable amount of Stuart woodwork in the benches and square pulpit, complete with back and sounding board supported on carved wall brackets. The holy table is also of the same period.

RINGSHALL

Dedication:	St Catherine	
No of Bells:	2	
Deanery 1836:	Bosmere	
Hundred:	Bosmere & Claydon	
Union house:	Barham	
Deanery 2000:	Bosmere	

4 miles S of Stowmarket
between Wattisham &
Needham Market: just off
the road on a bend, north of
the village.
O.S. grid ref TM 042528
Post Code: IP14 2HZ

The church dates back to Norman times and signs can be seen in the
south door and slit windows in the nave. The tower also has slit
windows and may have been defensible at one time. The porch is
timber with a tiled roof, sitting on a short wall of stone and flint.
Glance above the porch and you will notice the great tie-beam
protruding through the wall with a giant peg. This is repeated on the
north side. (This feature can also be seen at Frenze in Norfolk and at
Withersdale). The roof of the nave is 14th c. with supporting arch-
braces and king-posts. The chancel has a single hammerbeam roof
which was constructed 200 years later. The ancient font is arcaded
but unadorned to any extent. There are wall paintings but they are
very faded, representing the Seven Acts of Mercy.

RUMBURGH

Dedication: St Michaels & All Angels
No of Bells: 5
Deanery 1836: Dunwich
Hundred: Blything
Union house: Bulcamp
Deanery 2000: Halesworth

4 m NW of Halesworth
between Bungay &
Halesworth: set well back,
400 yards north of the
'Rumburgh Buck' PH.
O.S. grid ref TM 346818
Post Code: IP19 0NU

As you approach Rumburgh church for the first time, you would be forgiven for wondering what happened to the tower. It was built in the 13th c. and was roofed like this centuries ago. There is a fascinating history to the church: it was once a part of a Benedictine priory, but is far too involved to go into here. The font is late 14th c. and has a simple Stuart cover. The nave roof is arch-braced tie beams with king posts. What remains of the screen has very delicate tracery but has been varnished much to its detriment. The 17th c. pulpit stands on a single leg and is unusually high. The old four-wheeled bier has been retained for posterity, as has an old parish chest. A very interesting church. The antiquarian, David Elisha Davy was born here in 1769. He is buried at Yoxford.

RUSHMERE		3 m NE of Ipswich between
Dedication:	St Andrew	Ipswich & Martlesham: off
No of Bells:	6	the A1214 into Humber
Deanery 1836:	Carlford	Doucy Lane - right into
Hundred:	Carlford	Rushmere Street.
Union house:	Nacton	O.S. grid ref TM 196460
Deanery 2000:	Ipswich	Post Code: IP5 1DH

There are two Rushmeres, easily confused but they couldn't be more different. The alignment of this church is northeast / southwest, the opposite of Needham Market (page 194). The lovely 'Norman' south doorway has twisted columns and a chevron arch of two orders. But it, like most of the church, has been totally restored. Even the pinnacles on the 16th c. tower were copied from the weather-beaten originals. The church is built on Norman foundations and there is Norman work in the columns of the nave. It has a dreadful modern building protruding from the chancel and sheds of various descriptions around the north side. This is a lovely church, the appearance of which has been marred by lack of proper consideration for the aesthetic value. Poor show, Rushmere St Andrew's.

RUSHMERE

Dedication:	St Michael	
No of Bells:	2	
Deanery 1836:	Lothingland	
Hundred:	Mutford & Lothingland	
Union house:	Oulton	
Diocese:	Norwich	

5 m SW of Lowestoft
between Henstead &
Carlton Colville: on a four
crossways east of Mutford,
north of Rushmere Street.
O.S. grid ref TM 495880
Post Code: NR33 8ET

This Rushmere has a different type of church altogether. It is thatched, has a lovely round tower which has Norman work at the base, and Roman bricks built into the fabric. The ancient south porch is brick-built with a tile roof and a shallow niche above the door. Most of the walls are original Norman work, although some repairs have been made here and there. A banner stave recess is let into the west end of the nave; nearby, just inside the door, is a stoup. The pulpit is Stuart but the back and sounding board have been removed. There are piscinas on north and south walls; the latter, unusually, does not face inward, but west into the reveal of the dropped window sill sedilia. The font is the traditional East Anglian type with flowers, angels and the obligatory lions. Only 3 services a year unfortunately.

SAXMUNDHAM

		11 m NE of Woodbridge
Dedication:	St John the Baptist	between Yoxford &
No of Bells:	6	Wickham Market: east off
Deanery 1836:	Orford	the B1121 (High Street)
Hundred:	Plomesgate	into B1119 (Church Road).
Union house:	Wickham Market	O.S. grid ref TM 389629
Deanery 2000:	Saxmundham	Post Code: IP17 1ES

The church stands on the brow of a hill overlooking the town and the rivulet that joins the Alde at Snape. The 14th c. tower has Norman foundations. Above the nave is a clerestory with six windows north and another six to the south. The roof is of single hammerbeam construction and was plastered over until 1932, hiding the beautiful timbers. The wall plates had to be replaced but the figures carved into the wall-posts are mostly original. Restoration however also had an opposite effect. The rood screen was removed and only a small part salvaged. This was made into a credence table and is in the chancel. The font is basically early 15th c. but that too was re-cut. The 13th c. piscina had the same treatment. Worst of all the splendid porch was demolished to extend the south aisle westwards.

SAXTEAD

Dedication:	All Saints
No of Bells:	1
Deanery 1836:	Hoxne
Hundred:	Hoxne
Union house:	Stradbroke
Deanery 2000:	Loes

2 m NW of Framlingham between Framlingham & Monk Soham: 1 m north of Saxtead Mill up a driveway, before Church Cottage.
O.S. grid ref TM 262657
Post Code: IP13 9QP

You may pass the drive up to the church before you find it. When you do you'll still wonder if you've gone wrong again. You are greeted by the south porch and the flushwork of stone and dressed flint. Just inside the porch are the village stocks and whipping post. A tower was never built; whether one was intended is not known. The font is a simple 15th c. example with a plain cover of the Stuart period, as are the holy table and altar rails. The bench ends are 15th c. but most have been mutilated. The nave roof is a single hammerbeam construction with carved decoration. The reredos is made up of parts of the old rood screen and old pulpit and includes a 15th c. roof boss. The 14th c. piscina has a pillar supporting the corner which opens into the dropped window sill sedilia.

SHADINGFIELD

		4 m S of Beccles, between
Dedication:	St John the Baptist	Beccles & Blythburgh: on
No of Bells:	1	the A145 near Church Farm
Deanery 1836:	Wangford	on a bend, large car park
Hundred:	Wangford	opposite the church.
Union house:	Shipmeadow	O.S. grid ref TM 434837
Deanery 2000:	Beccles & S. Elmham	Post Code: NR34 8DE

The porch with its elaborate gable is Tudor, but the brick is soft, and the re-pointing is abominable. The church has Norman origins. The north door indicates this, and one of the quoins shows signs of 12th c. carving. The nave roof is now plastered, concealing a plain arch-braced roof. A banner stave cupboard in the north wall of the nave is built into the tower buttress. The octagonal 15th c. font is nicely carved and has eight engaged columns around the shaft. It sits on a double pedestal , the top step being in the shape of a Maltese cross. The piscina is very plain and is flanked by a dropped sill sedilia. The seat level clearly indicates, as in many other churches, that the floor of the chancel has at some time been raised. The Stuart holy table is of a higher quality than most.

SHELLEY

Dedication:	All Saints	
No of Bells:	5	
Deanery 1836:	Samford	
Hundred:	Samford	
Union house:	Tattingstone	
Deanery 2000:	Hadleigh	

3 m S of Hadleigh between   Hadleigh & Stratford St Mary: on a sharp bend near Shelly bridge.
O.S. grid ref TM 030384
Post Code: IP7 5QX

There are not many churches with the tower on the north of the nave. This is one, with very shallow crenulations on the parapet.   The tower, which was built in the 14th c. and postdates the church by about a century. It is unlikely that a church existed here before then. The half-timbered porch has seen better days and is in a poor condition. The outside of the church is not much better, especially the north side. It is in the nave where the interest lies. Lying on her tomb, hands in prayer, is Dame Margaret Tylney (1598), dressed in black and head resting on two cushions. In the Tylney chapel there are other memorials, but it is now utilised as a cupboard. The reveals are lined with carved panelling. Tylney heraldry is recorded on the chancel wall. The Royal Arms are of George III.

SHIPMEADOW

Dedication:	St Bartholomew	
No of Bells:	1	
Deanery 1836:	Wangford	
Hundred:	Wangford	
Union house:	Shipmeadow	
Deanery 2000:	Beccles & S. Elmham	

2 m W of Beccles, between Beccles & Bungay: on the B1062, behind a broad grass verge. Now a private residence.

O.S. grid ref TM 382899

Post Code: NR34 8HL

This church is of Norman origins. A slit window in the north wall of the nave and most of the wall at the lower levels are Norman. The west tower is Tudor and is built of flint and brick with stumpy pinnacles. It has a north porch, also of the same period. In the 14th c. the roof of the chancel was raised and larger windows inserted. The font was pre-Reformation and of the traditional type for the area, and the screen, of which only the lower part remains, was of the same date. The Arms of George III once hung on the wall. Either side of the chancel, just above the altar rail, two metres or so above the floor level there are vertically pierced stone corbels. H. Munro Cautley believes these to be used for the Lenten veil. I cannot disagree, but I do feel they are rather too robust for that particular purpose.

SHOTLEY

Dedication:	St Mary
No of Bells:	1
Deanery 1836:	Samford
Hundred:	Samford
Union house:	Tattingstone
Deanery 2000:	Samford

9 m SE of Ipswich, between Harwich & Felixstowe on the peninsular: just after houses turn off the B1456, north into Oldhall Road.
O.S. grid ref TM 237360
Post Code: IP9 1ES

I had expected to find a beautiful traditional parish church sitting on a prominence overlooking the estuary. What I actually found is ugly to the extreme. The squat tower is cement-rendered and looks like a toilet block. Enough about the outside, however inside it is a different matter. The nave roof is a superb double hammerbeam construction with some simple tracery in the spandrils. The rest of the church has been clinically sterilised but is not offensive. The walls have been replastered and whitened. The chancel arch has been oak-panelled. The east window is very modern but not somehow out of place here. Although it doesn't show it, the church is actually 14th c. but the chancel is four centuries later. The clerestory lights the interior to perfection. Despite the outward appearance, I'm glad I went in.

SHOTTISHAM		4 m SE of Woodbridge
Dedication:	St Margaret	between Woodbridge &
No of Bells:	1	Bawdsey: from the B1083
Deanery 1836:	Wilford	to The Street, at The Square
Hundred:	Wilford	turn north to Church Lane.
Union house:	Nacton	O.S. grid ref TM 321447
Deanery 2000:	Woodbridge	Post Code: IP12 3HG

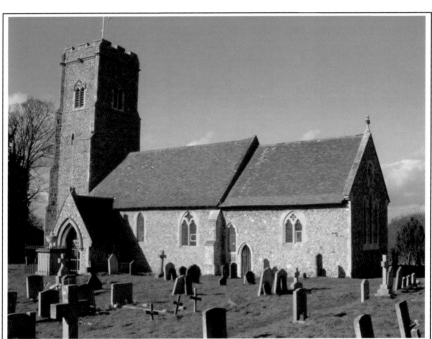

Looking very pleasant from a distance, as you near this church you notice the tower is suffering from the weather. It has been there for 500 or more years (notice the old roof line on the east side). The nave roof at one time was much higher pitched, and almost certainly thatched. The present roof dates from the 14th c.. The pier arcade which appears to be 13th c., was actually built in 1847. Nothing in this over-restored church is as it seems. Even the lovely old 13th c. octagonal Purbeck font bowl has not been overlooked, with eight modern multi-coloured marble columns around the base. The rood loft stairs are still open, top and bottom; beneath them is a small piscina. The simple piscina in the chancel has been restored and is adjacent to the dropped sill sedilia.

SIBTON
Dedication: St Peter
No of Bells: 5
Deanery 1836: Dunwich
Hundred: Blything
Union house: Bulcamp
Deanery 2000: Saxmundham

4 m N of Saxmundham
between, Yoxford &
Peasenhall: on the A1120
(Yoxford Road) east of the
village, near the village sign
O.S. grid ref TM 367695
Post Code: IP17 2NB

Immediately inside the small porch you are greeted by a late 12th c doorway with two engaged columns each side. The 13th c. structure and 15th c. tower were in good hands. Alterations have been made recently but everything is still intact. The attention is drawn upwards to the magnificent hammerbeam roof with shields on the ends of the hammers and 30 small figures look down. There are 100 bosses to count on the chancel roof. The 15th c. font, standing on a triple plinth, is well carved with animals, angels and wodewoses around the shaft, is quite complete. There are two canopied niches either side of the chancel arch and a nice monument to Sir Edmond Barker (1676) with his wife Mary. On the floor in the chancel is a portrait brass to Edmund Chapman and I think dated as 15 . 7 (1507 ?)

SNAPE

Dedication:	St John the Baptist
No of Bells:	3
Deanery 1836:	Orford
Hundred:	Plomesgate
Union house:	Wickham Market
Deanery 2000:	Saxmundham

3 m S of Saxmundham between Saxmundham & Aldeburgh: north side of the A1094, (1½ miles north of the maltings concert hall). O.S. grid ref TM 395593 Post Code: IP17 1QW

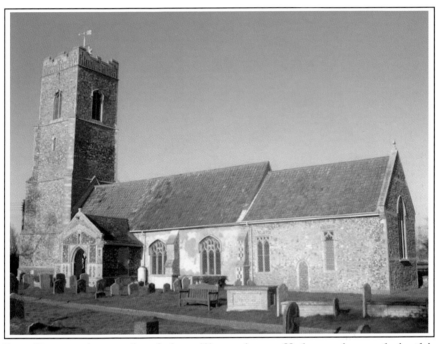

Standing to the north of the village, just off the main road, is this early but not original church. The porch has not been restored as well as it might have been. The south door has dragons carved in the spandrils. There is a blocked 12th c. doorway in the north wall. The 15th c. font is exceptionally well carved with various figures holding a banner signifying continuance; the corbel has angels and eight more figures surround the shaft. A badly worn inscription is to be found on the plinth. An old piscina had been hacked back to the wall and was rediscovered last century during renovations. A recess in the north wall was discovered at the same time and is believed to be an old tomb, utilised perhaps as an Easter sepulchre. Rebuilding of the east end can be verified by the incorrect placing of an old scratch dial.

SOMERLEYTON
Dedication: St Mary
No of Bells: 6
Deanery 1836: Lothingland
Hundred: Mutford & Lothingland
Union house: Oulton
Deanery 2000: Lothingland, Norwich

6 m NW of Lowestoft
between Lowestoft & St
Olaves: on the B1074
(Blundeston Road) up a
driveway.
O.S. grid ref TM 493972
Post Code: NR32 5PP

You will notice immediately that the tower above the roof line is a different material to the lower portion. Sir Morton Peto was responsible for the rebuilding, and creating a more elegant tower. Inside the church, immediately above the door, there is a carved stone panel depicting four of the emblems of the evangelists. The screen attracts the attention of the visitor and although very much restored it is well executed. On the panels are pictures of 16 Saints. The octagonal font is 15th c. but I think it must have been re-cut, or missed the attentions of the Puritans. The font cover is Stuart and is eye-catching in its simplicity. There are nicely carved busts on a wall memorial to Sir John Wentworth (1651) and his wife. Sir Thomas Gernegan's tomb is against the north wall of the chancel.

SOMERSHAM

		6 miles NE of Hadleigh
Dedication:	St Mary	between Ipswich & Offton:
No of Bells:	2	from (the) Main Road
Deanery 1836:	Bosmere	through the village turn
Hundred:	Bosmere & Claydon	south into Church Lane.
Union house:	Barham	O.S. grid ref TM 091484
Deanery 2000:	Bosmere	Post Code: IP8 4PJ

The 14th c. half timbered porch is possibly the oldest in the county, it sits comfortably against the south wall of the 14th c. church. (The other contender for oldest church porch is Boxford, which is certainly more elaborate). There is a scratch dial to be found on the buttress. The roof of the nave is constructed with braced tie-beams. There are wooden pegs fixed to the roof plate at the west end of the nave; no one knows for sure what their purpose is. The late Stuart holy table is contemporary with the altar rails. There are two sets of Royal Arms, those of Charles II have a fretted border, while the other is Hanoverian. The tie-beam above the altar rails still retains the ancient and rare example of the gallows for the sacring bell. The font is plain and uninteresting. Unless you're interested in plain fonts!

SOTHERTON

Dedication:	St Andrew
No of Bells:	1
Deanery 1836:	Dunwich
Hundred:	Blything
Union house:	Bulcamp
Deanery 2000:	Halesworth

4 m NW of Halesworth
between Blythburgh &
Shadingfield: 1 m NE of the
village centre, off the A145
near Church Farm. (signed)
O.S. grid ref TM 441794
Post Code: NR34 8ES

This small church is a mile away from the centre of the parish it serves. A single bell turret adorns the west gable, which has a central buttress flanked by two windows. Parts of the church have been rebuilt but in general the structure is Norman. In the 13th c. nave the arch-braced and collared roof is a good example. Set into the north wall is a recess in which lies a knight. Exactly who he is is uncertain, but he is most likely to be Walter de Bernham. The font is a traditional East Anglian type but the cover is more interesting. It is six feet high, pyramidal, and is surmounted by a small crown. It is suspended from the roof by a chain. Make sure not to miss the vestry door, which has early 16th c. panels from the rood screen attached to it, one of which is unique. Note the eagle at his feet!

SOTTERLEY with Willingham

Dedication:	St Margaret	
No of Bells:	2	
Deanery 1836:	Wangford	
Hundred:	Wangford	
Union house:	Shipmeadow	
Deanery 2000:	Beccles & S. Elmham	

5 m SE of Beccles
between Shadingfield &
Hulver Street: accessible
only by ½ m footpath, park
the car by the Village Hall.
O.S. grid ref TM 459852
Post Code: NR34 7TU

Sotterley was consolidated with Willingham in the middle of the 16th century. You have to be keen to get to this 15th c. church. Accessible for the visitor only by a footpath across potholed meadowland, the church is always open. The foundations and parts of the walls were built by Norman builders. The church has numerous memorials and portraits of the Playters family who lived in the nearby hall. One of the brasses to Sir Thomas dates from the 15th c.. The quality of the memorials is exceptional. An unusually large banner stave closet and a traditional octagonal East Anglian font are interesting but the piscina is more unusual. The cusped ogee arch springs from stone corbels, in the style of a hood-mould. The original pulpit has been removed to Framlingham Earl in Norfolk.

SOUTH COVE

Dedication:	St Lawrence	
No of Bells:	1	
Deanery 1836:	Dunwich	
Hundred:	Blything	
Union house:	Bulcamp	
Deanery 2000:	Halesworth	

3 m N of Southwold
between Kessingland &
Southwold: turn off the A12
at Wrentham onto B1127
(Southwold Road) for 1 m.
O.S. grid ref TM 500808
Post Code: NR34 7JD

At some time the Norman south doorway has been rebuilt or restored, because one of the stones has a scratch dial which is now upside down. The north doorway is also Norman and the door is 15th c. with three deeply carved panels. The nave roof is a simple arch-braced collar with arched braces giving additional support. Some of the benches are 15th c. and the piscina is from a century earlier. The pulpit is Stuart and not exceptional, unlike the painting of St. Michael on the door to the rood loft stairs which could so easily have been destroyed when the stairs were no longer used. Part of the screen remains on the south side and also retains some of the original colouring. The traditional East Anglian-type font is badly mutilated.

SOUTH ELMHAM ALL SAINTS

Dedication:	All Saints & St Nicholas	
No of Bells:	1	
Deanery 1836:	South Elmham	
Hundred:	Wangford	
Union house:	Shipmeadow	
Deanery 2000:	Beccles & S. Elmham	

4 m NW of Halesworth between Rumburgh & S.E. St Margaret: 1 m north-west of village turn south next to The Old Rectory. (signed) O.S. grid ref TM 329828 Post Code: IP19 0PB

This is one of our lovely Norman round tower churches. All Saints church is preserved by the Redundant Churches Trust. It remains a consecrated building and very occasionally a service is still held here. The Church of St Nicholas has long since disappeared. The south porch is 15th c. and there is a scratch dial on the face. The clerestory has 5 very small windows through which light weeps into the nave. There is a crude stoup just inside the door. The font is 13th c. Norman with a column at each corner and a large central pillar on a base. The square bowl is bevelled with a vertical scalloped design. The bench ends have amusing animals carved on them and the stalls have large poppyheads. The 14th c. piscina has recesses, one each side, the purpose of which is not fully understood.

SOUTH ELMHAM ST CROSS

Dedication:	St George	
No of Bells:	5	
Deanery 1836:	South Elmham	
Hundred:	Wangford	
Union house:	Shipmeadow	
Deanery 2000:	Beccles & S. Elmham	

7 m NW of Halesworth between Homersfield & South Elmham St Margaret: take the driveway near the bridge, signed 'Church'.
O.S. grid ref TM 299842
Post Code: IP20 0NX

No, it doesn't really lean like the tower at Pisa. The church is built on the side of a valley and is also sometimes referred to as South Elmham Sancroft. It is an unusually tall chancel with a clerestory giving a lofty appearance to the structure. In the 15th c. south porch is a 12th c Norman doorway upon which is carved a scratch dial, and some graffiti written in 1627. There is a lovely old iron-bound round-top parish chest in the nave just as you enter. The north doorway is also Norman but has been considerably damaged. The octagonal font is traditional East Anglian style and could be late 14th c.. The roof of the nave is an arch-braced type and still shows signs of the original painting. Some of the bench-end carvings depict various agricultural crops.

SOUTH ELMHAM ST JAMES

Dedication:	St James	4 m NW of Halesworth
No of Bells:	4	between Metfield & South
Deanery 1836:	South Elmham	Elmham All Saints; from
Hundred:	Wangford	The Street, turn south into
Union house:	Shipmeadow	Church Lane.
Deanery 2000:	Beccles & S. Elmham	O.S. grid ref TM 322812
		Post Code: IP19 0HL

This is the oldest of the South Elmham churches. Although the tower is square it is probably Saxon in the lower levels. The wall adjoining the tower and the west wall are definitely Norman. Inside the south porch is a tiny stoup in a pretty cusped and traceried recess. The font is contemporary with the church. Look carefully at the corners and see the arrow, a sign of the Trinity. The cover is 15th c.. There are some lovely interesting carvings. Almost all you see around you is Norman with one or two exceptions, such as the Jacobean parish chests and the screen. The small piscina has a detached shaft set at an angle and a moulded and cusped arch above. Next to it is a dropped sill sedilia. The bench end carvings are the work of local artisans, and the owls on the reading desk are by Sir Shafto Adair, the patron.

SOUTH ELMHAM ST MARGARET

Dedication:	St Margaret	
No of Bells:	5	
Deanery 1836:	South Elmham	
Hundred:	Wangford	
Union house:	Shipmeadow	
Deanery 2000:	Beccles & S. Elmham	

6 m NW of Halesworth between Homersfield & Rumburgh: the church is at the west end of the long, strung out village street.
O.S. grid ref TM 314839
Post Code: IP20 0PJ

This church, which sits by a bend in the road, was obviously Saxon in its beginnings. The south doorway with two engaged columns is Norman and the slit windows still feed light into the nave. On the porch door jamb is a scratch dial. The village stocks stand redundant inside, and above in the parvise, a barrel organ awaits a grinder. There is nothing exceptional about this church but it has its interesting points. The nave roof is simple arch-braced. The traditional East Anglian font has been restored. An old hour-glass holder is screwed to the wall near the pulpit. In the chancel there is a nicely carved Easter sepulchre set into a recess; the base has panels with tracery decoration and there are modest pinnacles either side of the arch. Part of the old gilded rood screen is in the chancel.

SOUTH ELMHAM ST MICHAEL
Dedication: St Michael
No of Bells: 1
Deanery 1836:   South Elmham
Hundred: Wangford
Union house: Shipmeadow
Deanery 2000:   Beccles & S. Elmham

5 m NW of Halesworth
between South Elmham St
Peter & South Elmham All
Saints: the water tower is a
good landmark to follow.
O.S. grid ref TM 341839
Post Code: NR35 1ND

This is one of the 31 'thankful' parishes and the only one in Suffolk.
Eleven men went to war in 1939 and all returned safely 6 years later.
To the right of the porch on the nave wall is a sundial which tells
you, 'Why stand gazing? Be about your business' and 'Only count
the sunlit hours'. Inside the porch is a nice Norman doorway with
engaged columns and three orders of decoration. Just inside the door
there is a stoup set deep into the wall. The roof of the nave is arch-
braced with tie-beams. The font is traditional East Anglian style, and
looking quite crisp, perhaps restored. The piscina in the chancel is as
ancient as the building but very simple in its form. Before you leave,
glance around at the headstones: some have decoration rarely seen
and one is fashioned from oak, but the inscription has long gone.

SOUTH ELMHAM ST PETER

		5 m NW of Halesworth
Dedication:	St Peter	between Ilketshall St
No of Bells:	3	Margaret & South Elmham
Deanery 1836:	South Elmham	St Margaret: quite easily
Hundred:	Wangford	recognised from a distance.
Union house:	Shipmeadow	O.S. grid ref TM 335848
Deanery 2000:	Beccles & S. Elmham	Post Code: NR35 1NG

As you enter the gate, on your right is the base of an ancient cross with traceried sides. The possible shaft is in the tower. The tower is peppered with wallflowers and most attractive when flowering. The porch is rubble-built and crude. On the door jamb are scratch dials. An early chapel which was north of the chancel has been dismantled. The chancel arch has niches either side, and beneath the arch is a rood screen which carries a modern rood or cross and is flanked by two carved figures. The roof of the nave and chancel are both a simple arch-braced design springing from stone corbels with carved bosses at the crossings. The font is in the traditional East Anglian style, but restored. Round the base are lions which look more like pussy cats. The benches are simple and austere.

SOUTHOLT

Dedication:	St Margaret
No of Bells:	1
Deanery 1836:	Hoxne
Hundred:	Hoxne
Union house:	Stradbroke
Deanery 2000:	Hoxne

4 m SE of Eye. between Thorndon & Worlingworth: situated at the west end of Southolt Street, near The Green & Yew Tree Cottage. O.S. grid ref TM 193688 Post Code: IP23 7QJ

Southolt's church can be easily passed without being noticed. It is set at the back of the village green and obscured by trees. There was once a tower but it fell centuries ago. The double buttresses where the tower stood form an arch at the top which supports the bell turret, which was built instead of reconstructing the tower. The simple framed and braced roof to the nave is boarded at the eastern end; it was once a canopy of honour to the rood but all signs of it having been so have been removed. The font is of the traditional East Anglian style and has a modest pyramidal cover. In the south-east corner of the nave is a consecration cross on the wall. The altar rails and holy table are dated around the Stuart period. The Royal Arms are of George III.

SOUTHTOWN

Dedication: St Mary
No of Bells: 1
Deanery 1836: Lothingland
Hundred: Mutford & Lothingland
Union house: Oulton
Deanery 2000: Lothingland, Norwich

6½ m N of Lowestoft
between Gorleston &
Great Yarmouth, Norfolk:
at the northern end of
Southtown Road, east side.
O.S. grid ref TG 521071
Post Code: NR31 0JB

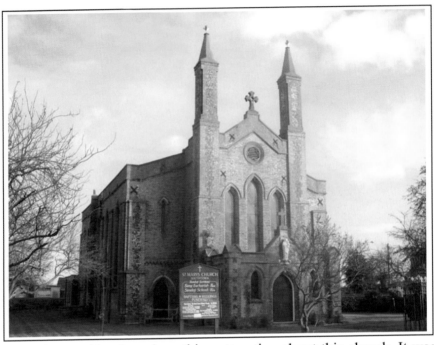

From the outside, there is nothing attractive about this church. It was built by the early Victorians in 1831 in white brick with dressed flint flushwork. There is no tower, but two fine pinnacles point skyward at the west end of the nave. Entrance to the nave is through the west porch; above, on the gable, is a Madonna and Child. Inside, it is spacious, without internal columnar supports for the roof. The tall windows north and south let the available light flood into this brightly decorated church. The small octagonal font is contemporary with the church and has carved decoration on the faces of the bowl. The pulpit also dates from the same period. There is a piscina and three-seat stepped sedilia, although they went out of use centuries before this church was built. Alas, it is only open during services.

SOUTHWOLD   *****

Dedication:	St Edmund	11 m S of Lowestoft
No of Bells:	8 + 2	between Lowestoft &
Deanery 1836:	Dunwich	Leiston (on the coast) from
Hundred:	Blything	the A1085 (Station Rd) turn
Union house:	Bulcamp	left near library & follow.
Deanery 2000:	Halesworth	O.S. grid ref TM 507763
		Post Code: IP18 6JA

Although a much earlier church stood on this spot for centuries, what is seen today is virtually all 15th c. The unbroken line of the copper-clad roof, the mid bell turret, and the unembattled parapet of the tower is probably the most recognisable in Suffolk. The complexity of the architecture also makes it one of the finest churches in the county. There is so much inside to attract the visitor that I cannot possibly mention everything here. Above the stone and flint porch is a chamber with a secret lock. The nave roof has hammerbeams with arch-bracing, that of the chancel is boarded and painted. The seven sacrament font has been badly mutilated. A jack-of-the-clock flanks the painted pulpit. Beautifully carved bench-ends and misericordes are a 'must see'. Allow at least a couple of hours here.

SPEXHALL

Dedication:	St Peter	
No of Bells:	1	
Deanery 1836:	Dunwich	
Hundred:	Blything	
Union house:	Bulcamp	
Deanery 2000:	Halesworth	

2 m N of Halesworth between Halesworth & Bungay: turn west at the crossroads on the A144 into Church Lane, follow ¾ m. O.S. grid ref TM 378801 Post Code: IP19 0RQ

A lovely little round tower church over a half mile from the Roman road of Stone Street. A blocked doorway under a flying buttress catches the eye, but take a look at the east wall before proceeding and examine the diaper-work in the brick and flint, and how it has been repaired over the centuries. The tower was almost totally rebuilt at the beginning of the 20th c.. Just inside the south door is a Norman stoup. The roof of the nave is an amalgamation of arch-braced scissor-beams and tie-beams. The piscina has a deep bowl, but very simple, with minimal cinquefoil decoration to the arch. The rood-loft stairs are blocked and the steps utilised as shelves for flowers etc.. In the chancel there are brasses to Silvester Browne and other members of the same family dated 1593. The Royal Arms are of George II.

SPROUGHTON

Dedication:	All Saints
No of Bells:	6
Deanery 1836:	Samford
Hundred:	Samford
Union house:	Tattingstone
Deanery 2000:	Samford

3 m W of Ipswich, between Ipswich & Burstall: next to Sproughton Bridge in Church Lane at the junction with Lower Street.
O.S. grid ref TM 125450
Post Code: IP8 3DB

This 15th c. church on the outskirts of Ipswich seems to be suffering from everyone having more important things to do than clean up the churchyard. But I have seen much worse. There are many interesting points outside to see. The glacial boulders built into the foundations and plinth, for example, are a sign of a very early church. The well executed stone tracery in the windows, and the thriftily built clerestory with a small east window and the sundial above the door of the porch are all worth your attention. Inside, the hammerbeam and arch-braced roof is supported on arches with clustered columns. There is a peephole in what was the north chapel through to the chancel where there are some old bench-ends. There is a very nice memorial to Elizabeth Bull, who died aged 76 in 1634.

STERNFIELD

Dedication:	St Mary Magdalene	
No of Bells:	4	
Deanery 1836:	Orford	
Hundred:	Plomesgate	
Union house:	Wickham Market	
Deanery 2000:	Saxmundham	

1 m S of Saxmundham
between   Saxmundham &
Snape: just off the B1121
turn east on Church Hill,
Sternfield into driveway.
O.S. grid ref TM 390615
Post Code: IP17 1RS

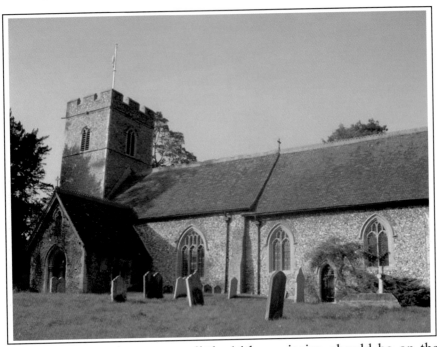

I have no idea why a pretty little 14th c. piscina should be on the north wall of this church, but there is and it is decorated with ballflowers. On the west face of the 14th c. tower there is an armorial shield of the de la Pole family. There are two more similar shields in the glass of the west window. There are three scratch dials, one still bearing the remains of a gnomon. As you pass through the 14th c. porch the two-light windows are worthy of note for their decoration. The font is 14th c. with a simply decorated octagonal bowl. The benches are mainly 15th c. and have grotesques and other carving worth closer inspection. The north chapel in the chancel has, like so many others, been transformed into a vestry and that may be why the piscina is now outside.

STONHAM ASPAL

Dedication:	Blessed Virgin Mary
No of Bells:	10
Deanery 1836:	Bosmere
Hundred:	Bosmere & Claydon
Union house:	Barham
Deanery 2000:	Bosmere

5 m E of Stowmarket between Stowmarket & Earl Soham: situated on the A1120 (The Street) opposite 'The Ten Bells' PH.
O.S. grid ref TM 133595
Post Code: IP14 6AF

The village is so proud of its church that the wooden 10-bell belfry is on the village sign, yet they hide it behind a screen of Irish yew trees. The tower had this wooden top specially constructed in 1742 to accommodate the 10 bells. Behind metal railings on the south side of the chancel is a sculptured memorial to Anthony Wingfield dressed in all his regalia. The tower also serves as a south porch, and inside the church the 16-window 15th c. clerestory lights the interior wonderfully. The font is 13th c. and has an interesting bowl. The pulpit is Stuart, the sounding board of which has been transformed into a table dated 1616. The chancel piscina is plain with a cusped head and is flanked by the dropped sill sedilia. The knight in the chancel tomb is from around 1330, but has been terribly mutilated.

STONHAM PARVA

Dedication:	St Mary	
No of Bells:	5	
Deanery 1836:	Bosmere	
Hundred:	Bosmere & Claydon	
Union house:	Barham	
Deanery 2000:	Bosmere	

4 m NE of Stowmarket between Mendlesham & Needham Market: west off the A140, ½ m north of the A1120 crossroads. Signed. O.S. grid ref TM 111601 Post Code: IP14 5JL

Otherwise known as Little Stonham (both are used but Parva is favoured). This lovely church has a beautiful flint and stone tower with delicate pinnacles and crenulations. If you have your binoculars, examine closely the detail of the panelling of the parapet. The crow-stepped gables complement the crenulations above the clerestory. The nave has a double hammerbeam roof with tracery in the spandrils and mutilated figures in the wall posts. The chancel roof is relatively modern with angels keeping an eye on those below. The traditional East Anglian font has pierced heart decoration in panels to the bowl and figures holding hands around the corbel. The Royal Arms are those of Queen Anne. A memorial tablet is set on the wall to Gilbert Mowse (1622) who is buried in Westminster Abbey.

STOVEN

Dedication:	St Margaret	
No of Bells:	1	
Deanery 1836:	Dunwich	
Hundred:	Blything	
Union house:	Bulcamp	
Deanery 2000:	Beccles & S. Elm-	

5 m NE of Halesworth
between Beccles &
Blythburgh: east off the
A145 at Brampton Dog B&B
follow for about 1 mile.
O.S. grid ref TM 448816
Post Code: NR34 8ER

This church was made redundant and later reprieved. Sadly it is now falling into decline. The fabric is in dire need of repair. The church is Norman, with Victorian restoration which has preserved it for us. The Norman tower has no buttresses and is capped by a tiled pyramidal roof. Around the soffit are 28 grotesque heads. The Norman doorways remain at north (rebuilt) and south entrances. Both have engaged columns and an arch of two orders. Inside, the chancel arch is in the Norman style but not, I think, original. The octagonal font is very different from most, being quite modern, and cut from one piece of stone, with marble engaged columns around the shaft. The piscina is very small and simple. The square pulpit is Victorian and part of the restoration.

STRADBROKE

Dedication: All Saints
No of Bells: 10
Deanery 1836: Hoxne
Hundred: Hoxne
Union house: Stradbroke
Deanery 2000: Hoxne

6 m E of Eye, between
Laxfield & Eye: in the
village centre in Church
Street, at the junction with
Queen's Street.
O.S. grid ref TM 232740
Post Code: IP21 5HG

The tower is over 100 feet high and dominates the town. The turret stairs extend above the crenulated and panelled parapet. The church was built in the 15th c. as a result of local prosperity. It was much restored during the Victorian period. Above the nave is a clerestory with a panelled roof with carved bosses. The font is of traditional East Anglian type with an inscription round the plinth, naming John Smyth and Joanna Rous. In the sanctuary there is a richly carved canopied niche which probably served as an Easter sepulchre. Even the rear wall has a diaper pattern. The holy table is of the Stuart period. The pulpit and benches are nicely carved but are all of the Victorian period. The Bishop who defied the Pope when Rome was taxing England dry, was born here, his name was Robert Grosseteste.

248

STRATFORD   3 m SW of Saxmundham
Dedication: St Andrew   between   Saxmundham &
No of Bells: 3, now removed   Wickham Market. turn off
Deanery 1836:   Orford   Main Road on bend.
Hundred: Plomesgate   Now a private residence.
Union house: Wickham Market   O.S. grid ref TM 357601
Deanery 2000:   Saxmundham   Post Code: IP17 1PZ

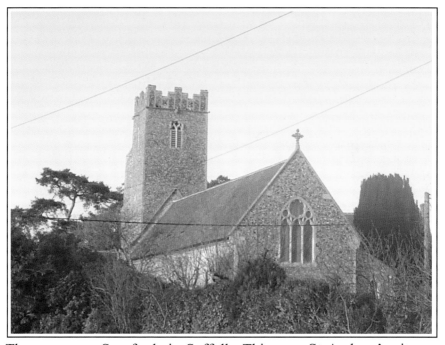

There are two Stratfords in Suffolk. This one, St Andrew's sits, on the west bank of the river Alde across the valley from Farnham. It was made redundant in 1991 and has been a private residence for some time. The church is 13th c. Norman in origin and a slit window in the south wall of the nave substantiates this. The typical font bowl is contemporary with the church. The piscina, which still retains its shelf, has been slightly modified from the original with two columns, one of them a century older than the other. The Stuart pulpit and holy table have been removed from the church along with the other religious paraphernalia. Perhaps in the hands of a private owner the structure will last longer than it may otherwise have done had it remained an empty building prone to damp and misuse.

STRATFORD
Dedication: St Mary
No of Bells: 6
Deanery 1836: Samford
Hundred: Samford
Union house: Tattingstone
Deanery 2000: Hadleigh

6 m S of Hadleigh
between Capel St Mary &
Colchester: on the Dedham
Road (B1029) immediately
off the A12.
O.S. grid ref TM 052346
Post Code: CO7 6LS

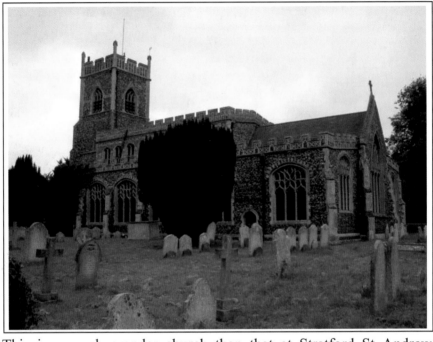

This is a much grander church than that at Stratford St Andrew. Coincidentally, sited on the bank of a river, this time the Stour, it is just a mile from the Essex border. The fine embattled clerestory and south chapel, together with the blackness of the flint alongside the contrasting stone make this a very imposing church. The stone-carver left all kinds of creatures crawling all over the building. As you pass through the 16th c. porch you enter a nave that has been re-built and very restored, but it contains many features of interest. The rood stairs now lead into the pulpit and a holy table, now not used as such, was all the work of Jacobean craftsmen. Much of the woodwork is modern, including the linen-fold choir stalls. The north aisle is a monument to Thomas Mors and Margaret, his wife.

STUTTON

Dedication:	St Peter
No of Bells:	6
Deanery 1836:	Samford
Hundred:	Samford
Union house:	Tattingstone
Deanery 2000:	Samford

6 m S of Ipswich, between
Holbrook & Brantham:
south off the B1080 into
Church Road or The Drift,
at the end of a cul de sac.
O.S. grid ref TM 161344
Post Code: IP9 2SD

The church overlooks Holbrook Bay, and the Royal Hospital School is close by. The tower, which was built in the 15th c., doubles up as a south porch. The church is only a little earlier, probably late 14th c. as can be determined from the ironwork on the south door. It was rebuilt making use of parts of the earlier 12th c. church. The little slit window, for example, and some of the stone in the buttresses, were first cut in Norman times. The font is quite plain with simple arcading to the octagonal bowl and is supported by eight columns around a central pillar. There are two similar-looking 17th c. monuments to Isaac and Jane Jermy and their son John and his wife. There are also memorials to two of the rectors who served for 111 years between them; Thomas Mills, and Tobias Rustat.

SUDBOURNE

Dedication:	All Saints
No of Bells:	1
Deanery 1836:	Orford
Hundred:	Plomesgate
Union house:	Wickham Market
Deanery 2000:	Woodbridge

9 miles NE of Woodbridge between Snape & Orford: from the five crossways on the B1084 the church can be seen to the east.

O.S. grid ref TM 420519

Post Code IP12 2AS

A well-proportioned tower with a neat spirelet or 'Hereford spike' pointing skyward over the embattled parapet greets you as you approach this lovely little church. Originally built by the Normans in the 12th c. it has been so restored that very little of the original remains. Since the Victorian rebuilding programme, the roof no longer differentiates between the nave and the chancel and it is the same inside. A north and south transept were also added; the former housing the organ, the latter, private pews. The south porch has been utilised as a vestry since the north door is nearer the entrance to the churchyard. The north wall of the sanctuary houses the enormous memorial and effigy to Sir Michael Stanhope (1621), who was privy councillor to Queen Elizabeth and James I

SUTTON

Dedication: All Saints
No of Bells: 1
Deanery 1836: Wilford
Hundred: Wilford
Union house: Nacton
Deanery 2000: Woodbridge

3 m SE of Woodbridge between Woodbridge & Bawdsey: of the B1083 at the northern end of village street near the Old School. O.S. grid ref TM 306464
Post Code: IP12 3DT

The tower of this church fell in 1642 and was never rebuilt. It originally stood south of the nave and served as a porch. A new bell was purchased in 1713 and is housed in a bellcote south of the junction of the nave and chancel. (It is rung from inside the church by means of underground levers.) The nave has a panelled wagon roof interspersed with timbers. The rood-loft stairs are open to the top, revealing the thickness of the wall. The first south window in the chancel has in the reveal a small mask fashioned in wet plaster by a mediaeval craftsman. The octagonal font is of the greatest interest. Early 15th c. carvers filled the panels with evangelistic emblems and figures of angels, a monk, a cardinal, and a priest. The corbel is decorated with tools used for the sacrament.

SWEFFLING

Dedication:	St Mary
No of Bells:	6
Deanery 1836:	Orford
Hundred:	Plomesgate
Union house:	Wickham Market
Deanery 2000:	Saxmundham

2 m W of Saxmundham between Saxmundham & Framlingham: in the centre of the village main street, hard to miss

O.S. grid ref TM 347638

Post Code: IP17 2BL

The church sits high on the brow of a hill with the street and houses below. The porch is panelled with stone and flint flushwork with three niches above the doorway, and George and Dragon in the spandrils. I was delighted when I entered the church through the 12th c. Norman doorway, for it is not just a church, it is also a museum. Beneath the tower there are photographs and paraphernalia depicting village life of the past. The font has a shallow arcading around the 13th c. bowl, the rest is modern. The simple piscina is utilised as a shelf to keep a prayer-book stand. The Arms of Queen Anne hang high on the north wall above the Commandments and Lord's Prayer of the same period. The church has in its possession a boiled leather 14th c. chalice case, unique in Suffolk. It is not on public display.

SWILLAND

Dedication:	St Mary	
No of Bells:	1	
Deanery 1836:	Claydon	
Hundred:	Bosmere & Claydon	
Union house:	Barham	
Deanery 2000:	Woodbridge	

6 m N of Ipswich, between Witnesham & Helmingham: not far off the B1077 in Church Lane (an unmade driveway) by Corner Cottage O.S. grid ref TM 187529 Post Code: IP6 9LP

What a strange thing, a Swiss cottage on top of a church tower! It was designed by J. S. Corder and added about 1897. A church has stood on this site since Saxon times. After the Conquest the Normans built a stone church here. The south doorway, protected by the little half-timbered porch, has two engaged columns each side. However, it is a re-build and the doorway has been altered. The arch above has four orders of sculpture but this too has been restored. The roof in the nave is a simple hammerbeam and arch-braced construction. The font has been painted in the past by Robert Faulconer, rector here 1892-1897. The reredos is the pride of the parish and is indeed very elaborate, but for me the Jacobean pulpit is far more interesting - seemingly of leather, so rich is the colour and depth of polish.

TATTINGSTONE

Dedication:	St Mary	
No of Bells:	6	
Deanery 1836:	Samford	
Hundred:	Samford	
Union house:	Tattingstone	
Deanery 2000:	Samford	

6 m S of Ipswich, between Capel St Mary & Holbrook: in Church Road close to the centre of the village. Near the playing field.

O.S. grid ref TM 136371

Post Code: IP9 2NA

The 14th c. church stands in a large churchyard in which there is a scattering of headstones and monuments. There are two porches: north, built in the 15th c., and south a century earlier. The tower has been horribly cement-rendered on the east face. A cheap option, instead of re-pointing in the proper manner. The gable of the south porch has had similar treatment. Inside is no better. The double hammerbeam roof of the nave has been boarded in pine and looks dreadful. The piscina in the chancel is being used as a bookshelf, next to that is a dropped sill sedilia. The modern pulpit stands on a stone plinth. The font at least, although simple 13th c., is the only genuine treasure this sad church has to offer. A marble memorial on the wall is for Thomas Western (1814) and his widow, Mary.

SYLEHAM

Dedication: St Mary
No of Bells: 3
Deanery 1836: Hoxne
Hundred: Hoxne
Union house: Stradbroke
Deanery 2000: Hoxne

5 m NE of Eye, between
Hoxne & Weybread: on the road
between Syleham Lodge &
Monk's Hall; opposite a road
junction, by Cross Cottage.
O.S. grid ref TM 204796
Post Code: IP21 4LN

A long muddy path leads down into the bottom of the Waveney Valley, where we find this charming little church. As I approached on a Sunday morning the congregation started to file out of the door. There were six cars in the car park and eight in the congregation, plus the vicar. The lower part of the tower is Saxon, as is much of the church. It was here in this very church that Baron Bigod met with Henry II in 1172 and swore submission to him and surrendered his two castles of Framlingham and Bungay. Inside the south porch the doorway has shields around the jambs. The base of the font is 12th c. and has volutes on the corners, with signs of an inscription round the base. The very plain font and shaft is later. The conical font cover is dated 1667. The 13th c. chancel has a contemporary piscina.

Dedication: St Ethelbert
No of Bells: 6
Deanery 1836:   Hoxne
Hundred: Hoxne
Union house: Stradbroke
Deanery 2000:   Hoxne

4 m NW of Framlingham
between Worlingworth &
Dennington: much closer to
Braiseworth Hall than
Tannington, at Church Corner.
O.S. grid ref TM 242674
Post Code: IP13 7LU

The south porch, with nice flushwork and niche, has an embattled parapet which complements the tower. The north doorway is Norman and has engaged columns, carved capitals and a well moulded arch. The chancel has a plain 13th c. piscina with a corner column set into the reveal of the dropped window sill sedilia. There is a portrait brass memorial to Anne Dade (1612). The simply decorated font is a typical 13th c. bowl sitting on a 12th c shaft. The 15th c. benches, with many different grotesques and figures are a delight to examine. They may have been carved by the same craftsman as did the ones at Athelington and Wilby. The roof of the nave is a wagon roof with the interest at the east end. It is rare to find a canopy of honour to the rood these days, but here there is one to see.

THEBERTON

Dedication:	St Peter	
No of Bells:	6	
Deanery 1836:	Dunwich	
Hundred:	Blything	
Union house:	Bulcamp	
Deanery 2000:	Saxmundham	

4 m NE of Saxmundham
between Yoxford &
Leiston: on the B1122 at
the western end of the
village in Church Road.
O.S. grid ref TM 437659
Post Code: IP16 4SA

A Norman round tower with a later octagonal top, a thatched nave and chancel roof. This is a charming little parish church. The tower is very thick at the base, over 5 feet. What used to be the north door is now protected inside the vestry. It has two engaged columns to each side and a chevron moulded arch. A large north Norman window is now blocked up. The south porch with flushwork panels is the same period as the south aisle. The arches in the south aisle have been painted in the manner as they would have been when the church was built. The typical East Anglian octagonal font has wodewoses around the base. The piscina is very simple and is flanked by a three-level sedilia. In the churchyard is the grave of 16 Germans whose zeppelin crashed here in 1917. Part of the wreckage hangs in the church.

THORINGTON

Dedication:	St Peter
No of Bells:	1
Deanery 1836:	Dunwich
Hundred:	Blything
Union house:	Bulcamp
Deanery 2000:	Halesworth

3 m SE of Halesworth between Blythburgh & Bramfield: turn west off the A12 at 'The Round House', and follow for 1 mile.
O.S. grid ref TM 422741
Post Code: IP19 9JG

This poor little Norman round-tower church is almost unable to breathe. It is totally surrounded by trees and suffering from damp. On the Norman tower there is shallow arcading around the middle stage, with loopholes interspersed and lovely round-arched windows. The brickwork forming the octagonal 'crown' is a Tudor addition. The tower arch at the west of the nave is restored. The nave roof is of arch-braced construction. with angels at each principal. The octagonal font bowl is typical of the 13th c. with arcading similar to that on the tower. The base is 200 years younger. The piscina is from the 14th c. and has flush tracery decoration. Some of the benches are more interesting than others. There are two parish chests, both of the 17th c., and the Royal Arms are those of George II.

TRIMLEY ST MARTIN

Dedication:	St Martin
No of Bells:	1
Deanery 1836:	Colneis
Hundred:	Colneis
Union house:	Nacton
Deanery 2000:	Colneys

2 m NW of Felixstowe between Ipswich & Felixstowe: turn off the bypass into 'The Trimleys' Two churches side by side. O.S. grid ref TM 276370 Post Code: IP11 OSW

The Trimleys, as they are known come together at their two churches. The parish boundary runs down the centre of the graveyard between them; they stand only 100 yards apart. St Martin is a 14th c. church. However, there are modern additions such as the battlements on the tower, and the nave and porch. The walls everywhere are rendered with horrible cement and no attempt at decoration or breaking up the plainness has been attempted. The font is 12th c. with a square bowl and chevron decoration on the angles. The holy table is of the Stuart period with carved legs. The Royal Arms, which are carved in oak are those of George I. Don't bother trying to go inside, it's more trouble than it's worth. The parish was consolidated with Stratton St Peter many years ago.

TRIMLEY ST MARY

Dedication: St Mary
No of Bells: 1
Deanery 1836: Colneis
Hundred: Colneis
Union house: Nacton
Deanery 2000: Colneys

2 m NW of Felixstowe
between Ipswich &
Felixstowe: turn off the
bypass into 'The Trimleys'
Two churches near Bus Stop.
O.S. grid ref TM 276369
Post Code: IP11 0SP

The tower was 14th c. but is a pitiful sight. The church is rendered in cement and not at all appealing to the visitor. The corbels of the windows depict the heads of a monk, nun, bishop and king. You are greeted by a grinning face over the door and inside on the tower arch there are more carvings, this time of angels. The sanctuary is panelled and has a richly decorated reredos against the east wall. The church is still consecrated but is used by a mother and toddler group and it is no more than a playroom. Don't try to have a look round, it isn't worth it. The only thing of real interest is standing beside the path; it is a 12th c. square font with a round bowl. I was told it was brought to this spot centuries ago, when the church of Alston St John the Baptist in Lower Trimley was demolished in around 1500.

TUDDENHAM ST MARTIN

Dedication: St Martin
No of Bells: 6
Deanery 1836: Carlford
Hundred: Carlford
Union house: Nacton
Deanery 2000: Ipswich

3 m NE of Ipswich
between Ipswich &
Grundisburgh: where The
Street meets High Street in
village centre. Parking poor
O.S. grid ref TM 191484
Post Code: IP6 9BS

Quite an interesting Norman church. Approaching from the north up a steep incline, through the kissing gate, the Norman doorway to the nave is original. Two columns to each jamb. All four have carved capitals and abacus, and one pair has twist decoration. The arch has a roll and chevron design moulding. The tower is 15th c.. The nave roof is an unpretentious hammerbeam construction. The 15th c. bench-ends are carved with various figures and still have the holders for rush-lights. The spectacular pulpit is of the same date, with canopied saints in the buttresses each side of the carved panels. The base is modern. The Tudor Arms are incorporated in the backboard. The beautifully carved font is dated 1443. The piscina is very low; the chancel floor having been raised to match that of the nave.

TUNSTALL

Dedication:	St Michael	
No of Bells:	6	
Deanery 1836:	Orford	
Hundred:	Plomesgate	
Union house:	Wickham Market	
Deanery 2000:	Woodbridge	

6 m NE of Woodbridge between Woodbridge & Snape: near the junction of the B1069 & B1078 (Orford Road) through the village. O.S. grid ref TM 363551 Post Code: IP12 2JN

It is sad to see the mess that so-called restorers have made of the tower and porch of this otherwise lovely church. The tower once had a spirelet, but this was removed 100 years ago. Inside the porch there is a stoup accommodating a bowl of flowers. The 13th c. octagonal font has two shallow arcades on each face; the shaft was replaced in the 16th c.. The priest's door in the chancel may be original 14th c. woodwork. Over the door is a hood-mould with ballflower decoration. The old four-wheeled bier is on display and maybe still used. The box pews have all been painted, and the pulpit has been lovingly decorated but to my eye this does not sit easily in an old mediaeval church. The Royal Arms are high-quality and of George III and dated 1764, the lion having the appearance of an angry yorkie.

UBBESTON

		6 m SW of Halesworth
Dedication:	St Peter	between Laxfield &
No of Bells:	2	Walpole: on a bend in the
Deanery 1836:	Dunwich	road up a driveway.
Hundred:	Blything	Now a private residence.
Union house:	Bulcamp	O.S. grid ref TM 323726
Deanery 2000:	Halesworth	Post Code: IP19 0ET

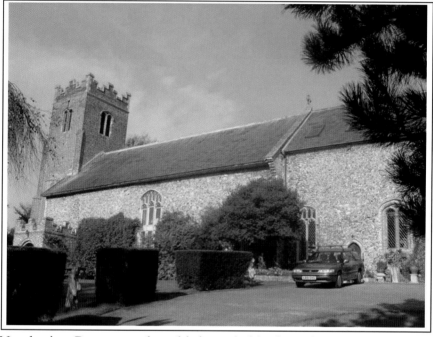

Nearby is a Roman road, and it is probable that Ubbeston church was built on the site of a roadside encampment or small settlement. The church was made redundant in 1971 and was in a poor state of repair. Although we can no longer visit the church it is more pleasing to look at than a pile of flint rubble and brambles. The Tudor porch still protects the 12th c. doorway with engaged shafts and a lovely chevron arch. The embattled tower is contemporary with the porch, built in the same style; both are built with red Tudor brick. The roofs are arch-braced and collar construction and arch-braced wall-posts hold it all together. The font, which was dated 1400, has been removed and is in use elsewhere. Most of the other interior furnishings have been moved to nearby Heveningham church.

UFFORD		3 m NE of Woodbridge
Dedication:	St Mary	between Woodbridge &
No of Bells:	8	Wickham Market: find
Deanery 1836:	Wilford	Church Lane off Barrack
Hundred:	Wilford	Lane & Lower Street.
Union house:	Nacton	O.S. grid ref TM 298521
Deanery 2000:	Woodbridge	Post Code: IP13 6DW

Outside the churchyard stand the village stocks. Not far from the River Deben is this 11th c. church. Parts of it are still recognisable as such: the north wall of the nave for instance. The south door may be just as early, but as it has been rebuilt it is difficult to be certain. The south porch is 15th c. with stone and flint panelling. Inside the door is a stoup. But your eye is caught by the sheer magnificence of the Tudor font cover, and for a while nothing else matters. It is unique, it is 18 feet tall, it is memorable. Even William Dowsing admired it. The font itself is late 15th c.. The nave roof is simple, arch-braced with hammer and tie-beams alternating. There are two misericorde stalls: one is inscribed with the Willoughby crest. This is well worth a visit for the font cover alone, and there is plenty more to see.

UGGESHALL

Dedication: St Mary
No of Bells: 1
Deanery 1836:   Dunwich
Hundred: Blything
Union house: Bulcamp
Deanery 2000:   Halesworth

4 m NW of Southwold
between Halesworth &
Wrentham: midway on the
road between Wangford &
Stoven near a road junction.
O.S. grid ref TM 455803
Post Code: NR34 8BD

Uggeshall church would not look out of place in a Saxon village.
There once was a tower but it fell quarter of a millennium ago. The
whole building is thatched, tower and porch, nave and chancel. The
south door is in the Norman style and may have replaced an original
but was built in the 14th c.. There is a poor-box on a pillar, almost
demanding a donation as soon as you enter. The nave roof is arch-
braced and collar type and originally carried a canopy of honour to
the rood at the eastern end. The roof of the chancel is a Victorian
restoration in the same style. The pulpit is 19th c. and neatly carved.
The font is octagonal traditional East Anglian type and has an
unusual cover: a pyramid formed from four corners and a pelican on
her nest at the apex. Modern? certainly different.

WALBERSWICK

Dedication:	St Andrew
No of Bells:	1
Deanery 1836:	Dunwich
Hundred:	Blything
Union house:	Bulcamp
Deanery 2000:	Halesworth

1 m SW of Southwold
between Blythburgh & the
coast: almost at the eastern
limit of the B1387, situated
on The Street.
O.S. grid ref TM 489747
Post Code: IP18 6UZ

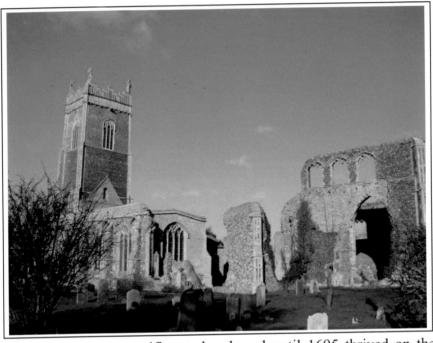

This was once a magnificent church and until 1695 thrived on the
wealth of the parish. The fabric was sold and a smaller church built
from the south aisle of the former. The 15th c. tower still dominates
the old walls. There was an even earlier church, but little is known of
its existence. Outside the porch is the base and socket for a stone
cross. The 15th c. south doorway is protected by the 18th c. porch
with a stone groined ceiling, and upper chamber. The font is a
traditional East Anglian type with lions and what I believe is a green
man around the base. The pulpit is mediaeval, with nicely carved
quatrefoil panels with foliage design. There are other carvings worth
finding. For me the interest lies in the ruins and imagining the
structure complete and majestic as it was in 1493, when first built.

WALDRINGFIELD

Dedication:	All Saints
No of Bells:	1
Deanery 1836:	Carlford
Hundred:	Carlford
Union house:	Nacton
Deanery 2000:	Colneys

3 m S of Woodbridge between Woodbridge & Kirton: south of the village in Mill Road (the road to Newbourne).
O.S. grid ref TM 282442
Post Code: IP12 4PY

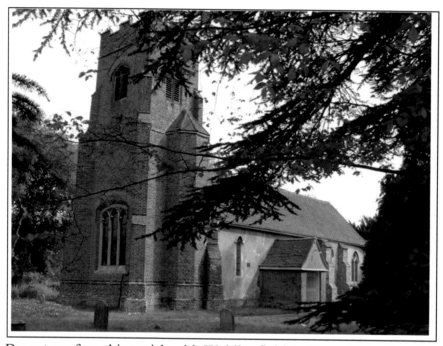

Do not confuse this parish with Waldingfield (with no 'R'). Standing close to the road, the tower catches the eye and immediately you wonder about the date. Well, it is Tudor and has turret stairs leading to the belfry. The walls of the church have been rendered with cement but the external character has not been lost. The porch is very simple. There is a good traditional East Anglian octagonal font with evangelical symbols around the bowl. Angelic faces peer down from the corbel and cross-legged figures pray around the shaft. Everything else is reproduction or new in 1864 when the Victorians 'restored' the church. The nave and chancel are austere and lack any warmth or character. On the south wall is a recent memorial to Sir William Bragg F.R.S. (1971). The best thing here is the view of the Deben.

WALPOLE

Dedication: St Mary
No of Bells: 1
Deanery 1836: Dunwich
Hundred: Blything
Union house: Bulcamp
Deanery 2000: Halesworth

3 m SW of Halesworth
between Halesworth &
Heveningham: on the
B1117 (Halesworth Road)
at the top of Church Hill.
O.S. grid ref TM 366746
Post Code: IP19 9AU

There has been a church here since the earliest days of Christianity. It is fitting that just up the road from the church is the oldest chapel in the county, converted in 1647, in the middle of the Civil War, from a 40-years-old meeting house. The parish church dates from the 14th c. but Saxon workmanship can still be seen today in the glacial erratics used as quoin stones in the walls of nave and chancel alike. The tower and spire are modern. The porch is 14th c. and has a scratch dial. The Norman doorway is rich in zigzag chevron decoration and inside there is a Norman stoup with broken bowl, now just a niche. The sedilia and piscina with cusped pediment are both 14th c.. The holy table is Jacobean. High on the wall of the nave are the gilded plaster Royal Hanoverian Arms.

WALTON

Dedication:	St Mary
No of Bells:	1
Deanery 1836:	Colneis
Hundred:	Colneis
Union house:	Nacton
Deanery 2000:	Colneys

now part of N Felixstowe between The Trimleys & Felixstowe: unmissable, in the High Street. 1½ miles south of The Trimleys. O.S. grid ref TM 295356 Post Code: IP11 9DS

In the churchyard near the porch is the remains of a buttress of the earlier church. Also constructed mainly out of septaria is the wall of the chancel, and it is still serving its purpose. A small Norman priest's door has been blocked up many years. Entry to the church is through the south door of the tower. There is a sketch of the church as it was about 1623. A black and white photograph shows the church without a tower. There is a rare King James bible under glass. The font is a traditional East Anglian octagonal bowl but the shaft has two lions, a wodewose and a green man. A small crude brass of a kneeling choirboy is to William Simond and states simply: 'Born 1601 - Died 1612'. A larger brass is to William and Agnes Tabard. In the tower are eight tubular bells hung in 1919 as a War Memorial.

WANGFORD

		3 m NW of Southwold
Dedication:	St Peter	between Lowestoft &
No of Bells:	5	Blythburgh: turn off the A12,
Deanery 1836:	Dunwich	- right into High Street, to
Hundred:	Blything	junction with Church Street.
Union house:	Bulcamp	O.S. grid ref TM 465791
Deanery 2000:	Halesworth	Post Code: NR34 8RW

This church has been re-built. Before the 1864 Victorian restoration, a spire atop the tower. Unusually the tower is at the north-east end of the church. It was rebuilt in 1875 and now has crocketted pinnacles on the embattled parapet and is easily recognisable from a distance. There are few earlier parts to the building: one is the porch which is 15th c., and the north wall of the nave is another. The font is late 14th c., the cover much more recent. The pulpit is 17th c. and retrieved from Henham Chapel with the reading desk; both have marquetry panels. (Henham Chapel was the private chapel of the Rous family at Henham Hall). There are many monuments to the Rous family. The building is suffering from damp and water penetration. There is another Wangford in Suffolk near Mildenhall.

WANTISDEN

Dedication:	St John
No of Bells:	1
Deanery 1836:	Orford
Hundred:	Plomesgate
Union house:	Wickham Market
Deanery 2000:	Woodbridge

4 m NE of Woodbridge, midway between Tunstall & Butley: ½ mile along unmade road 250 yds north of Dale Farm Estate offices. O.S. grid ref TM 362532 Post Code: IP12 3PG

To visit this church by car you will first have to obtain a key for the gate from Dale Farm Estate offices. It is so remote that it has been broken into as a place to sleep, probably more than any other church in the county. It is a lovely Norman church and the south doorway demonstrates this with an engaged shaft to each jamb and an arch of three orders. The dripstones on the hood-mould are heads. The tower is built entirely of coralline crag, which is abundant hereabouts. A slit window on the north side, and a chancel arch of two orders are further evidence. The round font is 12th c. and is unusual in being constructed from blocks of stone tied without mortar. The benches are of the 15th c. and most of the carvings are mutilated. The Royal Arms are those of George III.

WASHBROOK

Dedication:	St Mary
No of Bells:	1
Deanery 1836:	Samford
Hundred:	Samford
Union house:	Tattingstone
Deanery 2000:	Samford

3 m SW of Ipswich, between Chattisham & Copdock: from Washbrook Street, into Spring Lane, church is down a lane on a bend. Take care! O.S. grid ref TM 109425 Post Code: IP8 3HG

Buried deep in the dales of south central Suffolk, this lovely little Norman-built church is not easy to locate. There is a huge Sarsen stone at the base of the tower; which may or may not have been used by earlier religions on this spot. There are slit windows north and south of the nave. You may find the scratch dial on the buttress. The tower is 14th c. with a later embattled parapet. The nave roof is the original 14th c. braced tie beam roof with king posts and braced collar runners. The stone work and carving are quite exceptional in their execution. The 14th c. font is the traditional East Anglian type. There is a small chest which could be as early as 13th c. with iron strapwork on the lid and iron-bound. The Arms of Queen Victoria are set high on the wall.

WENHASTON

Dedication:	St Peter	5 m E of Southwold
No of Bells:	6	between Halesworth &
Deanery 1836:	Dunwich	Dunwich: on the opposite
Hundred:	Blything	side to the houses in The
Union house:	Bulcamp	Street. Park in Church Lane
Deanery 2000:	Halesworth	O.S. grid ref TM 424754
		Post Code: IP19 9EG

This is the home of the Wenhaston doom. Whitewashed to protect it from the Puritans, it was long forgotten and during restoration in 1892, it was thrown out to be burned. Heavy rain washed off the whitewash, the doom was revealed and saved for posterity. The church was built by the Normans on the site of a Saxon church and still has the evidence: a small slit window in the south wall of the nave. At least three distinct stages of building can be seen on the tower. Outside the porch is a small stoup. The door handle has been in use for 700 years. Just inside the door is a banner stave locker. The 15th c. font is badly mutilated and possibly once depicted the seven sacraments. A great deal of the woodwork in the church can be attributed to the Stuart period, including the pulpit and benches.

WESTERFIELD

Dedication: St Mary
No of Bells: 3
Deanery 1836:   Claydon
Hundred: Bosmere & Claydon
Union house: Wherstead Rd, Ipswich
Deanery 2000:   Ipswich

1 m N of Ipswich between
Ipswich & Witnesham: in
Church Lane, off the
crossroads on the B1077
(Westerfield Road).
O.S. grid ref TM 175476
Post Code: IP6 9BE

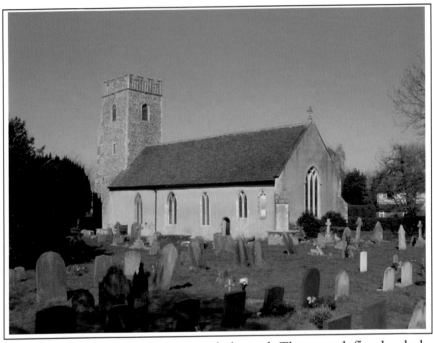

The single roof unites the nave and chancel. They are defined only by the moulded rood beam which ties north and south walls together. The roof structure is the original 14th c. fine single hammerbeam. Angels look down upon the visitors. This is a Norman church, and what was once the south doorway now forms part of the window with the chevroned arch mould incorporated into the sill and arch. More evidence of Norman origins can be seen at the base of the embattled tower and in the vestry. The font is of traditional East Anglian type. On the north side, a modern building has been erected, and while I hate this type of desecration of a graveyard, this one at least is in keeping with the church; or would be, if the church hadn't been cement-rendered.

WESTHALL *******

Dedication: St Andrew
No of Bells: 5
Deanery 1836: Dunwich
Hundred: Blything
Union house: Bulcamp
Deanery 2000: Beccles & S. Elmham

6 m S of Beccles between Halesworth & Brampton: 1½ miles SE of the village. off Strawberry Lane near Goodwins Cottages. O.S. grid ref TM 423804 Post Code: IP19 8NU

This church is a must for anyone interested in Norman architecture. H. Munro Cautley wrote extensively about it. What outwardly appears to be the south aisle is the 12th c. Norman nave. Beneath the 13th c. tower is what was once the west doorway. The ornamentation of this doorway exceeds anything in a church of these proportions anywhere. Above are three windows, two of which are blocked. On the south wall is another fine Norman doorway, and to the right what remains of a contemporary window. It is not just the building, the font is a rarity, showing the seven sacraments in original colour. This is only a small church but to me it has more to offer than the great edifice at Lavenham. For a model of how a church has progressed there is none finer.. A Bohun memorial reveals the family's history.

WESTLETON

Dedication:	St Peter	
No of Bells:	1	
Deanery 1836:	Dunwich	
Hundred:	Blything	
Union house:	Bulcamp	
Deanery 2000:	Saxmundham	

5 m NE of Saxmundham
between Yoxford &
Dunwich: just off the
B1125 turn into Darsham
Road by the War Memorial.
O.S. grid ref TM 439690
Post Code: IP17 3AF

Without a tower this church looks more like a thatched tithe barn. The church was rebuilt from the Saxon foundations in 1340. The tower, containing 8 bells, fell in 1770 and was rebuilt on failing foundations. Early in the 20th c it was dismantled and today has a single bell brick turret. The 13th c. piscina and sedilia are lovely examples, with detached columns with bases and capitals between each sedile. The arches are cusped and set back into the wall with the arch moulding covering the apex. The roofs have been plastered over and sterilised with white emulsion paint. The 15th c. octagonal font is of traditional East Anglian style and has been mutilated but still displays the ecclesiastical emblems. Beneath one of the south windows is a face below what appears to have been a corbel.

WESTON

		2 m S of Beccles between
Dedication:	St Peter	Beccles & Shadingfield:
No of Bells:	3	turn off the A145 at the
Deanery 1836:	Wangford	bottom of the valley,
Hundred:	Wangford	opposite Weston Hall.
Union house:	Shipmeadow	O.S. grid ref TM 429871
Deanery 2000:	Beccles & S. Elmham	Post Code: NR34 8TU

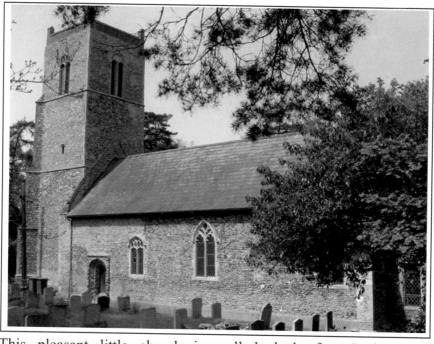

This pleasant little church is well looked after. It is nicely proportioned with a 15th c. tower and traces of the original Norman builders can still be found. A lancet window has been blocked and the doorways are 13th c.. Entry is through the porch and north doorway. The roofs of the nave and chancel are of a simple braced construction divided by the chancel arch. The tower arch has two small heads at the spring. The font is 15th c. seven sacrament type standing on an octagonal base divided into a Maltese cross. The shaft has been re-cut and has panels between the buttresses. There is a treat in store for those interested in the 15th c. art of bench-carving. A wonderful variety of fauna, flora and figures await you. The rare 17th c. Royal Arms of James II hangs on the north wall of the nave.

WEYBREAD

Dedication:	St Andrew
No of Bells:	6
Deanery 1836:	Hoxne
Hundred:	Hoxne
Union house:	Stradbroke
Deanery 2000:	Hoxne

7 m NE of Eye, between
Fressingfield & Harleston,
Nfk: from Harleston (Road)
(B1116) to King Street, turn
right into Church Road.
O.S. grid ref TM 240801
Post Code: IP21 5TR

The round western tower is out of proportion to the rest of the church. The clerestory, with its lofty windows, is the culprit. The whole church has in the past undergone such extensive restoration by the Victorians that little is worthy of note. The porch is a simple one with stone and flint panelled flushwork. The font is modern, but the 15th c. font remains in the south aisle with the bowl reduced to half its original height. The rood-loft stairs are still open and the corbels that support the roof are all different, as are the bench ends. There are two piscinas, the one in the south aisle is 13th c. and that in the chancel is 100 years later. There is a very recent memorial to Sergeant Alfred Ablett, the first man from Suffolk to be awarded the Victoria Cross.

WHERSTEAD

Dedication: St Mary
No of Bells: 3
Deanery 1836: Samford
Hundred: Samford
Union house: Tattingstone
Deanery 2000: Samford

2 m S of Ipswich, between Ipswich & Freston: turn east off A12 near Copdock interchange, into The Street, go straight on at junction.
O.S. grid ref TM 161406
Post Code: IP9 2AG

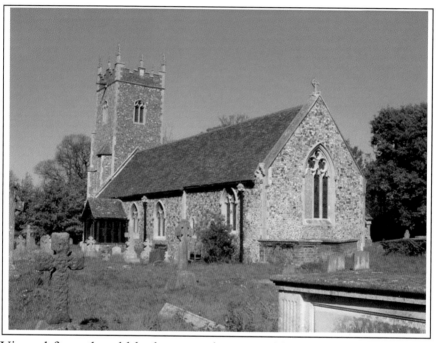

Viewed from the old lychgate at the west, this attractive little church has a crenulated brick parapet on top of the mediaeval tower and fine pinnacles reaching skywards. A mile to the east is the Orwell bridge. The little half-timbered south porch protects a Norman doorway with two engaged shafts and an arch of two chevroned orders. The north doorway, also Norman, has been blocked up. The nave is 15th c.. The chancel, with walls which are four feet thick in places, and the fine hammerbeam roof are 14th c.. The elegant piscina with slender columns is 14th c.. The stone pulpit was carved by the same artist who did much of the work in Ely Cathedral. A great deal of the church's history was discarded by Victorian 'restorers'. The bench ends with poppyheads are all 20th century workmanship.

WHITTON (cum Thurleston)
Dedication: St Mary
No of Bells: 1
Deanery 1836:   Claydon
Hundred: Bosmere & Claydon
Union house: Ipswich
Deanery 2000:   Ipswich

2 m NW of Ipswich
between Ipswich &
Claydon: Whitton Church
Lane is off Old Norwich
Road, - off A1156.
O.S. grid ref TM 149476
Post Code: IP1 6JL

This church was almost entirely rebuilt by the Victorians in the style of the late 13th, early 14th c.. The south aisle, tower and lovely broached spire were all constructed from the disused St Botolph's church at Thurleston, less than a half mile away across the fields. St. Botolph's fell into disrepair in 1528 and was eventually used as a barn until 1867. The rebuilt tower doorway is 13th c., and the single bell is dated 1441. Almost everything inside the church is post-1870; the date of the restoration. The piscina, however, is 13th c. and the roof of the chancel was also left as it was. The church owns an Elizabethan chalice but this is held elsewhere for safe keeping. The church is slowly being encroached upon by development, as are many suburban churches today.

WICKHAM MARKET

Dedication:	All Saints
No of Bells:	6 + a clock bell
Deanery 1836:	Wilford
Hundred:	Wilford
Union house:	Wickham Market
Deanery 2000:	Loes

10 m NE of Ipswich between Saxmundham & Woodbridge: turn off the A12 onto B1438 and follow to parish centre.

O.S. grid ref TM 302557

Post Code: IP13 0SB

Travelling down the A12, this church's beautiful leaded octagonal spire is clearly visible from miles away. When you attempt to photograph it close up it is impossible as the site is unfortunately surrounded by houses and trees. Approaching the church, you will notice the mass bell on the west of the spire. The whole church was very much restored in1875 but it is difficult to determine the old from the new. (the way it should be). Access to the nave is through the base of the tower, which serves as a south porch. Much of what you see is 15th or 16th c.. The font is probably the oldest thing in the church, being 14th c.. The roofs have been plastered. The piscina and three matching sedilia are 19th c. with elaborate arches. There is an older piscina with a simple cusped arch.

WILBY

Dedication:	St Mary
No of Bells:	8
Deanery 1836:	Hoxne
Hundred:	Hoxne
Union house:	Stradbroke
Deanery 2000:	Hoxne

6 m NW of Framlingham between Stradbroke & Dennington: beside the B1118 as it passes through the village. Unmissable. O.S. grid ref TM 241720 Post Code: IP21 5LE

A beautiful church, but large for the present size of the parish. The church was built in the 15th c. using dressed stone from the earlier Norman church which once stood on this spot. There are a dozen niches around the entrance to the stone and flint panelled porch; all are empty. The nave roof is of vaulted arch-braced design. The octagonal font is 15th c. and has an unusual decoration. Around the shaft are the apostles and their emblems. The benches are the items of real interest, having some unusual carvings. The seven sacraments are represented but most of the delicate figures have lost their heads. Animals and grotesques prevail. There are some faded wall paintings in the nave. The iron-bound chest is enormous. The pulpit is nicely decorated and from the Stuart period.

WILLISHAM

Dedication:	St Mary	
No of Bells:	1	
Deanery 1836:	Bosmere	
Hundred:	Bosmere & Claydon	
Union house:	Barham	
Deanery 2000:	Bosmere	

5 m S of Stowmarket
between Barking &
Somersham: between
Willisham Hall &
Strawberry Hall.
O.S. grid ref TM 070504
Post Code: IP8 4SL

A church has stood on this site for many hundreds of years. The dedication has always been to St Mary and that is about the only thing that hasn't changed. Unfortunately, nothing remains of interest in this charming little church. It was totally rebuilt in 1878, to an uncomplicated design by Herbert J. Green. Construction is of traditional undressed flints with stone quoins, sills and windows and doorways and a tiled roof. The total cost was £1400. The matching porch is contemporary, with two round windows which look totally out of place. The bell-cote for the single bell sits above the gable at the west end of the nave. The only thing of any age in the building is the traditional East Anglian 15th century font which was rescued from the old church before it was demolished.

WINGFIELD

Dedication:	St Andrew
No of Bells:	6
Deanery 1836:	Hoxne
Hundred:	Hoxne
Union house:	Stradbroke
Deanery 2000:	Hoxne

6 m NE of Eye between Hoxne & Fressingfield: turn south on Vicarage Road and follow for 300 yards.

O.S. grid ref TM 230768
Post Code: IP21 5RA

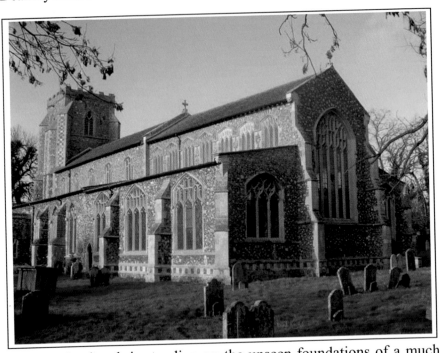

This lovely church is standing on the unseen foundations of a much earlier building. The tower is 14th c. and the rest of the structure is of the following 5 centuries. The font is the traditional East Anglian type with a restored cover first made when the font was new. There are effigies here of Sir John Wingfield (1360) founder of the college; John de la Pole (1491) and his wife Elizabeth Plantagenet, the sister of Edward IV and Richard III. Rare wooden effigies of Michael de-la-Pole (1415) and his wife Katherine. The chancel has many good misericordes and the carvings on the benches are numerous and interesting. There is also a very rare 'hudd', or hood, under which the priest would stand during a funeral in wet weather. The parish chest is a hollowed-out tree trunk. (the origin of the name trunk).

WINSTON

Dedication: St Andrew
No of Bells: 5
Deanery 1836:   Claydon
Hundred: Bosmere & Claydon
Union house: Barham
Deanery 2000:   Loes

1 m S of Debenham
between Debenham &
Framsden: just off the
B1077 on a bad bend, park
by the War Memorial.
O.S. grid ref TM 180616
Post Code: IP14 6LG

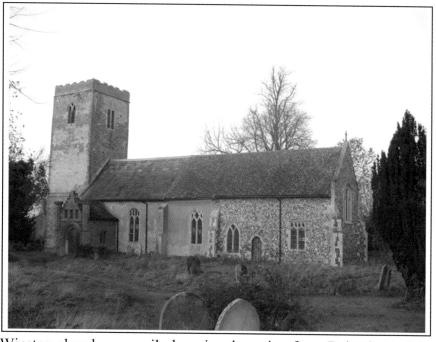

Winston church can easily be missed coming from Debenham. The 14th c. tower has shallow crenulations on a low parapet. The church is generally the same period with a few changes. The Tudor brick south porch adds a little colour: it has a crow-step gable and three empty niches flanked by turrets. The piscina is early 13th c. and has detached columns and an interestingly carved cusped arch. There is a peephole at the west end of the nave giving a view of the altar. The benches are worth inspection, carved with some quite unusual figures. The Royal Arms are those of George III. In 1556 Thomas Spencer was taken from here to Beccles and burned at the stake, with Edmund Poole and John Denny, for refusing to attend mass. (The Martyrs Memorial church, in Beccles is in their memorial)

WISSETT

			2 m NW of Halesworth
Dedication:	St Andrew		between Halesworth &
No of Bells:	6		Rumburgh: situated on The
Deanery 1836:	Dunwich		Street at the junction with
Hundred:	Blything		Lodge Lane.
Union house:	Bulcamp		O.S. grid ref TM 366792
Deanery 2000:	Halesworth		Post Code: IP19 0JG

The tower of Wissett church is 11th c., built about the time of the Conquest. Three of the windows are original. The 15th c. south porch protects the lovely Norman doorway with engaged columns and two orders of moulding. For an even better doorway go to the north. Here there are two finely carved columns to each jamb with chevron and spiral decoration and three orders of moulding to the arch. There are three scratch dials to look for. The 14th c. chancel has a barrel roof. The roof of the nave is arch-braced with alternate tiebeams. The octagonal font is 15th c. with evangelistic emblems around the bowl and lions and wodewoses around the shaft. The stairs to the rood-loft are still open to the top. The pulpit and holy table are both of the Jacobean Stuart period.

WITHERSDALE

Dedication:	St Mary Magdalene	
No of Bells:	2	
Deanery 1836:	Hoxne	
Hundred:	Hoxne	
Union house:	Stradbroke	
Deanery 2000:	Hoxne	

7 m NW of Halesworth between Halesworth & Harleston, Nfk: go east of the village on Withersdale Street & before Metfield. O.S. grid ref TM 283807 Post Code: IP20 0JR

This lovely little church has been thoroughly and sympathetically restored, leaving the inside very much mid-17th c. style. It sits snugly in the valley with a rivulet of the Waveney just a few yards away. A church has probably stood here since well before the Normans arrived. The small porch protects a narrow south doorway. The north doorway is Norman. The font bowl is 12th c. and nicely carved. The pulpit, complete with back and sounding board is on the north wall of the nave facing south. The box pews and benches surround the pulpit from east, west and south. The western gallery is 18th c.. The tie-beam at the east end which may have been used for the veil, pierces the wall and is pinned through outside. The timber bell-cote is said to have been given by Archbishop Sancroft.

WITNESHAM

Dedication:	St Mary
No of Bells:	6
Deanery 1836:	Carlford
Hundred:	Carlford
Union house:	Nacton
Deanery 2000:	Ipswich

4 m N of Ipswich, between Ipswich & Ashbocking: turn off the B1077 at the crossroads into Witnesham Church Lane.
O.S. grid ref TM 180509
Post Code: IP6 9JD

The south tower also serves as a porch to this 750-year-old church. On the tower is a scratch dial, probably deliberately placed; above it to the right, is a sundial, and in the centre of the tower is an old clock-face. The doorway to the nave is original, and inside the nave is a hammerbeam and arch-braced roof which has been panelled and plastered. The simple piscina is also contemporary with the building of the chancel. The clerestory, I am sure, is a later Tudor addition but with only two south facing windows of limited benefit. The re-cut font is extraordinarily large with the usual decoration of angels and lions and stands on a unusual crude base. The pulpit, supported by a slender central stem, holy table and two carved chairs in the sanctuary are Jacobean, the pulpit having two levels of panelling.

WOODBRIDGE

Dedication:	St John	
No of Bells:	1	
Deanery 1836:	Loes	
Hundred:	Loes	
Union house:	Nacton	
Deanery 2000:	Woodbridge	

8 m NE of Ipswich between Ipswich & Wickham Market: Situated at the junction of Castle Street & St John's Hill.
O.S. grid ref TM 274492
Post Code: IP12 1HP

This church was built between 1842 and 1845 out of necessity to support the increase in prosperity in the town. It was designed by J. M. Clark and built by Alfred Lockwood. Construction is in white brick, with a west tower, on top of which is a slender zinc covered spire. The windows are all tall and narrow, lancet-like. At the east is an apse. A tall stone pulpit was installed in 1888 as an afterthought and later lowered to its present height. It is an interesting exercise to wander round and compare this interior with mediaeval churches which have been adapted and altered trying to satisfy the fastidious requirements of the Victorian church-architect. Here they had a free hand, starting from scratch, with a pleasing result. Restorations of Norman and Mediaeval churches have not always been so agreeable.

WOODBRIDGE

Dedication:	St Mary
No of Bells:	8
Deanery 1836:	Loes
Hundred:	Loes
Union house:	Nacton
Deanery 2000:	Woodbridge

8 m NE of Ipswich between Ipswich & Wickham Market: At the top of Church Street and bottom of Theatre Street. O.S. grid ref TM 270490 Post Code: IP12 4LP

This is a grand 15th c. church with a tower 108 feet tall which dominates the town. Above the embattled parapet with attractive flushwork are pinnacles with weathercocks at each corner. The south porch has three niches, each with a Saint. The most spectacular item of interest is the monument to Jeffrey Pitman (1626). Situated to the east of the south aisle, above the monuments, are two 16th c. helmets. The 15th c. seven sacrament font, too, must not be missed. It still has faint traces of the original colouring. The parish chest is unusual in that it is in the form of an Ark, iron-bound and leather-covered and dated 1672. Fourteen beautifully painted panels of the old rood screen have been preserved and are hung on the wall. Sir Thomas Seckford, a great benefactor to the town, is buried here.

WOOLVERSTONE

Dedication: St Michael
No of Bells: 1
Deanery 1836:   Samford
Hundred: Samford
Union house: Tattingstone
Deanery 2000:   Samford

4 m S of Ipswich
between Ipswich &
Chelmondiston: turn north
off A1456 at crossroads
near Holbrook Lodge.
O.S. grid ref TM 190385
Post Code: IP9 1AY

Woolverstone's 14th c. church sits in the pleasant surroundings of Woolverstone Park. The tower peeps above the Irish yew trees and the well trimmed bushes with fine pinnacles pointing skyward. It was restored by Sir Gilbert Scott in 1862 but in 1888 was almost totally remodelled. The church progressed northwards; what was the nave became the south aisle and a new nave and chancel were constructed while the tower and 13th c. porch remained in situ. The design followed the example of the earlier structure. A piscina and sedilia were made new and set, as is the custom, in the south wall. The tower was given a parapet, battlements and pinnacles to complete the restoration. The work was paid for by Captain Berners who resided at Woolverstone Hall which was built in 1783 by his forefathers.

WORLINGHAM

		1 m E of Beccles between
Dedication:	All Saints	Beccles & Lowestoft: on
No of Bells:	6	the Lowestoft Road from
Deanery 1836:	Wangford	Beccles at the top of a rise.
Hundred:	Wangford	Car park in Rectory Lane.
Union house:	Shipmeadow	O.S. grid ref TM 445898
Deanery 2000:	Beccles & S. Elmham	Post Code: NR34 7RY

The Lych gate is the parish War Memorial 1914-18. The church was somewhat over-restored by the Victorians in 1874. The 13th c. building stands on the site of a much earlier church mentioned in Domesday. Worlingham was once divided into two parishes, Magna and Parva. Parva ceased to exist around the 15th c. when Worlingham Parva St Peter fell into disrepair. The building of a by-pass revealed its long-lost whereabouts. The 15th c. font is of traditional East Anglian style. The Sparrow memorial remembers two Roberts, one a General and the other his son. It was carved by Sir Francis Leggatt Chantry R.A. who has other pieces in Westminster Abbey and St. Paul's Cathedral. There is also a memorial to Nicholas Wrenne and his wife and another to members of the Duke family.

WORLINGWORTH

Dedication:	St Mary	
No of Bells:	8	
Deanery 1836:	Hoxne	
Hundred:	Hoxne	
Union house:	Stradbroke	
Deanery 2000:	Hoxne	

5 m NW of Framlingham
between Framlingham &
Horham: at the eastern end
of the main street through
the village, in Church Road.
O.S. grid ref TM 233686
Post Code: IP13 7NT

The church is strong and sturdy in appearance with the embattled tower rising above the trees. The porch has good flushwork and a George and Dragon are featured in the spandrils above the door. The nave roof is a super double hammerbeam construction with traceried spandrils. The East Anglian style font is belittled by the towering (25 ft plus) 15th c. font cover which is carved with the Greek palindrome 'Cleanse your sins and not your face only'. The Stuart pews are beautifully carved. The Stuart pulpit and holy table are of the same period. A graceful 14th c. piscina is flanked by a dropped sill sedilia. There is a collecting shoe dated 1622 and a poor-man's box dated 1699. The Royal Arms are Hanoverian and hang above the tower arch. There is a nice Henniker family memorial.

295

WRENTHAM

Dedication:	St Nicholas
No of Bells:	6
Deanery 1836:	Dunwich
Hundred:	Blything
Union house:	Bulcamp
Deanery 2000:	Halesworth

4 m N of Southwold between Lowestoft & Blythburgh: at a five-way junction on the B1127, well west of the parish.
O.S. grid ref TM 489830
Post Code: NR34 7LX

This pleasant little church is suffering from damp and only the western tower reveals its position; the rest is almost hidden from view by trees and shrubs. The church is decorated with stone and flint panels around the plinth and tower base. The walls of the chancel are 13th c., the nave 15th c.. From inside, the walls of the nave are battered outwards as they get thinner towards the top. There has been some restoration during the Victorian era, but it has been sympathetically executed. The lovely 15th c. font sits on a section of what appears to be a Greek column. The stone mensa is probably very early and still bears its original consecration crosses. There are two very good brasses in the church, one to Ele Bowet (1400) wearing a long dress and another to Humphrye Brewster (1593) dressed in armour.

YOXFORD

Dedication:	St Peter	4 m N of Saxmundham
No of Bells:	6	between Blythburgh &
Deanery 1836:	Dunwich	Saxmundham: on the
Hundred:	Blything	A1120 as it passes through
Union house:	Bulcamp	the parish, opposite shops.
Deanery 2000:	Saxmundham	O.S. grid ref TM 394689
		Post Code: IP17 3ER

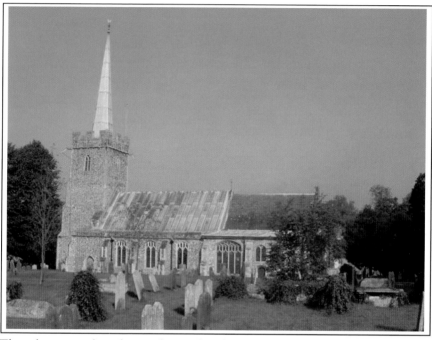

The elegant spire above the embattled tower is in perfect proportion to the rest of the building. Sitting very comfortably in a large churchyard a little higher than the road, the 14th c. church has been very much restored but retains a good few articles of interest. The font is dated to the early 15th c. and is quite unusual. A 16th c. altar tomb which once stood in the chancel has been badly mutilated. The pulpit and holy table are both Stuart period. Many notable locals are remembered here, many in brasses others in wall plaques. They include David Elisha Davy; Ann More aka Ann Candler; Sir Charles Blois, wounded at Waterloo, buried here 40 years later; Tomasine Tendryng; John Norwiche; Anthony Cooke; Joan Brooke and Christian Foxe.

Ruins and known sites of churches not mentioned elsewhere

Parish	Consolidated with :	OS MR
Alston St John the Baptist	Trimley St Martin	TM 265368
Brickett Parva St Lawrence	Offton	TM 051501
Capel St Andrew	Butley	TM 375479
Dunningworth St Mary	Tunstall	TM 382572
Engate St Mary (Beccles)	Beccles	TM 430892
Fordley Holy Trinity	Middleton	TM 430678
Gedgrave St Andrew	Orford	TM 405486
Hazelwood St Mary	Aldeburgh	TM 448591
Ipswich St Mildred	Ipswich	TM 162446
Loudham (dedication unknown)	? Pettistree	TM 311541
Oakley St Andrew	Oakley St Nicholas	TM 147785
Redisham Parva	Ringsfield	TM 402864
South Elmham St Nicholas	Sth Elmham All Saints	TM 322829
Stratton St Peter / St Mary	Trimley St Martin	TM 241388
Thorpe St Mary	Aldringham	TM 472599
Thurleston St Botolph	Whitton	TM 154482
Walberswick (dedication unknown)	Walberswick St Andrew	?TM 491742
Washbrook Velchurch (ded'n u/k)	Washbrook	TM 126431
Willingham St Mary	Sotterley St Mary	TM 445864
Worlingham Parva St Peter	Worlingham Magna	TM 460893

There are many other churches where the site is uncertain or unknown.
For this reason they are not listed here.

Note:
Norman Scarfe has compiled a more comprehensive list of churches which were
mentioned in Domesday and elsewhere.

Index of names on memorials etc. mentioned in the text.

North, Dudley	Little Glemham
Norwiche, John	Yoxford
Parker, Sir Philip	Erwarton
Pennyng, Arthur & 2 wives	Kettleburgh
Pitman, Jeffrey	Woodbridge St Mary
Plantagenet, Elizabeth	Wingfield
Playters, Sir Thomas	Sotterley
Poley, Dorothy	Badley
Pollock, (Bishop)	Blyford
Preston, Peter & wife	Mickfield
Reeve, Clara	Kirton
Reve, Thomas	Monewden
Revers, John & Mary	Chattisham
Revett, John	Boyton
Riley, Dorothy	Gunton
Rogers, Samuel	Otley
Rope, Dorothy	Blaxhall
Rope, Ellen Mary	Blaxhall
Rope, Michael	Blaxhall
Roskin, Sir William	Ipswich St Margaret
Rous family	Wangford St Peter
Rous, Edward	Badingham
Rous, Joanna	Stradbroke
Rustat, Tobias	Stutton
Sancroft, William (Archbishop)	Fressingfield
Sancroft, William (Archbishop)	South Elmham St Cross
Sayer, Samuel & Thomasine	Nettlestead
Seckford	Great Bealings
Seckford, Sir Thomas	Woodbridge St Mary
Seckford, Thomas & Margaret	Henley
Sherwood, John, Sarah, Hannah	Ashby
Simond, William	Walton
Smyth, John	Stradbroke
Southwell	Barham

GLOSSARY of Terms, Architectural & Ecclesiastical

Abacus	flat portion on top of a capital.
Aisle	space between an arcade and the outer wall.
Ambulatory	aisle round an apse.
Apse	rounded end (usually of chancel or chapel).
Arcade	row of arches, free-standing and supported on piers or columns; a blind arcade is known as a dummy.
Arch	can be round-headed; pointed, two-centred or drop, i.e. an arch struck from centre on the springing-line; ogee pointed arch with double curved sides, upper arcs convex, lower concave; lancet pointed arch formed on an acute-angle triangle; and depressed flattened or elliptical.
Arms	heraldic bearings, heraldic crest.
Ashlar	worked stone with flat surface, usually of regular shape and square edges.
Aumbry	recess to hold sacred vessels, usually with a light or lit candle close by.
Back board	a board behind a pulpit giving support to a sounding board or tester.
Baluster	small (usually circular) supporting columns or posts - as seen on 17th c. communion rails.
Baptistery	a part of the church set aside to accommodate the font.
Barrel roof	like a covered wagon, or inverted ship; barrel vault is a plain vault of uniform cross-section.
Bastion	solid masonry projection.
Batter	inclined face of wall; hence battered and battering.
Battlements	parapet with indentations or embrasures, with raised portions (merlons) between; the gap is called a crenulation.
Bays	internal divisions of building, marked by roof principals or vaulting piers.
Belfry	chamber where the bells are hung in a tower.
Bell chamber	where bells are hung whether or not in a tower.
Bell turret	open stone structure above the roof line containing one or more bells.
Bell cote	small wooden cage like structure containing (usually) one bell.
Billet	log-shape decoration forming part of a moulding.
Bond	arrangement of bricks or stone in courses.
Box pew	a pew surrounded by a wooden partition with an entrance door for private worship usually for those of higher rank or status than the great unwashed.
Brattice	timber tower, or projecting wooden gallery.
Broach(ed)	having the shape of a spike, with the angle at top more acute

than the angle at the bottom.

Buttered / Buttering   interior walls that appear to lean outwards. Enabling the wall to be narrower at the top without the outer wall being out of plumb.

Buttress   projection from wall etc. for additional support.

BVM   Blessed Virgin Mary.

Candle beam   a beam forming part of the rood loft upon which candles are lit to illuminate the rood.

Canopy of honour   highly decorated roof beams above and behind the rood.

Capital/cap   the top of a pier or column, upon which the arch rests. also called a 'celure'.

Chamfer   surface made by smoothing off the angle between two stone faces.

Chevron   zigzag moulding (Norman, twelfth century).

Cinquefoil   five-lobed.

Clerestory   the part of the nave roof above the side aisles with windows to allow more light into the church, particularly onto the rood.

Clunch   hard chalk material.

Cob   unburnt clay mixed with straw.

Corbel   a piece of carved stone or wood which supports a hood-mould or part of a roof.

Cornice   decorative projection along top of wall.

Course   level layer of stones or bricks.

Crenel   gap in battlemented parapet.

Crenulated   embattled or to fortify.

Crocket   carved decoration on the sloping side of a spire or pinnacle usually thorn shaped and pointing skyward.

Cupola   a small domed turret on a roof or top of a tower, usually with a door.

Cusped /cusping   an upwardly pointed figure created by the intersection of two or more arcs or foils.

Decorated   architectural style around 13th – 14th century. 1280 - 1377.

Diaper work   decoration of squares or lozenges. Trellis-like

Dogtooth   diagonal indented pyramid or triangle.

Dormer   window placed vertically in sloping roof.

Dressing   carved stonework around openings.

Drystone   un-mortared masonry.

Early English 1175 - 1280.

Easter sepulchre   always on the north wall, originally a timber framework representing the cave in which Jesus' body was placed, into which the cross from the altar

was transferred from Good Friday to Easter morning.
These were later constructed of stone. Sometimes
tombs were utilised; some intentionally situated for
the purpose.

Embattled   battlemented; with battlements; crenulated.

Engaged   (column) refers to being attached to the jamb along
its length. not free-standing. (opp of detached).

English Renaissance Period 1625 - 1700.

Fillet   narrow flat band.

Finial   carving at the apex of an arch, pinnacle spire or roof

Fleche   a slender spire, esp. on a church above an
intersection of the nave and transept.

Fleuron   a carved flower.

Flushwork   patterns made in the masonry using flint or stone,
neither sunken nor raised.

Fluting   concave mouldings in parallel.

Flying buttress   buttress which is not attached to the wall it
supports at the lower portion, to allow passage
through, or to save weight, or look more elegant

Foils   lobes used to embellish the head of an arch or a
circular opening. Trefoil. quatrefoil, cinquefoil.

Foliated   carved with leaves.

Footings   bottom part of wall.

Freestone   high-quality sandstone or limestone.

Fresco   painting on wet plaster wall.

Gable   wall covering end of roof-ridge.

Gallery   long passage or room.

Galilee   a small chapel or porch at the west end of some
mediaeval churches

Gargoyle   a carved stone usually with a spout to throw
rainwater well clear of the foundations.

Georgian   period 1700 - 1825

Gnomon   that part of a sundial which casts the shadow.

Gothic   architectural period 12th - 16th century.

Grisaille   a glass monochrome picture in shades of grey

Groined   roof with sharp edges at intersection of cross-vaults.

Grotesques   outlandish, distorted or bizarre characterisations of
people or animals, not necessarily ugly as in
gargoyles.

Half-shaft   roll-moulding on either side of opening.

Hammer-beam   beam jutting out horizontally at right angles at the
top of a wall to support other beams and arch braces.

Hanoverian   pertaining to the reign of the house of Hanover, 1714

- 1917

Hatchments	Lozenge shaped frames bearing the coat of arms of a deceased person, made for the funeral and retained in the church as a memorial.
Headstock	The wooden beam which carries the weight of a bell.
Herringbone	brick or stone laid diagonally.
Holy table	the table forming the altar, usually 17th c. after the original stone altars were destroyed by the puritans.
Hood	arched covering.
Hoodmould	a hood when used to throw off rainwater.
Hourglass	two vertically connected glass bulbs containing sand taking an hour to pass from upper to lower bulb. Usually fixed by a bracket to the wall adjacent to the pulpit as a guide for the clergy as to the length of the service.
Impost	wall bracket to support arch.
Ionic	order of Greek architecture characterized by a column with scroll-shapes on either side of the capital.
Jacobean	1603 - 1625
Jamb	side of arch, door or window against which the door/ window closes.
Joist	timber stretched from wall-to-wall to support floorboards.
Lancet	(window) long, narrow window with pointed head. (1190 - 1280 in date).
Laudian	Pertaining to Archbishop William Laud (1573 - 1645).
Lintel	horizontal stone or beam bridging opening.
Loop	narrow opening in a wall
Louvre / louver	(Bell) louver – to allow the sound of bells to escape through the tower wall.
Lucarne	A small slit or opening to allow light into spires and towers.
Mass dial	see Scratch dial.
Mensa	a table usually of stone on stone pillars.
Merlon	solid part of embattled parapet.
Misericord	projection under a choir stall seat serving (when the seat is turned up) to support a person standing, usually carved.
Moulding	masonry decoration.
Mullion	vertical division of window.
Mural	wall or a painting on a wall

Nailhead	pyramidal moulding.
Newel	centre-post of circular staircase.
Niche	a recess usually arched, made in a wall to contain a statue or other object.
Nookshaft	shaft set in angle of jamb or pier.
Norman	1066 – 1190 Romanesque.
Ogee-headed arch	moulding showing in section a double continuous curve, concave below passing into convex above, back to front S.
Oolite	granular limestone.
Open joint	wide, un-mortared space between faces of stones.
Oriel	projecting window in wall; originally a form of porch, often of wood.
Parclose screen	a screen to delineate a private area or to enclose part of the nave for whatever reason, usually privacy for the upper classes.
Parapet	low wall on outer side of main wall.
Parish chest	the 'safe' of the parish normally with three locks and three different key holders to prevent theft or fraud.
Parvise	room or chamber above a porch. (orig. balcony).
Pediment	low-pitched gable over porticos, doors, windows, etc.
Perpendicular	English architectural style, circa. 1377 - 1547.
Pier	support for arch, usually square as opposed to pillar (round).
Pilaster	shallow pier used to buttress a wall.
Pinnacle	ornament crowning spire, tower etc. or small spire on top of building.
Piscina	basin, usually set in or against wall, with drain for washing vessels after the sacrament.
Pitch	the slope of a roof .
Pitching	rough cobbling.
Plinth	projecting base of wall.
Pointing	mortar or cement in joints between brickwork.
Poppyheads	ornamental carving at the end of church benches and / or pews. *[Endless variations on a theme]*
Principal	a main truss or rafter that supports a roof.
Pulpit	wooden or (later) stone raised enclosed platform from which the preacher delivers a sermon.
Purlin	horizontal timber in a roof supporting rafters.
Quatrefoil	four-lobed.
Quoin	dressed corner stone at the angle of a building.
Refectory	communal dining-hall.
Reredos	decorative screen of wood or stone behind the altar.

Glossary

Respond/s	half-piers found in the jambs of arches.
Reveal	the thickness of the wall from the inside edge, to the window or door.
Rib	raised moulding dividing vault.
Romanesque	prevailing architectural style, eighth to twelfth century, with rounded arches.
Rood	A cross, [Saxon] object of veneration usually surmounting a screen which divides the chancel from the nave.
Rood loft	a platform above the roof screen to permit access to light candles to illuminate the rood.
Rood screen	a decorative wooden screen dividing the nave from the chancel and supporting a rood or cross centrally above.
Rood stairs	stairs that allow access to the rood loft, usually within the thickness of a wall, sometimes within a turret.
Roofridge	summit line of roof.
Royal Arms	the Royal Crest attributed to the Monarch of the day.
Rubble	un-squared stone/s not laid in courses.
Rustication	worked ashlar stone, with faces left deliberately rough.
Sacring bell	a bell rung at the time the sacrament is taken.
Saltire	a diagonal; equal-limbed diagonal cross. St Andrew's style cross.
Sanctuary	the part of a church nearest to the altar, usually behind the altar rail.
Saxon	pre 1066.
Scratch dial	a crude sundial with central hole (into which is inserted a gnomon) with rays usually scratched on a buttress or quoin-stone of a church to show the time of the next service, also mass-dial.
Sciapus	legendary Scandinavian figure with enormous feet which shelter him from the sun.
Sedilia (pl.)	seats for clergy during parts of long mediaeval masses (usually in or on the south wall of the sanctuary, often a dropped window sill.)
Septaria	A semi-hard brownish clay-like stone with calcite bonding.
Serpent	18th c. deep-toned wind instrument,
Seven sacraments (the)	Baptism, Holy Communion, Confirmation, Holy Orders, Reconciliation, Matrimony & Anointing of the sick.

Shaft　　　　narrow column. i.e. supporting the font.
Shingle　　　a wooden tile, usually of cedar.
Soffit　　　　underside of arch, opening or eaves.
Sounding board　　see Tester.
Spandrel　　 the space (roughly triangular in shape each side)
　　　　　　 between an arch and it's square hood-mould.
Splay　　　　chamfer, or sloping face. Window reveal, wider on
　　　　　　 the inner wall than at the window.
Squint　　　 observation hole in wall or room.
Stoup　　　　a carved bowl for holding holy water to purify
　　　　　　 oneself before, or as, entering the church.
Stringcourse　continuous horizontal mouldings on a wall-face.
Stuart　　　　pert. to the reign of house of Stuart, 1603 - 1707.
Sundial　　　 to indicate the time (of the next service), usually on
　　　　　　 the south porch gable or on the tower.
Tester　　　　a suspended canopy over a pulpit also 'sounding
　　　　　　 board'.
Tie beam　　 large horizontal beam at the base of a roof (or top of
　　　　　　 a wall) to stop the walls spreading outwards with the
　　　　　　 weight of the roof. Occasionally piercing the wall and
　　　　　　 pinned-through outside.
Tracery　　　 intersecting rib-work in upper part of window or
　　　　　　 decoratively carved in wood.
Transept　　 either or both of the arms of a cross-shaped church
　　　　　　 at right angles to the main body of the church.
Transom　　 horizontal division of window.
Trefoil　　　 three-lobed.
Tudor　　　　Elizabethan　1547 - 1600.
Turret　　　　small tower, round or polygonal, tapered or straight.
Tympanum　 the stonework filling the space between the
　　　　　　 horizontal lintel of a doorway and the arch above it.
Victorian　　 pert. to the reign of Queen Victoria, 1837 - 1901.
Volute　　　　decorative spiral scroll in stonework found on some
　　　　　　 Ionic capitals.
Voussoir　　 wedge-shaped stone in arch, not the keystone.
Wag(g)on roof　　see Barrel roof.
Wall-stair　　staircase built into thickness of wall. as rood-stairs.
Weathering　 sloping surface to throw off rainwater on buttresses
　　　　　　 and battlements etc..
Wodewose　 or Woodwose. Wild man with beard carrying a club
　　　　　　 usually found on the shaft of a font and associated with
　　　　　　 lions. Probably to ward off evil spirits.

Notes

Notes

East Suffolk
as defined by the
Archdeaconry of Suffolk 1836

Map courtesy of
Suffolk Record Office